CINEMATERNITY

CINEMATERNITY

FILM,

MOTHERHOOD,

GENRE

Lucy Fischer

PRINCETON UNIVERSITY PRESS

PRINCETON, NEW JERSEY

Library of Congress Cataloging-in-Publication Data
Fischer, Lucy.
Cinematernity : film, motherhood, genre / Lucy Fischer.
p.   cm.
Includes bibliographical references and index.
ISBN 0-691-03775-2 (cloth : alk. paper). — ISBN 0-691-03774-4
(pbk. : alk. paper)
1. Mothers in motion pictures.   2. Women in motion pictures.   3.
Film genres.   I. Title.
PN1995.9.W6F565   1997
791.43'6520431—dc20   96-12452 CIP

This book has been composed in Galliard

Princeton University Press books are printed on
acid-free paper and meet the guidelines for permanence
and durability of the Committee on Production
Guidelines for Book Longevity of the
Council on Library Resources

Printed in the United States of America
by Princeton Academic Press

10 9 8 7 6 5 4 3 2 1

(pbk.)
10 9 8 7 6 5 4 3 2 1

For my son, David Ethan Wicclair

AMNESIA

I almost trust myself to know
when we're getting to that scene—
call it the snow-scene in *Citizen Kane*

the mother handing over her son
the earliest American dream
shot in a black-and-white

where every flake of snow is incandescent
with its own burden, adding-

up, always adding-up to the
cold blur of the past
But first there is the picture of the past

simple and pitiless as the deed truly was
the putting-away of a childish thing

Becoming a man leaving
someone, or something—
still, why

must the snow-scene blot itself out
the flakes come down so fast
so heavy, so unrevealing

over the something that gets left behind?

(Adrienne Rich [1974], from *The Fact of a Doorframe: Poems Selected and New, 1950–1984*)

Contents

Acknowledgments

AS EVER, there are many people to thank for assistance in the writing of this book. Once more, I have found Marcia Landy and Dana Polan exemplary colleagues in the Film Studies Program at the University of Pittsburgh. They have each read assorted chapters of the book and have generously offered their suggestions for revision. Phillip Smith and David Bartholomae, Chairs of the Department of English during the period in which I composed this book, provided me both the reduced course load necessary to complete my work and funds for purchasing some of the book's illustrations. Several Graduate Student Assistants in my department aided me on the project: Mary Savanick, Julie Cramer, Alison Cuddy, Bethany Ogden, and John McCombe. Thanks as well to Sandy Russo for assistance in acquiring videotapes and stills for the book and support in running the Film Studies Program. Several other individuals at the University of Pittsburgh helped with audiovisual resources for the book—especially Cindy Neff, Max McGee, and Jeff Cepull of the University Center for Instructional Resources. A grant from the University of Pittsburgh allowed me to purchase videotapes and film stills necessary for the writing and publication of the book.

Mary Corliss of the Film Stills Archive of The Museum of Modern Art (MOMA) was extremely patient and helpful in locating illustrations for the manuscript, as was Bridget Kinally of the British Film Insitute's (BFI) Department of Stills, Posters and Designs. Charles Silver of MOMA's Film Study Center provided me with relevant clipping files and arranged screening of the newly restored version of *Way Down East*. Beyond that, through his graciousness, Charles always manages to make me feel, upon my return to MOMA, that I stopped working there only a few days ago. Thanks, as well, to Camille Billops and James Hatch for the still from *Finding Christa*.

I had the opportunity to present talks on various topics in the book at such places as the University of Southern California (1988), the Society for Cinema Studies conference in Los Angeles (1991), Loyola University (1992), the Modern Language Association meeting in Toronto (1993), the American Psychoanalytic Association meeting in New York City (1993), the Canadian Film Studies Association (1993), the University of Michigan (1994), and the University of Augsburg (Germany) (1995). I would like to thank all those individuals who arranged for such presentations: Krin Gabbard, Andrew Horton, Ira Konigsberg and Stuart McDougal, Robert Burgoyne, Marsha Kinder, Barry Grant, Klaus Post.

Several sections of the book have been published previously, although in different forms. Chapter 2 was originally published as "The Lady Vanishes: Women, Magic and the Movies," *Film Quarterly* 33, no. 1 (Fall 1979): 30–40. Chapter 4 was originally published as "Birth Traumas: Parturition and Horror in *Rosemary's Baby*," *Cinema Journal* 31, no. 3 (Spring 1992): 3–18. Chapter 5 was originally published as "Mama's Boy: Filial Hysteria in *White Heat*," in *Screening the Male*, edited by Steven Cohan and Ina Rae Hark (New York and London: Routledge, 1993), 70–84. Chapter 6 was originally published as "'Sometimes I Feel Like a Motherless Child': Comedy and Matricide," in *Comedy/Cinema/Theory*, edited by Andrew Horton (Berkeley and Los Angeles: University of California Press, 1991), 60–78. I am grateful to all the journal and anthology editors who commented on the revision of those essays, as well as to Mary Murrell of Princeton University Press who has been extremely helpful with (and patient about) the completion of this manuscript.

Finally, my gratitude and affection go toward my husband, Mark Wicclair, and my son, David Ethan Wicclair—both of whom I managed to lure upon an ocean journey around the world during the course of writing this book. As ever, they both humored me and provided me the proverbial "ballast" and "anchor" with which to enjoy the experience and complete my work.

CINEMATERNITY

1 _____

Introduction

MOTHERHOOD AND FILM: A CRITICAL GENEALOGY

The Mother of Invention

> [T]he peak of Victorian aesthetic activity, with its highly pic-
> torial bias in the arts . . . coincided with the final phase in the
> invention of the motion picture. The relationship suggested
> by these chronological parallels is significant. *It would suggest
> the well-known adage: "Necessity is the mother of invention."*
> The motion picture . . . was deeply rooted, even during its
> long period of *incubation*, in the social needs of the times. . . .
> Cinema was not *born* simply with the invention of Eastman's
> celluloid film nor with the arrival of the motion-picture cam-
> era . . . its *conception* . . . occurred simultaneously with analo-
> gous advances in the theatre of realism and romance.
> (A. Nicholas Vardac, my italics)[1]

As this quotation from *Stage to Screen* reveals, artists, theorists, and historians have long conjured metaphors of motherhood to explicate or
situate the cinema. In Vardac's case, he casts the motion picture as the
"child" of a "maternal" cultural necessity—the alleged "need" for creating machines of realism in the nineteenth century. Alternatively, Sergei Eisenstein fashions an image of parturition to proclaim cinema's ties
to the other arts. As he notes, "It is only very thoughtless and presump-
tuous people who . . . [proceed] from the premises of some incredible
virgin-birth of this art!" (232). Likewise, Siegfried Kracauer fancies the
photographic process (upon which cinema is based) as developing "like
the embryo in the womb" from a variety of social and scientific sources
(7). Finally, for poet Philip Dacey, it is the cinematic apparatus that is
maternal. He imagines sitting with his children before a theater screen as

Something large enough
to be our mother
embraces us
with light, shadow and sound,
making us one.

(23)

[1] A list of works cited follows each chapter.

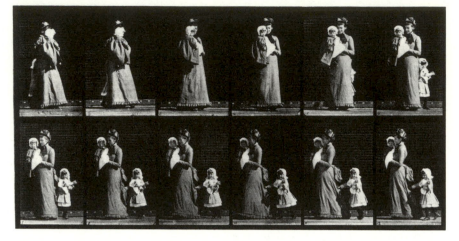

1. The perfect Victorian mother. Plate 52 (1887) in Eadweard Muybridge's *Animal Locomotion*, © Addison Gallery of American Art, Phillips Academy, Andover, MA

Significantly, some of the first cinematic images that people would have seen had, as Dacey imagines, a decidedly maternal cast. Among Eadweard Muybridge's famous "animal locomotion" studies were three apparently on the theme of motherhood—ones that seem, retrospectively, to lay bare central cultural and psychic conceptions of maternity.

In his Plate 52 (1887), we find a sequence of images depicting the perfect Victorian mother—formally coutured, with her two costumed children. In Plates 465 and 527 (both 1887), however, we find maternal polarities worthy of the childhood Unconscious. In the former, a bare-breasted "Good Mother" receives a bouquet from a little girl, whom she kisses in gratitude. In the latter, an unclothed "Bad Mother" (surveyed in a 360-degree "pan") spanks a naked boy unrelentingly. If we envision the animation of these photographs by Muybridge's zoopraxiscope, we have a scene of the very "mother" of cinematic invention producing the first (yet archetypal) maternal images.

Cinematernity (a title that bespeaks the cultural "fusion" of film and motherhood) seeks to extend and examine the relationship between these terms through an investigation of the mother's status as a figure in fiction, experimental, and documentary film. As its subtitle indicates, the book places this issue within a broader context. While it makes no claims to be a study of genre, per se, it makes "strategic" use of that notion as a fundamental *organizing principle*—as a means of structuring the text beyond the framework of a formless series of essays. The sense of genre that the study employs, however, is an open one that acknowledges the limits of proposing rigid definitions. As Andrew Tudor has written,

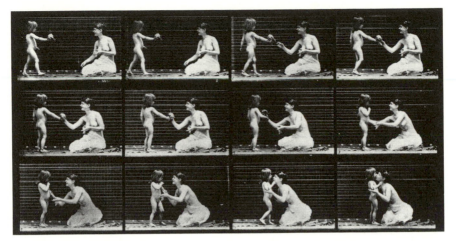

2. The "Good Mother" of the childhood unconscious. Plate 465 (1887) in Eadweard Muybridge's *Animal Locomotion*, © Addison Gallery of American Art, Phillips Academy, Andover, MA

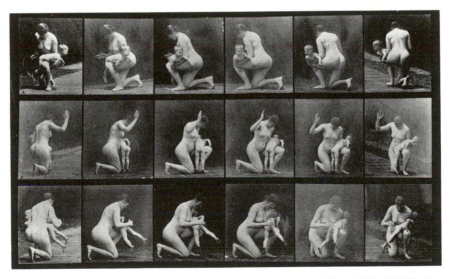

3. The "Bad Mother" of the childhood unconscious. Plate 527 (1887) in Eadweard Muybridge's *Animal Locomotion*, © Addison Gallery of American Art, Phillips Academy, Andover, MA

"*genre* is a conception existing in the culture of any particular group or society; it is not a way in which a critic classifies films for methodological purposes, but the much looser way in which an audience classifies its films" (Nichols, 123).

With this "commonsense" notion of genre in mind, we will pursue certain analytical avenues. If, as Thomas Schatz informs us, "a genre film involves familiar . . . one-dimensional characters acting out a predictable story pattern within a familiar setting" (6), we will want to trace the outline of the maternal heroine and delineate the narrative and mise-en-scène she regularly inhabits. At every turn, though, we will be cognizant that not all cases fit the mold and that stereotypes are culturally and historically determined.

This book's invocation of genre also reflects the perception of a certain paradoxical absence (yet excess) within film studies. Where issues of motherhood have been confronted, work has primarily attached itself to the realm of the *maternal melodrama*—to the exclusion of other modes. This tendency is, of course, logical, given that the "woman's picture" has been one of the few commercial paradigms to authorize a complex female protagonist.

Nonetheless, *Cinematernity* seeks to move beyond the privileged generic circle of melodrama by querying the status of motherhood in *other* established cinematic modes: the trick film, the horror film, the crime film, the comedy, the thriller, the postmodern film, the documentary, and the experimental film. While there has been pioneering work in many of these areas (Tania Modleski on mothering and comedy ["Three Men and Baby M"]; Barbara Creed on reproduction and horror; Robin Blaetz on motherhood and war films ["You're Going to Live"]; Lori Shorr on childbirth and the documentary), no *single text* has systematically explored the representation of maternity across diverse generic patterns, nor argued for the centrality of the subject beyond the confines of melodrama. Where certain genres are omitted (science fiction, for example), it is because they have already been analyzed rather thoroughly by other feminist critics.

Gender and Genre

> The relationship between gender and genre is at present only vaguely perceived. . . . once these two concepts are together opened to inquiry, they become central to the process of interpretation and their changing relationships afford a key to understanding.
> (Mary Gerhart)

In implicating numerous genres, *Cinematernity* reveals an interest in the broader question of gender and genre: how narrative and cultural forms imply a specific sexual politics. In confronting this issue, my work builds upon a body of research that has transpired in the fields of both cinema and literature. Writing on the latter, Mary Gerhart highlights the etymological connections between the words *genre* and *gender*:

> When we locate the term[s] etymologically in a family of meanings across several disciplines, we find that they share family resemblances. The family to which both *genre* and *gender* belong includes words such as *general, gender, genre, genes, genus, generic, generation* and *generative*. This family of *genre* and *gender* carries two general senses: the categorical and the productive. The categorical sense pertains to the meaning "of a kind or sort." . . . The productive sense means "of or pertaining to the act of rooting, begetting, bearing, producing." (98)

For Gerhart, the sense of genre as "classification" has eclipsed its valence as "production," a fact she views as a critical "aberration" (98). Clearly, in the repressed sense of genre as "rooting, begetting, bearing," we find an intimation of maternity at the very *heart* of the word. Significantly, the privileging of genre's scientific cataloging role has been seen by certain critics as aligned with a masculine perspective. As Paula Rabinovitz notes:

> genre is inevitably linked to the order of genealogy . . . and to the patriarchal order—to the Law of the Father, to masculine authority. The law of genre, then, is also the law of gender: that system which demarks the boundaries of and ascribes meaning to sexual difference. And anything that steps outside of those boundaries risks "impurity," it becomes bastardized, a "monstrosity"— or put more politely, "implausible" within the codes of difference of either genre or gender. (68)

One finds a rather rigid view of genre and gender implicit in traditional film scholarship. In his seminal work on Hollywood cinema, Thomas Schatz links particular genres to either masculine or feminine poles. Western, gangster, and detective films are characterized by a male hero and a "macho" ethic of violence and isolation. By contrast, musicals, melodramas, and screwball comedies are "female dominant." They are marked by a couple-hero and by a "maternal-familial code" valorizing emotion, domestication, civilization, and community (35). While we recognize the validity of Schatz's assertions (which are echoed by numerous other scholars), his neat classification, so easily reduced to a chart, tends to calcify forms, and to mask their potential interrelations. Hence, the schema may encourage the critic to ignore the role of the mother in the crime film, or to miss a maternal subtext in the masculine "thriller."

Countering such established binarisms, Stephen Neale ends his book *Genre* with a section titled "Genre and Sexuality" (56–62). In it, he reminds us that while mainstream cinema has always aimed its work at a gendered audience (women for musicals, men for westerns), it has also attempted (for economic reasons) to please *both* groups at the same time, thus maximizing profits. Hence we cannot so easily diagram genres along sexual lines. Citing one example, he notes how the western (conventionally aligned with machismo) is actually a site to "privilege, examine and celebrate the body of the male" (57). Likewise, melodrama (traditionally linked to the female) requires a "feminized" male at its center (59–60). Thus Neale argues for a more fluid conception of genre, one released from stark gender stereotypes.

Primary among those voices to confront gender and genre have been feminist scholars, who have insisted on introducing the "woman question" into critical discourse. E. Ann Kaplan edited an innovative anthology entitled *Women in Film Noir* (1978), opening up a discussion of the crime film's resonant femme fatale. Diane Waldman investigated the Gothic subgenre of the thriller—a form centered on a female victim rather than on a male detective. Judith W. Hess mocked the classic western for offering only "bar girls" and "eastern school teachers" (56).

But early work on film genre nonetheless favored Schatz's "masculine" forms. Attention was first drawn to the western and crime film (Warshow, Kitses, Cawelti [*Adventure, Mystery, and Romance* and *The Six Gun Mystique*], Buscombe, Tudor, Collins, Braudy [*The World in a Frame* and "Genre"], MacArthur, Griffith). Later, it shifted to the musical (Altman, Fischer [*Shot/Countershot*, 132–71], Feuer) and to romantic comedy (Gehring, *Screwball Comedy: Defining* and *Screwball Comedy: A Genre*)—more egalitarian narratives in their gender orientation. Most recently, feminist criticism claimed the melodrama as the preferred site of generic interrogation.

Cinematernity argues for a broader exploration of filmic categories, whereby questions of maternity can be located outside of their assumed generic "home." For, as Brenda O. Daly and Maureen T. Reddy write: "The boundaries between genres are fluid. . . . Therefore . . . in the process of redefining mothering it is also necessary to redefine genres and their conventions" (12).

Motherhood and Mass Culture

There is another issue in the dynamics of genre and gender that bears scrutiny—one that exists below the more obvious surface. While criticism has superficially privileged male paradigms (westerns, policiers, war epics, sports sagas), ironically, the genre text *itself* has been seen as a "feminized" cultural form. Here, again, we veer away from genre's "patriarchal" role as cataloger to its "maternal" task of endless propagation and proliferation.

Several critics have commented on the ties between popular entertainment and the "feminine." Andreas Huyssen writes that "mass culture is somehow associated with woman while real, authentic culture
remains the prerogative of men" (191). Significantly, in the film studies
literature, genre is linked to such "feminine" qualities as innocence,
emotion, equivocation, moral instruction, and communality. For Leo
Braudy, "Classics set up a distance between themselves and their audience, compounded of awe and emotional disdain, but genre films, in
their unpretentious and often ambivalent way can be more effectively
didactic. . . . The success of genre films argues a community of feelings
about the world" (*The World in a Frame*, 181).

Beyond such broad feminine references, a submerged association between genre reception and motherhood is found in a critical discourse
that positions the film consumer as an anxious, insecure child. First,
there is the way that scholars connect genre to "the familiar," configuring it as the comforting aesthetic "home." Stanley Solomon writes that
"[g]enre . . . has much to do with the familiar" (6–7). Leo Braudy finds
that "[t]he genre film lures its audience into a seemingly familiar world,
filled with reassuring stereotypes of character, action, and plot"
("Genre," 449). John Cawelti asserts that "[a]udiences find satisfaction
and a basic emotional security in a familiar form" (*Adventure, Mystery,
and Romance*, 9).

Second, many critics have linked genre works to modes of storytelling
performed by mother for child. As Braudy observes, "In genre films the
most obvious focus of interest is neither complex characterization nor
intricate visual style, but pure story . . . [l]ike fairy tales or classical
myths" ("Genre," 452). (Significantly, in *White Heat*, Cody Jarrett's
plan to rob an oil refinery by hiding his gang inside an empty tank trunk
is inspired by the myth of the Trojan horse, a tale told to him as a youth
by his mother.)

Scholars have also likened the reader's engagement with genre to a
naive, ludic fascination. As Cawelti notes, "[T]he escapist aspect of formulaic art makes it analogous to certain kinds of games of play" (*Adventure, Mystery, and Romance*, 19). Finally, critics like Braudy have employed the word *infantile* to describe the response of the gullible genre
audience: "Genre films essentially ask the audience, 'Do you still want to
believe this?' Popularity is the audience answering, 'Yes.' Change in
genre occurs when the audience says, 'That's too infantile a form of
what we believe. Show us something more complicated'" (*The World in
a Frame*, 179).

If the genre audience is childlike, the genre author is procreative. As
Cawelti remarks, "For creators, the formula provides a means for the
rapid and efficient production of new works. . . . Thus formulaic creators

tend to be extremely *prolific*. . . . Others have an even more spectacular record of *quantity and production*" (*Adventure, Mystery, and Romance*, 9, my italics).

Hence, while genre works and their critics have favored masculine perspectives (obscuring issues of womanhood and maternity), the concept of genre has been feminized in its theorization—and subject to a series of maternal/familial metaphors. Thus the category of genre has been positioned in the realm of the cinematic Imaginary, outside the sphere of the masculine Symbolic.

Motherhood and Film Criticism[2]

While it is likely that, throughout film history, critics have touched upon the issue of maternity in the course of discussing particular movies (*Sunrise* [1927], *The Miracle of Morgan's Creek* [1944], or *Penny Serenade* [1941]), the topic has often been ignored. Hence critical discourse has suffered the same kind of "amnesia" about the mother as that which poet Adrienne Rich (quoted in the book's epigraph) detects in *Citizen Kane*. Only recently has serious attention been paid to motherhood. And, clearly, this scrutiny coincided with the rise of the women's movement and of feminist film criticism, two fields that burgeoned in the early 1970s. But, as Maureen Turim has noted, early scholarship often "implicitly or explicitly attacked motherhood . . . as a by-product of the attack on marriage as institution." Only later did feminist criticism valorize issues of "maternal creativity and power" (24).

The Maternal Melodrama

Pioneering work on this subject was done by Molly Haskell in *From Reverence to Rape* (1974)—a book that surveyed the image of women in American film from the teens through the contemporary period. Most noteworthy was Haskell's chapter "The Woman's Film," one of the first attempts to theorize melodrama and the female spectator. In the course of probing a wide range of thematics (the housewife, the career woman, the showgirl), Haskell touches on the topic of motherhood. For her, maternity is depicted on-screen as a strict cultural requirement: melodrama bespeaks "a conviction that children are the reason for getting married

---

[2] In the survey that follows of criticism on issues of motherhood and the cinema, I will not discuss in any depth the literature which I examine in future chapters.

. . . or the only thing holding marriage together . . . , or women's ultimate *raison d'être*, her only worth-confirming 'career'" (169). Ultimately, the genre presents a rather grim picture, while apparently endorsing the status quo. As Haskell writes, "The persistent irony is that [a
woman] is dependent for her well-being and 'fulfillment' on institutions—marriage, motherhood—that by translating the word 'woman'
into 'wife' and 'mother,' end her independent identity" (159–60). Hence
most maternal melodramas focus on "'ordinary' women . . . whose options have been foreclosed by marriage or . . . by children" (160).

One of Haskell's most important insights is to link the maternal melodrama with the theme of *sacrifice* (163). She finds this maudlin motif
most prevalent in Hollywood film: "Children are an obsession in American movies—sacrifice of and for children, the use of children as justification for all manner of sacrifice—in marked contrast to European films
about love and romantic intrigue, where children rarely appear at all and
are almost never the instruments of judgment they are in American
films" (168). Rather than interpret this fixation as evincing a sincere national dedication to parenthood, she sees it as revealing the opposite—
thereby executing one of the first feminist readings of film "against the
grain":

> The surrender of the children for their welfare . . . is a maneuver for circum
> venting the sacred taboo, for getting rid of the children in the guise of ad
> vancing their welfare. (The sacrifice of oneself for one's children is a more
> subtle and metaphorical means to the same end: of venting hostility on the
> children through approved channels.) Both of these transactions represent
> beautifully masked wish fulfillments, suggesting that the myth of obsession—
> the love lavished, the attention paid to children, their constant inclusion in
> the narratives where their presence is not required—is compensation for
> women's guilt, for the deep, inadmissible feelings of not wanting children, or
> not wanting them unreservedly, in the first place. (170)

Building on Haskell's work, later feminist critics explored the genre
in greater depth. In "Who Is without Sin? The Maternal Melodrama in
American Film, 1930–39" (1979), Christian Viviani analyzed a broad
spectrum of films, identifying certain dramatic elements within the
"master" narrative (separation, disgrace, social decline, and the like).
Viviani also focused upon the genre's import for screen actresses: "[A]ny
star worth her salt gave in at least once in her career to the ritual of maternal suffering . . . it was a kind of rite of passage, an ordeal whereby the
actress proved she was a True Actress" (84). The role also served as a
"bridge" for the aging star "between playing the seductress and playing
the 'heavy'" (84). As Viviani's title makes clear, the maternal melodrama

wallows in guilt and retribution: "[I]n its American vein [it] is an apologia for total renunciation, total sacrifice, total self-abnegation" (96).

On the heels of such theorization, certain melodramatic films achieved canonical status and gained selective scholarly recognition. *Mildred Pierce* (1945) is a case in point. Beginning in 1977 with Joyce Nelson's essay "*Mildred Pierce* Reconsidered," there arose a virtual cottage industry dedicated to critiquing this film. Not all the writing, however, centered on issues of maternity.

Nelson, for example, focuses her analysis on the "missing" shot of Mildred's homicidal daughter, Veda (Ann Blyth), in the film's opening murder sequence of Monte Beragon (Zachary Scott). In place of this shot, the narrative "sutures in" an image of Mildred (Joan Crawford) which leads the viewer to believe that she is the culprit. For Nelson, this is one of many ways in which the text annihilates woman's discourse. Further supporting her argument is the manner in which the diegesis "frames" Mildred's domestic story within a drama of male crime detection, and the way it establishes equivalences between Mildred (an independent working mother) and her devious child.

A year later, in Kaplan's *Women in Film Noir*, Pam Cook published "Duplicity in *Mildred Pierce*." Drawing on Nelson's work, she argues that the film involves a stylistic struggle between the masculine genre of film noir and the feminized maternal melodrama—a battle that mirrors the heroine's attempts to achieve independence from patriarchal authority. For Cook, Mildred is ultimately defeated in the film, as an entrepreneurial heroine who is coerced to return to a life as conventional wife and homemaker. Cook is also interested in pursuing the mythic resonances of the text, comparing its dramatic trajectory to J. J. Bachofen's model for the ancient transition from mother- to father-right.

In 1980, Albert J. LaValley published *Mildred Pierce*, a volume in the Wisconsin/Warner Brothers Screenplay Series. While his introduction emphasizes the film's production history (the contributions of its producer, studio, screenwriter, lead actress), he references its status as a "woman's picture" and rehearses the critical debates the film has engendered.

More germane to the concerns of the present study is Andrea Walsh's *Women's Film and Female Experience: 1940–1959* (1984), which includes the chapter "The Evolution of the Maternal Drama in the 1940s" (89–136). While Walsh pursues a variety of themes and texts (female courage in *The Grapes of Wrath* [1940]; the home front in *Since You Went Away* [1943] and *Mrs. Miniver* [1942]; the maternal muse in *I Remember Mama* [1948]), she also examines *Mildred Pierce*. For her, the film is atypical of its genre—darker and more "obsessional" than the usual fare. Relating it to the social context, Walsh sees *Mildred Pierce* as critical of the "overinvested" mother of the 1940s, a pernicious female stereotype.

In Janet Walker's "Feminist Critical Practice: Female Discourse in *Mildred Pierce*," (1982) she critiques the rather negative positions of Nelson and Cook and argues that the tie between Mildred and her daughter Veda represents an icon of female power, despite its perverse valence within the narrative. What is crucial about Walker's work is that she gives *primary* consideration to the issue of maternity, drawing on the insights of Nancy Chodorow to explain the overwhelming love that Mildred feels for her child. Walker's emphasis on this topic attests to the fact that motherhood had by this time achieved more prominence within studies of the woman's picture.

In "Feminist Film Theory: *Mildred Pierce* and the Second World War" (1988), Linda Williams surveys the voluminous literature amassed on *Mildred Pierce* and contends that it frequently ignores the film's historic specificity. For her, what is interesting about the text is its refusal to deal openly with its wartime context—despite its invocation of such timely themes as working women and departing men. For Williams, such "evasion" allows the film to celebrate woman's independence in a manner forbidden in the righteous, war-related dramas.

In "Structural Irony in *Mildred Pierce*, or How Mildred Lost Her Tongue" (1990), Pamela Robertson concerns herself with the film's acoustic dimension. While Mildred's voice-over narration (with its feminine "grain," its womanly earnestness, its talk of domesticity) highlights a female perspective, the film's visual track undercuts that focus, creating a "gendered gap" between sound and image (43). It does so by suggesting that Mildred's look (which is focused on her daughter) is tainted by incestuous longing, hence criticizing her maternal stance.

Finally, in "Too Much Guilt Is Never Enough for Working Mothers: Joan Crawford, *Mildred Pierce* and *Mommie Dearest*" (1992), Mary Beth Haralovich considers the biographical aspects of the film. In a manner consonant with my own prior work on *Imitation of Life* (*Imitation*, 3–28), she connects the screen persona of Mildred Pierce to the star image of Joan Crawford—detailing how the media condemn the working mother, be she actress or restaurateur. As part of this discussion, Haralovich also cites *Mommie Dearest* (a biography by Crawford's adopted daughter) as well as its 1981 filmic adaptation.

It is intriguing to consider precisely *why Mildred Pierce* functioned as an idée fixe within the feminist critical community. Clearly, the film's focus on the mother-daughter bond was suggestive, even before theoretical discourse had given priority to questions of maternity. Furthermore, the film's apparent blame of the working woman allowed a generation of young, female scholarly professionals to confront the ideology of their parents' culture and to comprehend how film had contributed to its dissemination. Finally, the fact of the movie's release during World War II made it resonant for tracing the interrelations of sexism and history.

Several other maternal melodramas have achieved exemplary status within the field. In 1983–1984, a debate surfaced around King Vidor's *Stella Dallas* (1937). What was especially intriguing to scholars was how the film invoked questions of class in relation to standards of mothering. In "The Case of the Missing Mother: Maternal Issues in Vidor's *Stella Dallas*," E. Ann Kaplan sees the text as "perpetuating . . . oppressive patriarchal myths" (127). The film punishes Stella (Barbara Stanwyck) for her refusal to be consumed by parenting and for her desire to maintain her sexual allure. Furthermore, it opposes her to a more ideal, upper-class mother in the form of her ex-husband's second wife. Finally, it requires Stella to relinquish her daughter in the name of martyrdom, moving Stella from a stance of "resistance to passive observ[ation]" (129).

Taking exception to Kaplan's interpretation, Linda Williams (in "'Something Else besides a Mother': *Stella Dallas* and the Maternal Melodrama") finds the text more salutary. Rather than read its ending as oppressive—Stella, now separated from her child, tragically watches her daughter's wedding as an anonymous spectator—Williams finds it resonant with contradictions. Drawing on Chodorow's theories, she sees a parallel between the female child (who must identify with both mother and father) and the female spectator (who identifies with multiple protagonists and subject positions within a film). Hence the viewer of *Stella Dallas* must "alternate between a number of conflicting points of view"—those that criticize Stella and those that renounce that very criticism (155). Central to Williams's argument is the fact that such spectatorship is inscribed within the drama, both in Stella's moviegoing and in her voyeuristic apprehension of her daughter's nuptials.

While Williams seeks to demonstrate the complexity of *mainstream* maternal melodrama, other critics have focused on the work of Douglas Sirk, known for its campy excess. In 1991, I edited a volume on *Imitation of Life* (1959), another text to enter the feminist maternal "pantheon." In my introduction, I characterize the film as an encyclopedic treatise on the working mother—as registered both within and without the diegesis. The film's narrative counterposes two maternal heroines: Lora Meredith (an actress) and Annie Johnson (her maid). Both women are blamed for their parental inadequacies: Lora for being absent and placing career above motherhood; Annie (Juanita Moore) for being omnipresent and suffocating her child. Playing Lora in the film is Lana Turner, a star who (like Joan Crawford) had well-publicized problems

4. *Imitation of Life* (1959). An encyclopedic treatise on the working mother.
MOMA

with her daughter. Also central to the film is a discourse on race, delineating how the role of mothering is farmed out by wealthy white women
to black domestics. Included in the volume are additional articles by
Marina Heung, Paul Willemen, Sandy Flitterman-Lewis, Charles Affron, Michael Stern, Jeremy Butler, and Richard Dyer.

Another work that has achieved privileged status within the canon of
maternal melodrama is Josef von Sternberg's *Blonde Venus* (1932). In
Women and Film: Both Sides of the Camera (1983), E. Ann Kaplan investigates the fetishization of its maternal heroine, Helen (played by
Marlene Dietrich). Kaplan finds this characterization at odds with the
character's parental position and "a way of repressing Motherhood"
(53–54). Kaplan also remarks on von Sternberg's reluctance to cast his
beloved leading lady in a maternal role.

In *The Wages of Sin: Censorship and the Fallen Woman Film, 1928–
1942* (1991), Lea Jacobs confronts *Blonde Venus* for a dual purpose: to
locate aspects of the work that caused censorship problems (the heroine's

status as cabaret performer, adulteress, and prostitute); and to examine how these violations affect the protagonist's figuration as mother (85–105). What Jacobs argues is that industry censors attempted to "rationalize" the film's textual offenses through locating their motivation in conventions of maternal sacrifice. Like Kaplan, however, she finds that the visual and dramatic eccentricities of von Sternberg's text (such as Marlene Dietrich's arch performance and immoderate costuming) refuse any easy accommodation of transgression and maternity.

For Gaylyn Studlar, *Blonde Venus* represents a "subversive" woman's picture in its portrayal of an "eroticized relationship of mother and child." As she notes, Helen's treatment of Johnny infantilizes him: "Although he is said to be five years old, he sleeps in a crib [and she] feeds him by hand and carries him." Given the portrayal of Helen's husband as metaphorically "impotent," Johnny's perverse "assumption of power within the Oedipal triangle" is clear (*In the Realm of Pleasure*, 76).

More recently, the career of Marlene Dietrich has been placed within a biographical frame similar to that constructed around Crawford or Turner. With the publication of a "tell-all" memoir by Dietrich's daughter, the star's screen portrayal as dedicated mother has been juxtaposed with Maria Riva's sordid version of the backstage domestic scene. This issue is made still more intriguing by Riva's claim that *Blonde Venus* was modeled on her own relationship with Dietrich (141), and by the fact that Riva later appeared on-screen with Dietrich in *The Scarlet Empress* (1934) as her mother's younger self (275–80).

Another melodrama that has received much attention is *Now Voyager* (1942). For most critics, the interest of the film lies in the pernicious relationship betweeen Charlotte Vale (Bette Davis) and her mother (Gladys Cooper)—as seen from the filial point of view. Andrea Walsh finds the film paradoxical since it concludes with Charlotte's figuratively adopting her lover's daughter. As Walsh notes, the film is a "tale of liberation from maternal domination and fulfillment through vicarious motherhood" (116). For Maria LaPlace, Mrs. Vale stands for sexual repression, as she prevents Charlotte from having any passionate liaisons. The narrative trajectory of the film charts Charlotte's move toward personal autonomy through separation from her destructive parent. According to LaPlace, the romantic hero of the woman's picture is a mother-substitute—"a 'maternal' man, capable of nurturing the heroine" (159). Lea Jacobs makes a related point in focusing upon the issue of the heroine's tenuous control of the discourse. In the beginning of the film, "Mrs. Vale effectively reduces her daughter to silence." While later in the narrative Charlotte gains access to speech, "[t]his form of enunciation becomes available to [her] through the male characters in the film" ("*Now Voyager*," 93). E. Ann Kaplan sees *Now Voyager* in relation to aspects of cultural history. Produced when psychoanalytic theories were being popularized in the United States, it displays a "Freudian awareness of Oedipality" as well as a sense of the "split" between good mother and bad (*Motherhood and Representation*, 110, 112). Furthermore, Kaplan sees its sadistic treatment of Mrs. Vale as a perverse reaction to the growing power of women during World War II.

Another maternal melodrama, *Letter from an Unknown Woman* (1948), has been frequently analyzed—in my own work (*Shot/Countershot*, 89–110), and in that of Modleski ("Time and Desire") and Virginia Wright Wexman (*Letter from an Unknown Woman*). What interested me about the film was the heroine's stance as an unwed mother who, when abandoned by her paramour, stoically and silently bears his son. Thus Lisa (Joan Fontaine) creates, through procreation, a male child-substitute for her callow, absent lover, Stefan (Louis Jourdan). Modleski is less interested in issues of motherhood than she is in the film's invocation of both male and female forms of hysteria. For Wexman, the import of *Letter* is its engagement of turn-of-the-century Vienna (the locus of many films by Max Ophüls). It is within this context that she understands the rebellious maternal heroine, a woman "[r]ejecting . . . traditional norms . . . yearn[ing] for the new world of ineffability represented by Stefan. . . . Unlike Stefan, however, Lisa's sexuality has consequences: pregnancy, marriage, and years that she would 'prefer not to remember'" (7).

While *Blonde Venus*, *Mildred Pierce*, *Stella Dallas*, *Now Voyager*, *Letter from an Unknown Woman*, and *Imitation of Life* have received selective attention, other films have also inspired critics on the topic of maternity: *Reckless Moment* (1949) has been examined by Mary Ann Doane (92–96) for its conjunction of maternal melodrama with the film noir mode. *Hard, Fast and Beautiful* has been considered by Wendy Dozoretz for its depiction of the mother-daughter bond—which eclipses the maternal voice by substituting a set of male nurturers (father and lover). In her book *All That Hollywood Allows: Re-Reading Gender in 1950s Melodrama*, Jackie Byars includes a section titled "Stories of Mothers and Daughters" (146–58). Focusing on such classic films as *Magnificent Obsession* (1954), *All That Heaven Allows* (1955), *Picnic* (1956), and *Peyton Place* (1958), she sees the maternal "woman's picture" as one in which a heroine begins by being involved in a "communit[y] of women and children" (147); she then, "for personal reasons, strives to create or recreate a triad" (148). This closure comes through the inclusion of a "sensitive" male figure whom Byars terms the "intruder-redeemer" (149, 155). Hence the maternal melodrama is, ironically, a form in which a male protagonist is central. In a chapter of her book on Alfred Hitchcock (*The Women Who Knew Too Much*, 43–55),

Tania Modleski focuses on *Rebecca*, a film that is not, superficially, about motherhood. Nonetheless, Modleski finds within the work's narrative a submerged maternal discourse. In the drama of a young newlywed who confronts her obsession with her husband's awesome deceased wife, Modleski sees a symbolic replay of the female Oedipal crisis, whereby a daughter must transcend her mother's realm to be free for heterosexual union.

Beyond the original impact of these diverse feminist essays, they have had a secondary life and influence through republication within important anthologies. Texts by Viviani, Williams, Kaplan, Doane, Modleski, LaPlace, and myself were incorporated into Christine Gledhill's *Home Is Where the Heart Is: Studies in Melodrama and the Woman's Film*, Patricia Erens's *Issues in Feminist Film Criticism*, and Marcia Landy's *Imitations of Life: A Reader on Film and Television Melodrama*.

Aside from analyzing individual films, critics have continued to theorize the broader genre of maternal melodrama. In *The Desire to Desire* (1987), Mary Ann Doane examines the woman's picture of the 1940s and offers an entire chapter entitled "Pathos and the Maternal" (70–95). In comparison to Haskell's earlier study, Doane's is more informed by film theory and psychoanalytic discourse. As her chapter title indicates, Doane sees the maternal melodrama as ruled by the "pathetic"—an affect that entails a fundamental disproportion "between desires and their fulfillment or between [a] transgression . . . and the punishment associated with it" (86). Doane finds the poignancy of the form augmented by its various dramatic strategies: blockages of expression and frustrating delays (90). As she notes, "Pathos is . . . related to a certain construction of temporality in which communication or recognitions take place but are mistimed" (91). Doane also deems maternal representation a discourse of the "obvious" (70), well suited to the melodramatic form, which is "immediately readable" and almost "*too* explicit" (71). Often, maternal love is counterposed to romantic longing, marking it as "a sign of the impossibility of female desire" (94). Finally, Doane illuminates how maternal melodrama is transformed by the exigencies of its cultural milieu. During the war, for example, the theme of "separation and return" was displaced from its usual mother-and-child locus onto the dynamic of husband and wife (78). Likewise, the sin of excessive mothering was tied to a politics of international isolationism (81).

Certainly E. Ann Kaplan has been one of the premier scholars to foreground motherhood in the cinema. While she broached this topic in her first two books, her central work on the subject is *Motherhood and Representation: The Mother in Popular Culture and Melodrama* (1992).

Kaplan begins by surveying the historical field (from 1830 to 1960) for its conceptions of maternity, identifying discourses around the "early modern, high-modernist and postmodern mother" (20). She then explores psychoanalytic models of motherhood, drawing on the theories of Sigmund Freud, Jacques Lacan, Melanie Klein, Nancy Chodorow, Hélène Cixous, and Julia Kristeva. But the major part of her study is devoted to close analyses of literary and filmic texts, which she links to certain psychodramatic "paradigms." As the book's subtitle indicates, the focus is, once more, on the maternal *melodrama*. Among patriarchy's favored female portrayals is that of the sacrificing madonna, and Kaplan traces its inscription in the novelistic and filmic versions of Mrs. Henry (Ellen) Wood's *East Lynne*. On the opposite end of the traditional spectrum is the pernicious "phallic" mother, a figure whom Kaplan examines in *Now Voyager* and *Marnie* (1964). For Kaplan, the texts in which such malign stereotypes circulate are "complicit" ones, reinforcing patriarchal assumptions. Contrasted to these are works that "resist" such misogynist underpinnings, opening up "a space for critical appraisal of *how* women are constructed or positioned" within conventional society. Under the rubric of resistant works, Kaplan names literary texts, including *Uncle Tom's Cabin* (1861) and *Herland* (1915); and such cinematic works as *The Blot* (1921), *The Crowd* (1928), *Applause* (1929), *Christopher Strong* (1933), *Craig's Wife* (1936), *Imitation of Life* (1934/1959), and *Stella Dallas*. In her final chapter, Kaplan brings the discussion around to the 1980s and finds dramatic shifts in society's conception of motherhood. Among the changes she documents are the growing media prominence of the "nurturing" father, the problematic depiction of the working mother, and the complications wrought by modern reproductive technologies. She articulates her points by reference to such films as *Baby Boom* (1988), *Parenthood* (1989), and *Look Who's Talking* (1990).

Other critics have confronted questions of reproductive rights as narrativized in the cinema. In "The Way We Weren't: Abortion 1950s Style in *Blue Denim* and *Our Time*" (1992), Nina C. Leibman examines two films—one made in the 1950s (when abortion was illegal) and one made in the 1970s (in the wake of the *Roe v. Wade* decision). She finds that in *Blue Denim* (1959), the struggle around a young girl's decision to terminate a pregnancy is transposed to her boyfriend, thus reframing "abortion as a choice for men" (33). While *Our Time* (1974) sets out to be more progressive (in its retrospective look at barbaric abortion conditions of the 1950s), Leibman finds that it finally represents the act as a "fatal punishment"—"the ultimate comeuppance for promiscuous women" (41). In the course of her investigation, Leibman not only analyzes the two films but discusses the 1956 lifting of Production Code restrictions on the depiction of abortion. She also examines the films' promotional campaigns and their critical receptions.

While most Anglo-American work on maternal melodrama has privileged the Hollywood tradition, some research has taken a more international perspective. In *Shot/Countershot: Film Tradition and Women's Cinema* (1989), I examine Ingmar Bergman's *Persona* (1966), a work that might be deemed a postmodern woman's picture (63–80). While on the surface *Persona* is a study of insanity, social masquerade, and theatricality (and has little to do with motherhood), appearances are deceptive. For the film implies that actress Elisabeth Vogler (Liv Ullmann) has gone mad because she is a cold and rejecting parent. Likewise, her neurotic nurse Alma (Bibi Andersson) is tortured by the memory of an abortion in her youth. Hence female derangement is tied to the refusal of motherhood—an "unnatural" position for woman.

In *Kino and the Woman Question: Feminism and Soviet Silent Film* (1989), Judith Mayne analyzes Vsevolod Pudovkin's *Mother* (1926), based upon a novel by Maxim Gorky. What she finds provocative about the film is that it charts the politicization of a figure usually seen "outside of production, and outside of political life in general" (93). While that aspect of the work is progressive, Mayne finds it significant that the mother's transformation comes only on behalf of her revolutionary son. As Mayne notes, "[S]he is a social being only *because* she is a mother" (105). Likewise, Mayne finds both the maternal and revolutionary discourses of the film inscribed within the framework of the natural—a cliché that dulls the work's radical potential.

In both her books on national cinema, Marcia Landy examines the maternal melodrama. In *British Genres* (1991), she notes how "the British cinema offers [only] a few instances of the genre" (203). She then proceeds to analyze *Illegal* (1932), a work about a mother who must endure the exploits of a gambler-husband and struggle to support her daughters. Like its Hollywood counterparts, the film stresses themes of sacrifice, "discipline and progressive isolation" (204). In *Fascism in Film* (1986), Landy finds strains of the maternal melodrama in the Italian cinema of the 1930s and 1940s. As she remarks: "Where the image of the mother . . . is dominant, the emphasis is on the bond between the mother and the daughter as a guarantor of nonpromiscuous relations. Everywhere is inscribed the subordination of the woman: to parental figures, to children, and . . . to the cause of fascism" (115).

In "Preliminary Thoughts on the *Haha-mono* Films of Japan," Patricia Erens confronts an Asian genre that is comparable to the Hollywood maternal melodrama. For Erens, the popularity of the *haha-mono* film is tied to the Japanese emphasis on the mother-child relation (especially

5. *Persona* (1966). Female derangement is tied to the refusal of motherhood. MOMA

that of mother and son). In comparing the genre to its American counterpart, Erens finds that the *haha-mono* film differs in its refusal to introduce a love story into the maternal discourse. Erens then goes on to apply her theoretical insights to an analysis of Keisuke Kinoshita's *A Japanese Tragedy* (1953).

In "Nursery/Rhymes: Primal Scenes in *La Maternelle*," Sandra Flitterman discusses a French film about an orphaned child who becomes emotionally attached to a young cleaning woman employed at the nursery school she attends. Flitterman analyzes how the child's spurned affections for her mother are transferred to the maid. Also transposed, however, are the child's feelings of hostility toward any man who separates her from a real or surrogate maternal figure. While most maternal melodramas foreground the mother, Flitterman finds it significant that *La Maternelle* aligns its perspective with the child—playing and replaying, through a series of point-of-view sequences, versions of the traumatic primal scene.

Other Genres

While it is clear how the maternal melodrama has claimed center stage, critics have begun to query other genres on the topic of maternity.

Recently, Virginia Wright Wexman (in *Creating the Couple*) has returned to one of the earliest genres considered in film criticism: the *western*. Rather than focus exclusively on the macho cowboy hero, she discloses a maternal discourse in the form:

> Because of their importance as the bearers and nurturers of children, women are almost invariably seen in Westerns as mothers or potential mothers. The protagonists of these films rarely have fathers, but they frequently have mothers, and "Ma" is a revered figure. The schoolmarm character, who often becomes identified as an ideal marriage partner, is seen as fit for this role largely because of her identification with children and nurturance. (83)

Other feminist critics have considered the *horror film*, uncovering its own maternal discourse. For Barbara Creed, the genre represents female deviance in "relation to [woman's] mothering and reproductive functions." As such, this vision wears a variety of faces: "the archaic mother; the monstrous womb; the witch; the vampire; and the possessed woman" (7). Hence Creed analyzes such issues as grotesque procreation in *The Brood* (1979) and the castrating mother in *Psycho* (1960). Carol Clover has also lent a feminist reading to the horror film in *Men, Women, and Chain Saws* (1992). While the focus of her work is not on motherhood, the subject does enter in her reading of certain films. In Brian De Palma's *Carrie* (1976), she sees the heroine as a victim of a "monstrous mother" (4). In such slasher films as *Psycho* (1960) and *The Eyes of Laura Mars* (1978) (to be discussed in chapter 7 below), she sees the texts' psychopathic heroes as "in the grip of boyhood" and the maternal (26, 28).

One of the major areas in which motherhood has been considered is *science fiction*. In "Time Travel, Primal Scene, and the Critical Dystopia," Constance Penley reads films like *The Terminator* (1984) and *Back to the Future* (1985) as dramatizing infantile curiosity about the mother. As she states, "The desire represented in the time travel story, of both witnessing one's own conception and being one's own mother and father, is similar to the primal scene fantasy" (72). She also sees science fiction heroines (like Ripley in *Aliens* [1986]) as fitting a maternal paradigm: "What we get finally is a conservative moral lesson about maternity, futuristic or otherwise; mothers will be mothers, and they will *always* be women" (77). Similarly, Ellen Bishop, in examining *Brazil* (1985), finds that despite the film's progressive gender reversals, it ultimately favors a vision of "dichotomously structured sex vested in woman-as-Mother for the panic-stricken, postmodern male" (91). Turning back to silent film history, Roger Dadoun examines Fritz Lang's *Metropolis* (1926), reading the doubled character of Maria as an incarnation of the archetypal Good and Bad Mother. Furthermore, he finds, in several scenes of the film, a replay of the primal scene, whereby a child discovers the mother engaged in sexual activity.

In a special issue of *The Velvet Light Trap*, *Parenting and Reproduction* (1992), scholars consider the *documentary* mode as it represents the act of childbirth. In "Performing Birth: The Construction of Female Bodies in Instructional Childbirth Videos," Lori Shorr contrasts two sets of works: mainstream "natural childbirth" videos (available at commercial rental stores) and "underground" midwife videos (accessible only through a circuit of practitioners). While the former texts focus on public, institutional space (the hospital) and emphasize the presence of the husband-coach, the latter are set in the private sphere (the home) and engage a community of women. While the first group almost pornographically segment and objectify the female body, the second frequently align the camera with the mother's vision. Finally, the midwife films refuse to employ extensive editing to excise the protracted process of childbirth. Instead, they celebrate the disturbing confusion between the birthing and birthed bodies. In "In Search of the Mother Tongue: Childbirth and the Cinema," Robin Blaetz highlights the aural elements of reproduction, drawing on the work of Kaja Silverman (discussed below). Blaetz contends that while the birthing female voice, with its unruly screams, moans, and sighs, is potentially a source of nonpatriarchal language ("the mother tongue"), it has been consistently suppressed within classical cinema. Pointing to films like *Stagecoach* (1939) or *Stella Dallas*, she describes how childbirth takes place offscreen, with its acoustic register silenced. In contrast to these works, she examines such feminist documentaries as Marjorie Keller's *Misconception* (1977) and Joyce Chopra and Claudia Weill's *Joyce at 34* (1976)—both of which offer the sounds of childbirth as part of their treatment of the process.

On occasion, avant-garde cinema has been the site of an investigation of maternity. In *Women and Film: Both Sides of the Camera*, Kaplan considers two such works (171–88). *Riddles of the Sphinx* (1976), made by Laura Mulvey and Peter Wollen, is noteworthy for its identification with the point of view of the mother—a rather uncommon phenomenon, even in feminist art. While raising material questions about woman's domestic labor, the film invokes the mythic dimension of patriarchy, counterposing the pedestrian mother to the fantastic Sphinx.[3] In Michelle

---

[3] I also discuss *Riddles of the Sphinx* in *Shot/Countershot* (49–62).

Citron's *Daughter Rite* (1978), Kaplan finds the child's perspective central, as the film regales us with a litany of complaints against Mother. While Kaplan appreciates Citron's location of such filial anger in a context of social constraints, she critiques the work for executing a "double negation" of the maternal voice (187).

Maureen Turim also considers motherhood and the avant-garde in confronting the experimental videotape *Born to Be Sold: Martha Rosler Reads the Strange Case of Baby S/M*—a wry commentary on the infamous case of a surrogate mother (Mary Beth Whitehead) who refused to relinquish her birth child to Bill and Elizabeth Stern. While Turim admires the "spunk" of Rosler's video essay (22), she takes exception to aspects of its style and politics: its occasional flippancy (transforming the initials of the baby's dual names [Sarah/Melissa] into "S and M"); its reification of childbirth as the site of maternal truth; its failure to acknowledge feminist support of Whitehead; its refusal to investigate the relation between surrogacy and general practices of adoption. Turim concludes by calling for a "theory of pregnancy, childbirth, and child-rearing [that is] adequate to our current technology and society" (23).

Film Theory and the Maternal

While the aforementioned literature locates a maternal discourse in genre criticism and/or in the explication of individual cinematic texts, a maternal theme is also evident in the broader corpus of film theory.[4]

Some critics have invoked the maternal in their investigation of the structure of *filmic narrative*. Raymond Bellour, for instance, sees classical diegesis as ruled by a familial drama. In a 1979 interview, he advances the notion that mainstream cinema (inspired by the nineteenth-century novel) is fueled by an Oedipal trajectory that locates the hero's heterosexual desire in a dislocated longing for the mother. As he notes:

> My constant surprise . . . was to discover to what degree everything was organized according to a classical Oedipal scenario which inscribed the subject, the hero of the film, in a precise position in relation to parricide and incest, and to observe that his itinerary, his trajectory . . . corresponded to a strict psychic progression and had as their function to engage the hero in the symbolic paths of Oedipus and of castration: namely . . . to make him accept the symbolization of the death of the father, the displacement from the attach-

---

[4] First, it should be noted that I do not wish to make a hard and fast distinction between film criticism and theory. Many of the works already discussed have a significant theoretical component, though it is focused on a particular text or genre. Second, the theme of maternity within film theory will also be considered in chapter 3 on *Way Down East*.

ment to the mother to the attachment to another woman. Which simply
means accepting the place of the subject in the Western family. (Quoted in
Bergstrom, 93)

Hence, for Bellour, the mother (in narrative) occasions the hero's psychic detour: she is a figure to be avoided in the name of another. If the
mother is desired at all, it is only as mediated through her surrogate—
the proper love object who may bear her obscure traces.

Building on these observations, Teresa de Lauretis, in *Alice Doesn't*
(1984), offers a feminist critique of such paradigms (103–57). Crucial
to her argument is the identification of the female/maternal figure with
the hero's "obstacle," which he overcomes in the course of his adventure. As she writes, "[B]ecause the obstacle, whatever its personifica-
tion, is morphologically female [it is] indeed, simply, the womb" (119).
Hence the "cinema works for Oedipus" (153), and woman can either
passively "take her place where Oedipus will find her awaiting *him*" (the
princess) or actively function as the pernicious barrier to his quest (the
Sphinx).

Still other critics have seen *film viewing* as tied to infantile psychic
processes. In his essay "The Apparatus" (1976), Jean-Louis Baudry examines the ideological implications of the cinema setup: the darkened
room, the projected light, the shadows on the screen, the audience.
Baudry finds a parallel between this situation and Plato's myth of the
cave, in which prisoners (chained there since birth) watch shadows projected on the wall and mistake them for the real world. Baudry links
both Plato's cave and the cinema to yet another text—Freud's theories
of dream and the unconscious. Like the prisoners in Plato's womblike
cave, Baudry configures film spectators as engaged in a regression toward an infantile state that reestablishes an illusory dyad with the
mother.

On one level, Baudry sees this state as almost prenatal. He tells us that
cinema replicates the dream, and that, according to Freud, "[s]leep . . .
is *a revivescence of one's stay in the body of the mother*" (Baudry, 114). But
on another level, the cinema (and dream) also hark back to the oral stage.
Here Baudry draws on Bertram Lewin's notion of the dream screen, a
phenomenon that presents "itself in all dreams as the indispensable support for the projection of images." Ultimately, Lewin sees this dream
screen as a "hallucinatory representation of the mother's breast on
which the child used to fall asleep after nursing" (Baudry, 116). Thus
the cinema apparatus may be likened to the mother not only in its repli-
cation of a dream/womb state, but in its presentation of a surface for
imagery, like the maternal breast on which the dozing infant once projected its fantasies. For Baudry, the presuppositions of the cinema, the

exhibition circumstances and equipment themselves, solicit and answer the spectator's need for regression toward maternal union and, in this sense, constitute a device of wish fulfillment.

As I indicated in *Shot/Countershot* (70–80), there is no film that so embodies Baudry's notion of the "maternal" film screen as Bergman's *Persona*. This work is also of great interest to Robert Eberwein in his book *Film and the Dream Screen: A Sleep and a Forgetting* (120–39). Eberwein reworks Lewin's seminal theory by stressing how film "makes us babies again, and reverses the process of ego differentiation by plunging us back in memory to that moment of identification with the source of nutrition," that is, the mother (42). For him, the cinema's capacity for close-up functions "in a most important way as a revival of our experience of the archetypal mass we recall only dimly—the breast, the face, the combination of these. . . . The face in the close-up is, in essence, the mother's face, the breast, the primal unity of infancy" (42).

One of the most influential treatises in feminist film theory is Laura Mulvey's 1975 essay "Visual Pleasure and Narrative Cinema" (reprint, 1989)—an essay that, like Baudry's, attempts to describe the psychodynamics of film viewing. While Mulvey does not speak directly of the mother, she does tie male spectatorship to infantile experience, thus implying a maternal presence. Primary among the phenomena operant in film spectatorship is the syndrome of fetishism. According to Freud, this orientation occurs when a young boy sees his mother naked and is shocked by her anatomical "omission." Fearing castration, he (as part of his Oedipal fantasy) compensates for his mother's "lack" by fixating on objects that substitute for her missing penis and which come to have an erotic charge. For Mulvey, many female film stars (like Marlene Dietrich in the works of Josef von Sternberg) are imbued with a fetishistic aura in their costuming and photographic treatment. Hence we might surmise that the specter of the mother manquée haunts the cinema, even in the apparent plenitude of its premier actresses. Furthermore, Mulvey sees the narratives of many films (*Vertigo, Rear Window, Marnie*) as driven by fetishistic metaphors. Mulvey also addresses the dominance in the cinema of scopophilia—a related syndrome whereby the look is eroticized and the film image is transformed "into something satisfying in itself" (21). In this dynamic, the male is the active bearer of the gaze and the female is its passive recipient.[5] As a complex, voyeurism also has ties

---

[5] Following "Visual Pleasure and Narrative Cinema," Mulvey rethought her ideas on film spectatorship in an article entitled "Afterthoughts on 'Visual Pleasure and Narrative Cinema' Inspired by King Vidor's *Duel in the Sun* (1946)." There she focused not on situations that relate to the position of the mother but on issues of bisexuality in female childhood development. She cites those tendencies to explain how the female viewer can actually identify, to some degree, with both male and female characters on-screen.

to the maternal figure since, according to Freudian theory, it is first prac-
ticed in the primal scene, as the child spies on his parents while they are
having sex.

A maternal discourse is also central to Gaylyn Studlar's analysis of the
cinematic aesthetics of Josef von Sternberg (whose *Blonde Venus* we
have earlier considered). In "Visual Pleasure and the Masochistic Aesthetic" (1985), she counters Mulvey's claim that classical cinema is
ruled by a male voyeuristic dynamic, asserting that a masochistic dimension is also present. Drawing upon the work of Gilles Deleuze, she shifts
the focus from the Oedipal to the pre-Oedipal stage—when the infant is
especially tied to the mother. During this period (before the intervention of the father and the patriarchal Symbolic), the mother represents
no phallic Lack but an awesome presence. As Studlar notes, "[T]he
child perceives the mother not an auxillary [*sic*] to the father, but an
independent, powerful, and even threatening figure" (7). For her, this
dynamic is best encapsulated in von Sternberg's cinema, in which a passive male (e.g., Professor Rath in *The Blue Angel* [1930]) succumbs to
the cruel machinations of a femme fatale (Lola Lola) who stands in for
the Primal Mother. While in Studlar's formulation, woman assumes a
kind of power unavailable to her in Mulvey's conception, that force is
seen as largely pernicious.

Although most theorists of the filmic apparatus have concentrated on
the image track, some have explicated the acoustic dimension. In *Unheard Melodies: Narrative Film Music* (1987), Claudia Gorbman relates
sound to maternity. Writing on the topic of spectatorial response to the
film score, she summarizes the literature in the field (citing, among others, Nancy Wood, Guy Rosolato and Didier Anzieu): "The underlying
pleasure of music can be traced to originary hallucinations of bodily fusion with the mother, of nonseparation prior to the Oedipal crisis of
language and interdiction" (64). For many critics, such reverberations
make film music function as a means to bypass psychic censorship: "In
practical terms this means . . . a lowered threshold of belief, a greater
predisposition for the subject to accept film's pseudo-perceptions as
his/her own" (64). Hence, according to canonical criticism, the maternal voice seduces the viewer (through a musical surrogate) into a naive
fusion with the fictional screen world.

Drawing on the same French theory, Kaja Silverman focuses more
emphatically on the maternal position in *The Acoustic Mirror: The Female Voice in Psychoanalysis and Cinema* (1988). In reviewing the literature, she finds that the maternal voice has been conceived in two major
ways. For Michel Chion, it has a rather "sinister inflection" (Silverman,
72). If it is the first voice that the developing human hears, it is also
associated with the "terror of an 'umbilical night'" (Silverman, 72). For

Guy Rosolato, on the other hand, the maternal voice is a "sonorous envelope" that "surrounds, sustains and cherishes the child" (Silverman, 81) in an "operatic" manner. Making an analogy to cinema spectatorship, Silverman conceives the maternal voice as a "voice-off" for the fetus. She then traces a maternal thematic discourse in such films as *Diva* (1982), wherein a young man "steals" the voice of an older opera singer by surreptitiously taping her concert. Silverman also examines the sexual politics of vocal synchronization and nonsynchronization, noting that feminist film often favors the latter since it breaks cinema's obsession with female embodiment.

Thus while the theorization of a maternal discourse in film originally focused on the image (and ignored "abject" sound), it eventually comes around to consider the acoustic domain. In a sense this "discovery" of sound as a vital and complex cinematic element replays the recent revelation of the maternal figure's role as central to filmic representation.

Cinematernity

Having summarized the literature in the field, I will draw upon it to consider the representation of motherhood in diverse cinematic forms. In chapter 2, I concentrate on turn-of-the-century "trick films," the genre around which I first confronted the issue of motherhood in 1979. I realize now—with some embarrassment for my prior obtuseness—that, at the time, I was beginning (almost unconsciously) to consider having a child myself. This retrospective insight has made me aware of how one's intellectual work is related, sometimes obliquely, to one's personal and emotional life. In successive chapters, I examine, in turn, silent melodrama, the horror movie, the crime film, screen comedy, the thriller, the postmodern film, and the documentary.

Although each chapter will be unified by a concentration on a specific genre, I will make no sweeping generalizations about the *entire* mode. Rather, I will identify resonant patterns that obtain for an important subgroup within the overall category (for example, the absence of the maternal figure in film comedy, the play with maternal transvestism in postmodernism). Furthermore, I will interrogate the relationship between such thematic structures and the nature of the genre per se, examining, for instance, why horror may be a popular and "appropriate" form in which to register childbirth anxieties.

While many of the chapters examine a *series* of films or videos (the magic film in chapter 2, the comedy in chapter 6, the thriller in chapter 7, the documentary in chapter 9), some sections concentrate on an in-depth analysis of a *single* work (the melodramatic text in chapter 3, the horror film in chapter 4).

Most of the films that I have chosen to examine are from the American cinema (e.g., *Rosemary's Baby, Way Down East, The Kid, Brats, His Girl Friday, White Heat, The Hand That Rocks the Cradle, The Guardian, Grey Gardens, The Ties That Bind, History and Memory*). In a few cases, European films are discussed, but it is generally within the context of a broader group that includes American film. In the chapter on comedy, for instance, I examine the French film *Three Men and a Cradle*, but partly because it is the basis for the later American farce *Three Men and a Baby*. In the chapter on postmodern film, I analyze the Spanish film *High Heels*, but only because it is a remake of the American classic *Imitation of Life* (1959). In the chapter on documentary, I discuss Belgian filmmaker Chantal Akerman's *News from Home*, but only because it is a work that she made in the United States. In the chapter on the trick film, I examine the work of Georges Méliès, but I discuss his American counterparts as well (e.g., Edison, Porter). In the chapter on the thriller, I discuss the British films *The Nanny* (1965) and *The Chalk Garden* (1964), but only in relation to two American films of the 1990s. Clearly, the conclusions I reach are applicable only to the Western film tradition, and additional work must be done to explore their relevance to other cultures. Within the Anglo-American sphere, however, I do engage issues of race and nationality. In the chapter on feminist documentaries concerning the mother-daughter bond and in the epilogue, I consider works by black American and British artists, as well as by Asian Americans.

Over the course of the book, I employ diverse methodologies to examine the genre text—often drawing on several approaches within one section. In numerous chapters (like those on the trick film, the thriller, and the documentary), I invoke psychoanalytic models. In others (like that on the trick film), I draw on anthropological material. In many chapters, I bring to bear sociohistorical research (on the treatment of the unwed mother in chapter 3, on the history of childbirth in chapter 4, on the plight of the returning World War II veteran in chapter 5, on the legacy of child care and wet-nursing in chapter 7). In several chapters, I place texts within a film historical frame (as in my discussion of comedy, of the thriller, and of the postmodern). In all essays, I employ strategies of close textual reading—both formally and thematically.

Beyond a diverse generic focus, each chapter will address a *different aspect of the issue of motherhood*, moving the book along on a broader sociohistorical level. Thus the chapter on the "trick film" examines the notion of male "womb envy"; the chapter on melodrama studies attitudes toward illegitimate birth; the chapter on the horror film surveys the psychology of parturition; the chapter on the crime film confronts the mother-son relationship; the chapter on comedy investigates related fantasies of "male mothering"; the chapter on the thriller explores contemporary hysteria around child care; the chapter on postmodern film tackles the notion of the "remake" and its metaphoric implications regarding cinema and birth; the chapter on the documentary illuminates the mother-daughter bond and its intersection with questions of race and nationality. Hence the study progresses on a *thematic* as well as on a generic basis. As the above topics suggest, the book addresses not only issues of film history, genre, and theory but broader questions of cultural studies. In investigating such subjects as illegitimate birth, the psychology of pregnancy, the mother-child relation, the problems of child care, issues of motherhood and race, I seek to place each work within a social-historical context and to draw from the fields of history, psychoanalysis, sociology, medicine, feminist studies, critical theory, and entertainment studies.

In general, the book confirms feminist perceptions that motherhood in the cinema has been a site of "crisis." In many films, the mother is blamed for her transgressions or for the ills she visits upon her offspring (birthing a bastard in *Way Down East*, child neglect in *High Heels*, raising a deviant in *White Heat*, and so forth). Significantly, while both *High Heels* and *White Heat* chastise the mother for producing a murderer, in the former film the maternal sin is absence, while in the latter it is overinvolvement—a paradox that instances how motherhood is continually imbricated in a series of conundrums and double binds. In other films, the heroine's experience of maternity is fraught with hysteria and anxiety (*Rosemary's Baby*, *News from Home*, *The Hand That Rocks the Cradle*). In some works, the mother is, essentially, excluded from the text (as in the male-mothering escapades of classic comedy, the prestidigitation of trick films, and the transvestism of the postmodern text). While a certain misogyny appears to be pervasive, there are works that address the female spectator more progressively. While, on the surface, *Rosemary's Baby* paints a picture of childbirth as satanic terror, on a deeper plane, it facilitates the expression of *legitimate* female concerns and worries about parturition, countering more accepted Pollyanna attitudes. Similarly, in the genre of feminist "matrilineal" cinema, we find daughters celebrating and speaking for their mothers, removing them from the realm of essentialism and locating them within the frames of race and history.

I conclude the book with a chapter that focuses on metaphors of procreation and artistry, a trope that has dominated the literary and filmic imagination. But while in the theoretical literature creation has been seen as figuratively analogous to childbirth, in the material world maternity and cultural production have been perceived as social "contradictions"—a destructive dichotomy that has plagued and silenced women. Thus I will end the book by examining how female writers and directors have imagined the connection between motherhood and creation in order to trace this theme through a body of films in which the heroine struggles to be an artist and a parent, including *Finding Christa* (1991), *High Tide* (1987), *The Sandpiper* (1965), and *Applause* (1929).

If truth be told, this struggle has bedeviled me as well, as an author/mother (and high melodramatic protagonist) who has tried to calibrate both aspects of her life. Paradoxically, the tension has been both a stimulus and a challenge to my work. But if I believed (as so many films proclaim) that the mother could not, dare not, or ought not, speak—or should wait for the feminist daughter to ventriloquize her—in what voice could I, the parent of a son, have written this book?

My autobiographical musings remind me of the words of novelist Jamaica Kincaid, who once quipped that by writing at home amid her family, she "managed to make the way [she] earn[s] a living into a domestic activity" (quoted in Lee, C10). I have, apparently, been more clever yet: in theorizing motherhood, I have managed to make "a domestic activity" into "the way I earn a living."

In the poem "Amnesia" that serves as this book's epigraph, Adrienne Rich bemoans how, in *Citizen Kane* (1941), the young Charles is forced to leave his mother, as snow falls on his childhood home. Rich queries, "[W]hy must the snow-scene blot itself out . . . over the something that gets left behind?" Though, on one level, the "something" to which she refers is, clearly, Charles's sled (his beloved "Rosebud"), on another, it is also his female parent. *Cinematernity* is an attempt to confront the cultural and artistic "anmesia" around mother that Rich, so eloquently, decries—to "recall" the importance of the maternal register within cinematic discourse.

Works Cited

Altman, Rick, ed. *Genre: The Musical*. London, Boston, Henley: Routledge and Kegan Paul, 1981.

Anzieu, Didier. "L'enveloppe sonore du soi." *Nouvelle revue de psychanalyse* 13 (Spring 1976): 161–79.

Bachofen, J. J. *Myth, Religion and Mother Right*. Princeton, NJ: Princeton University Press, 1973.

Baudry, Jean-Louis. "The Apparatus." *Camera Obscura*, no. 1 (1976): 104–26.

Bergstrom, Janet. "Alternation, Segmentation, Hypnosis: Interview with Raymond Bellour." *Camera Obscura*, nos. 3–4 (1979): 71–103.

Bishop, Ellen. "Feminism, Postmodernism, and Science Fiction: Gendered Logics and Structures of Thought." Ph.D. diss., University of Pittsburgh, 1995.

Blaetz, Robin. "In Search of the Mother Tongue: Childbirth and the Cinema." *Velvet Light Trap*, no. 29 (Spring 1992): 15–20.

———. "You're Going to Live If I Have to Blow Your Brains Out: War, Childbirth, and *The Big Red One*." Paper delivered at the meeting of the Society for Cinema Studies, Pittsburgh, PA, April 1992.

Braudy, Leo. "Genre: The Conventions of Connection." In *Film Theory and Criticism*, 2d ed., edited by Gerald Mast and Marshall Cohen, 443–68. New York: Oxford University Press, 1979.

———. *The World in a Frame: What We See in Films*. New York: Anchor-Doubleday, 1976.

Buscombe, Edward. "The Idea of Genre in the American Cinema." In Grant, 24–38.

Byars, Jackie. *All That Hollywood Allows: Re-Reading Gender in 1950s Melodrama*. Chapel Hill and London: University of North Carolina Press, 1991.

Cawelti, John G. *Adventure, Mystery, and Romance: Formula Stories as Art and Popular Culture*. Chicago and London: University of Chicago Press, 1976.

———. *The Six Gun Mystique*. Bowling Green, OH: Bowling Green University Popular Press, 1984.

Chion, Michel. *La voix au cinéma*. Paris: Editions l'Etoile, 1982.

Clover, Carol. *Men, Women, and Chain Saws: Gender in the Modern Horror Film*. Princeton, NJ: Princeton University Press, 1992.

Collins, Richard. "A Reply to Ed Buscombe." In Nichols, 157–63.

Cook, Pam. "Duplicity in *Mildred Pierce*." In Kaplan, *Women in Film Noir*, 68–82.

Creed, Barbara. *The Monstrous Feminine: Film, Feminism, Psychoanalysis*. London and New York: Routledge, 1993.

Dacey, Philip. "Taking My Children to the Movies." In *Movieworks: Stories and Poems about Movies*, edited by John W. Blanpied, 23. Rochester, NY: The Little Theatre Press, 1990.

Dadoun, Roger. "*Metropolis* Mother City—'Mittler'—Hitler." *Camera Obscura*, no. 15 (Fall 1986): 137–63.

Daly, Brenda O., and Maureen T. Reddy, eds. *Narrating Mothers: Theorizing Maternal Subjectivities*. Knoxville: University of Tennessee Press, 1991.

de Lauretis, Teresa. *Alice Doesn't: Feminism, Semiotics, Cinema*. Bloomington and Indianapolis: Indiana University Press, 1984.

Doane, Mary Ann. *The Desire to Desire: The Woman's Film of the 1940s*. Bloomington and Indianapolis: Indiana University Press, 1987.

Dozoretz, Wendy. "The Mother's Lost Voice in *Hard, Fast and Beautiful*." *Wide Angle*, no. 3 (1984): 50–57.

Eberwein, Robert. *Film and the Dream Screen: A Sleep and a Forgetting*. Princeton, NJ: Princeton University Press, 1984.

Eisenstein, Sergei. "Dickens, Griffith and the Film Today." In *Film Form: Essays in Film Theory*, edited and translated by Jay Leyda, 195–255. New York: Harcourt, Brace and World, 1949.

Erens, Patricia. "Preliminary Thoughts on the *Haha-mono* Films of Japan: Politics and Psychoanalysis." Unpublished manuscript.

———, ed. *Issues in Feminist Film Criticism*. Bloomington and Indianapolis: Indiana University Press, 1990.

Feuer, Jane. *The Hollywood Musical*. London: BFI Publishing, 1982.

Fischer, Lucy. *Shot/Countershot: Film Tradition and Women's Cinema*. Princeton, NJ: Princeton University Press, 1989.

———, ed. *Imitation of Life*. New Brunswick, NJ: Rutgers University Press, 1991.

Flitterman, Sandra. "Nursery/Rhymes: Primal Scenes in *La Maternelle*." In "Women, Representation and Cinematic Discourse," 191–219. Ph.D. diss., University of California, Berkeley, 1982.

Gehring, Wes. *Screwball Comedy: A Genre of Madcap Romance*. Westport, CT: Greenwood Press, 1986.

———. *Screwball Comedy: Defining a Film Genre*. Muncie, IN: Ball State University Press, 1983.

Gerhart, Mary. *Genre Choices, Gender Questions*. Norman and London: University of Oklahoma Press, 1992.

Gledhill, Christine, ed. *Home Is Where the Heart Is: Studies in Melodrama and the Woman's Film*. London: BFI Publishing, 1987.

Gorbman, Claudia. *Unheard Melodies: Narrative Film Music*. Bloomington and Indiana: Indiana University Press, 1987.

Grant, Barry, ed. *Film Genre: Theory and Criticism*. Metuchen, NJ, and London: Scarecrow Press, 1977.

Griffith, Richard. "Cycles and Genres." In Nichols, 111–18.

Haralovich, Mary Beth. "Too Much Guilt Is Never Enough for Working Mothers: Joan Crawford, *Mildred Pierce* and *Mommie Dearest*." *Velvet Light Trap*, no. 29 (Spring 1992): 43–52.

Haskell, Molly. *From Reverence to Rape: The Treatment of Women in the Movies*. Baltimore: Penguin Books, 1974.

Hess, Judith W. "Genre Films and the Status Quo." In Grant, 53–61.

Huyssen, Andreas. "Mass Culture as Woman: Modernism's Other." In *Studies in Entertainment: Critical Approaches to Mass Culture*, edited by Tania Modleski, 188–207. Bloomington and Indianapolis: Indiana University Press, 1986.

Jacobs, Lea. "*Now Voyager*: Some Problems of Enunciation and Sexual Difference." *Camera Obscura*, no. 7 (1981): 88–105.

———. *The Wages of Sin: Censorship and the Fallen Woman Film, 1928–1942*. Madison: University of Wisconsin Press, 1991.

Kaplan, E. Ann. "The Case of the Missing Mother: Maternal Issues in Vidor's *Stella Dallas*." In Erens, *Issues*, 126–36.

———. *Motherhood and Representation: The Mother in Popular Culture and Melodrama*. London and New York: Routledge, 1992.

Kaplan, E. Ann. *Women and Film: Both Sides of the Camera*. New York and London: Methuen, 1983.

————. *Women in Film Noir*. London: BFI Publishing, 1978.

Kitses, Jim. *Horizons West*. Bloomington and London: Indiana University Press, 1970.

Kracauer, Siegfried. "From *Theory of Film*." In *Film Theory and Criticism: Introductory Readings*, edited by Gerald Mast and Marshall Cohen, 7–20. 3d ed. New York and Oxford: Oxford University Press, 1985.

Landy, Marcia. *British Genres: Cinema and Society, 1930–1960*. Princeton, NJ: Princeton University Press, 1991.

————. *Fascism in Film: The Italian Commercial Cinema, 1931–1943*. Princeton, NJ: Princeton University Press, 1986.

————, ed. *Imitations of Life: A Reader on Film and Television Melodrama*. Detroit: Wayne State University Press, 1991.

LaPlace, Maria. "Producing and Consuming the Woman's Film: Discursive Struggle in *Now Voyager*." In Gledhill, 138–66.

LaValley, Albert J. *Mildred Pierce*. Madison: University of Wisconsin Press, 1980.

Lee, Felicia R. "Dark Words, Light Being." *New York Times*, 25 January 1996, C1, 10.

Leibman, Nina C. "The Way We Weren't: Abortion 1950s Style in *Blue Denim* and *Our Time*." *Velvet Light Trap*, no. 29 (Spring 1992): 31–42.

Lewin, Bertram. "Sleep, the Mouth and the Dream Screen." *Psychoanalytic Quarterly* 15 (1946): 419–34.

MacArthur, Colin. "The Iconography of the Gangster Film." In Grant, 118–23.

Mayne, Judith. *Kino and the Woman Question: Feminism and Soviet Silent Film*. Columbus: Ohio State University Press, 1989.

Modleski, Tania. "Three Men and Baby M." *Camera Obscura*, no. 17 (May 1988): 69–81.

————. "Time and Desire in the Woman's Film." *Cinema Journal* 23, no. 3 (Spring 1984): 19–30.

————. *The Women Who Knew Too Much: Hitchcock and Feminist Theory*. New York and London: Methuen, 1988.

Mulvey, Laura. "Afterthoughts on 'Visual Pleasure and Narrative Cinema' Inspired by King Vidor's *Duel in the Sun* (1946)." In *Visual and Other Pleasures*, 29–38. Bloomington and Indianapolis: Indiana University Press, 1989.

————. "Visual Pleasure and Narrative Cinema." 1975. In *Visual and Other Pleasures*, 14–26. Bloomington and Indianapolis: Indiana University Press, 1989.

Muybridge, Eadweard. *Complete Human and Animal Locomotion: All 781 Plates from the 1887 Animal Locomotion*. New York: Dover, 1979.

Neale, Stephen. *Genre*. London: BFI Publishing, 1980.

Nelson, Joyce. "*Mildred Pierce* Reconsidered." *Film Reader* 2 (1977): 65–70.

Nichols, Bill, ed. *Movies and Methods*. Berkeley, Los Angeles, and London: University of California Press, 1976.

Penley, Constance. "Time Travel, Primal Scene, and the Critical Dystopia." *Camera Obscura*, no. 15 (Fall 1986): 66–85.

Rabinovitz, Paula. *Labor and Desire: Women's Revolutionary Fiction in Depression America*. Chapel Hill and London: University of North Carolina Press, 1991.

Riva, Maria. *Marlene Dietrich*. New York: Knopf, 1993.

Robertson, Pamela. "Structural Irony in *Mildred Pierce*, or How Mildred Lost Her Tongue." *Cinema Journal* 30, no. 1 (Fall 1990): 42–54.

Rosolato, Guy. "La voix: Entre corps et langage." *Revue française de psychanalyse* 38, 1 (January 1974): 75–94.

Schatz, Thomas. *Hollywood Genres: Formulas, Filmmaking and the Studio System*. New York: Random House, 1981.

Shorr, Lori. "Performing Birth: The Construction of Female Bodies in Instructional Childbirth Videos." *Velvet Light Trap*, no. 29 (Spring 1992): 3–14.

Silverman, Kaja. *The Acoustic Mirror: The Female Voice in Psychoanalysis and Cinema*. Bloomington and Indianapolis: Indiana University Press, 1988.

Solomon, Stanley. *Beyond Formula: American Film Genres*. New York, San Francisco, Chicago, and Atlanta: Harcourt, Brace, Jovanovich, 1976.

Studlar, Gaylyn. *In the Realm of Pleasure: Von Sternberg, Dietrich, and the Masochistic Aesthetic*. Urbana: University of Illinois Press, 1988.

———. "Visual Pleasure and the Masochistic Aesthetic." *Journal of Film and Video* 37, no. 2 (Spring 1985): 5–26.

Tudor, Andrew. "Genre and Critical Methodology." In Nichols, 118–26.

Turim, Maureen. "Viewing/Reading *Born to Be Sold: Martha Rosler Reads the Strange Case of Baby S/M* or Motherhood in the Age of Technological Reproduction." *Discourse* 13, no. 2 (Spring–Summer 1991): 21–38.

Vardac, A. Nicholas. *Stage to Screen: Theatrical Origins of Early Film: David Garrick to D. W. Griffith*. Cambridge: Harvard University Press, 1949. Reprint, New York: Da Capo, 1987.

Viviani, Christian. "Who Is without Sin? The Maternal Melodrama in American Film, 1930–39." *Les Cahiers de la Cinémathèque*, no. 28 (July 1979). Reprinted in Gledhill, 83–99.

Waldman, Diane. "'At Last I Can Tell It to Someone': Feminine Point of View and Subjectivity in the Gothic Romance Film of the 1940s." *Cinema Journal* 23, no. 2 (1984): 29–40.

Walker, Janet. "Feminist Critical Practice: Female Discourse in *Mildred Pierce*." *Film Reader* 5 (1982): 164–72.

Walsh, Andrea. *Women's Film and Female Experience: 1940–1959*. New York: Praeger, 1984.

Warshow, Robert. *The Immediate Experience: Movies, Comics, Theatre, and Other Aspects of Popular Culture*. Garden City, NY: Doubleday, 1964.

Wexman, Virginia Wright. *Creating the Couple: Love, Marriage, and Hollywood Performance*. Princeton, NJ: Princeton University Press, 1993.

———, ed. *Letter from an Unknown Woman*. New Brunswick, NJ: Rutgers University Press, 1986.

Williams, Linda. "Feminist Film Theory: *Mildred Pierce* and the Second World War." In *Female Spectators: Looking at Film and Television*, edited by E. Deidre Pribram, 12–30. London: Verso, 1988.

———. "'Something Else besides a Mother': *Stella Dallas* and the Maternal Melodrama." In Erens, *Issues*, 137–62.

Wood, Nancy. "Text and Spectator in the Period of the Transition to Sound." Ph.D. thesis, University of Kent, Canterbury, 1983.

2

The Trick Film

THE LADY VANISHES: WOMEN, MAGIC, AND

THE MOVIES

Prologue: Birth Pangs

> Woman is the other, she is all man aspires to be and does not
> become. . . . Therefore he endows woman with her nature:
> the Other—opposition whom he can touch, conquer, pos-
> sess, take comfort from, be inspired by, and yet not have to
> contend with. She is *mystery*.
>   (Simone de Beauvoir, my italics)

In October and November of 1896, Star Film Company's first year of
production, Georges Méliès shot a film entitled *The Vanishing Lady*,
which is credited as displaying the director's first use of a cinematic
"substitution trick" (Hammond, 30). The "plot" of the film is simple:
a lady, in full Victorian garb, is seated in a chair, against the background
of an ornate, elaborately molded wall. A magician (played by Méliès)
drapes her body with a fabric cover. When the cloth is removed, the lady
has disappeared, and, much to our horror, in her place is a skeleton.
Though the occurrence portrayed is, of course, extraordinary, there is
nothing exceptional about the film. It is one of hundreds of such magic
films that Méliès produced between the years 1896 and 1912, films that
were imitated by Pathé in France and by Edison in the United States.

It is, in fact, precisely the commonplace quality of the film that is at
issue—its status as a cinematic archetype, or even a cliché. By 1896 the
trick film paradigm had been established: such works would frequently
involve a *male* magician performing acts of wonder upon a *female* subject. To make a lady vanish was, after all, Méliès's first idea for a substitution trick.[1] In subsequent films he would elaborate upon this basic situa-

---

[1] In her article "Film Body: An Implantation of Perversions" (published two years after
an earlier version of this chapter appeared in *Film Quarterly* [33 no. 1 (1979): 30–40]),
Linda Williams remarked that I asserted that the disappearance of female bodies was the
"primary function of women's bodies in Méliès' films" (30). I believe, however, that this
is a misconstrual of my point. In citing *The Vanishing Lady* as exemplary of the Mélièsian

6. *The Vanishing Lady* (1896). Woman is the occasion for Méliès's first "substitution trick." BFI

7. *The Vanishing Lady* (1896). A woman is turned into a skeleton. BFI

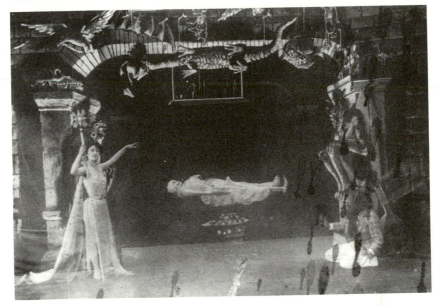

8. *L'Enchanteur Alcofrisbas* (1903). The levitation of a skeleton. MOMA

tion. Thus in *Apparitions fugitives* (1904) Méliès would levitate a female assistant and in *Extraordinary Illusions* (1903) reconstitute her out of a mannequin's parts. In *L'Enchanteur Alcofrisbas* (1903) Méliès would conjure women out of flames and in *Extraordinary Illusions* turn them into men. From film to film the superficial persona of the male magician figure would tend to vary—from the traditional nineteenth-century stage magician in *Ten Ladies in an Umbrella* (1903) to the Roman god in *Jupiter's Thunderbolts* (1903)—but his function would remain the same: to perform feats of wonder upon a female.

Though we are all accustomed to crediting Méliès with the "birth" of film magic, the implications of that genre for the image of women have not been adequately examined. In addition to being the "father" of film fantasy, Méliès may also have to stand as the inadvertent patriarch of a particular cinematic vision of women.

In this chapter I will investigate the precise nature of that vision and argue that the rhetoric of magic—in its theatrical and cinematic varie-

---

trick film, I was not focusing on the act of disappearance per se, but on the paradigm of male magician and female assistant. What I meant to imply by favoring that film (in the title of that essay) was that "the lady" always disappears in Méliès's films—in that woman (as woman) is gone, with only her male-fabricated image remaining. On this point Williams and I would seem to agree.

ties—constitutes a complex *drama of male-female relations*. In the guise
of the magician figure, man enacts a series of symbolic rituals upon
woman in which, among other things, he expresses his desire to control
her, to employ her as decorative object, to cast her as sexual fantasy.
Moreover, the discourse of magic evinces an obsession with *maternity*.
In some films, the male trickster confronts a female who resembles an
awesome mother, and attempts to exorcise her powers. In other works,
a symbolism of procreation obtains, as the male magician seeks to appropriate the force of female creativity. Hence Méliès may have "birthed"
not only cinematic fantasy but the very theme of birth in film.[2]

The Magician's Assistant: Conjuring and Control

In all fairness to Méliès, however, his personal role in authoring such a
vision is highly qualified. For, as we know, many of the screen creations
associated with him are, in truth, derived from the antecedent tradition
of *theatrical* magic. Méliès himself was a stage magician; prior to making
films he had purchased the Théâtre Robert-Houdin in 1888. Thus it is
to the legacy of theatrical magic that we must turn to find the roots of
this cinematic image of woman—a vision that Méliès and others eventually "grafted" onto the screen.

When one begins to examine the history of stage magic, one finds that
the trope of male magician and female assistant—so common to the trick
film genre—is simply a convention borrowed from theatrical magic. In
the course of an entire book on the history of stage magic (*The Magic
Catalogue* by William Doerflinger) only three female magicians are mentioned (21–41). Adelaid Herrman, who originally served as magician's
assistant to her husband Alexander, assumed his role when he died;
Dorothy Dietrich and Celeste Evans worked together and specialized in
"dove illusions." Clearly, this text does not constitute a definitive study
of stage magic, and one would assume that other female magicians have,
indeed, existed and performed. But the paucity of references to women
magicians at least makes clear the exceptional nature of that status and
the tenacity with which the model of male magician and female subject
is maintained. It is precisely the dominance and immutability of that paradigm that makes one begin to suspect that sexual role-playing is *itself* at

---

[2] In an unpublished paper, Donald Crafton argues that the image of women in turn-of-
the-century trick films is related to the eugenics movement in France, which sought, at the
time, to extol female fecundity in the face of a declining birthrate. Hence he sees the procreative imagery in a more positive, celebratory light.

issue in the rhetoric of magic, and that perhaps in performing his tricks upon the female subject, the male magician is not simply accomplishing acts of prestidigitation but is articulating a discourse on attitudes toward women.

To begin our investigation, let us return to the basic archetype of male magician working wonders upon the female subject, and commence to read it for its implications. Perhaps the act most typical of trick films is that of simply *conjuring* a woman. In Edison's *Mystic Swing* (1900), a series of women are made to appear on a moving trapeze; in Biograph's *Pierrot's Problem* (1902), a clown-magician produces two girls from behind his voluminous pantaloons. In *Ten Ladies in an Umbrella*, Méliès makes women appear and vanish with the help of an unlikely prop; in *The Ballet Master's Dream* (1903), a sleeper conjures women as part of an oneiric fantasy. Accustomed as we are to this particular magical trope, it is easy to accept it as a mere "given" of the rhetoric of magic, and therefore to neglect to pursue its implications. But if we regard it as meaningful and begin to consider its significance, various issues come into focus.

On the most obvious level, the male magician's act of conjuring women is simply a *demonstration of his power over the female sex*. Woman has no existence independent of the male magician; he can make her appear when he wants to and disappear when (to paraphrase de Beauvoir) he wishes no longer "to contend" with her. Woman is thus a function of male will. In the rhetoric of magic, the conjured woman is also a *decorative object* to be placed here and there like a throw pillow or piece of sculpture. Thus in countless trick films (like *Jupiter's Thunderbolts*), women appear in tableaux "arrangements"—like dried flowers or fruit.

On another level, the act of conjuring and "vanishing" ladies tends to *dematerialize and decorporealize the female sex*, to relegate woman to the level of "spirit." Thus, to paraphrase de Beauvoir again, magical practice literalizes the notion of woman as "Other," as unfathomable "mystery."

Often, however, in these trick films, woman's immaterial status takes on a particular inflection. Rather than function simply as spirit, she is cast specifically as a *figment of the male imagination*. In Méliès's *The Clockmaker's Dream* (1904), for example, the main character falls asleep and dreams of a bevy of women who emerge from a grandfather clock. Similarly, in *The Ballet Master's Dream*, a man dreams about a series of dancing women. In these films the narrative openly situates the women within the male imagination and casts them as sexual fantasies.

Birth Fears: The Awesome Mother

But perhaps, from another viewpoint, the male's need to exert control over the female can be seen as betraying the *opposite* impulse: rather than evince his sense of strength in relation to women, might it not bespeak his perception of relative weakness? In other words, the gentleman "doth protest too much." If our male magician is so sure of his own power over woman, why must he so relentlessly subject us to repeated demonstrations of his capability?

Might it be that in addition to demonstrating male power over the female, the practice of magic also evinces certain deep-seated male anxieties concerning the *female's power over him*? According to this reading, the male magician is not so much attempting to demonstrate his potency over the female as he is to *defuse or exorcise hers over him*. What aspects of magical practice might corroborate such a reading? Furthermore, what psychological and cultural evidence is there to support such a notion of male "anxieties" regarding women?

As a starting point for this investigation, it is useful to examine the reverse situation of the magic "paradigm"—that is, the rare model of a female magician performing tricks upon the male. Several films of this kind do exist, and their portrayal of the female magician is most telling.[3] There is, for example, a marvelous Edison film of 1905 entitled *A Pipe Dream*, which opens with a medium close-up of a woman smoking a cigarette, seated against a black background. She begins rather playfully to blow smoke into her outstretched hand, and out of nowhere, a tiny man appears, on bended knees, upon her palm. The homunculus seems to be pleading with the woman, as though asking for her hand in marriage. She laughs at him cruelly and begins to close her palm: her homunculus disappears. Perplexed, she tries again to conjure her little man but cannot repeat the trick.

What is interesting about this film is its characterization of the female "magician"—a characterization fraught with anxiety and ambivalence toward woman. Unlike the camera setup for most magic films, that of *A Pipe Dream* renders the scale of the woman huge, particularly in com-

---

[3] My research was based largely on the Library of Congress Paper Print Collection as well as on those trick films available through commercial distribution. Further research would have to be done into archival holdings and published trick film descriptions to ascertain precisely how uncommon female magicians were in this genre. Eileen Bowser and Bob Summers informed me that, based on their screenings at the FIAF Brighton Conference, female magician figures were most common in Pathé films. This has been borne out by my examination of *The Red Spectre* and *Transformation*, discussed in this chapter.

9. *A Pipe Dream* (1905). An awesome woman conjures a homunculus. MOMA

parison to her diminutive man. She is a literalization of the fearsome, domineering mother, as seen by a child-man. Thus she is a figure of considerable terror. Psychologists might have something to say about her as well, particularly about how her depiction evinces certain classic male fears concerning women. In her article "The Dread of Woman" (1932), for example, Karen Horney speaks of the psychic importance of the male child's anxieties regarding his mother, and Horney's language seems custom-made for the film. She discusses the young boy's perception that his genitalia are "much too small for his mother's" and how he "reacts with the dread of his own inadequacy, of being rejected and derided" (142). Such, of course, is the fate of our homunculus.

The film has other implications as well. The fact that the woman smokes a cigarette marks her, according to Victorian mores, as dangerously loose and "masculine" and thus invests her magician status with a degree of perversity. Furthermore, it is significant that when she tries to repeat her trick, she fails, as though her magical powers were accidental, or beyond her control.

Another film of the period, *The Red Spectre* (Pathé, 1907) is interesting to examine in this regard as well. The narrative of this film involves a competition between a male magician (dressed as a devil, in skeleton costume) and a female sorcerer (outfitted in courtly attire). Ultimately, the woman magician reduces the male to a limp, folded costume and appropriates his black cape. Again, a certain anxiety regarding the figure of the female magician is apparent, particularly her perceived ability to kill the male.

In point of fact, throughout the history of myth and religious practice, when women have been "granted" magical powers by men, those powers have most often been regarded as evil or dangerous. We rarely find an image of a harmless female magician, playfully conjuring people or objects. Rather, she is cast as a figure of great perversity. According to Greek legend, for example, the magical Circe turned the companions of Ulysses into pigs; and in Venezuelan mythology, the love goddess, Maria Leonza, turned men into stone (Lederer, 57). Similarly, the legendary Sirens were bird-women who played magical music on their lyres and lured sailors to a watery grave. Even in contemporary mythos, the tainted figure of the prostitute is said to turn "tricks" upon her "Johns." (Amusingly, when a magician's assistant, carrying caged doves, is mistakenly arrested as a hooker in Susan Seidelman's *Desperately Seeking Susan* [1985], a streetwalker inside the paddy wagon assumes that the woman is a "compatriot" and asks what sexual "tricks" she performs with the birds.) Thus, in all of these cases, women who practice magic seem to do so at the expense of men.

In terms of the history of the Christian religion, the most compelling female "magician" is, significantly, the witch—clearly a figure of great terror. Though male demons, or incubi, were thought to exist, the notion of witchcraft was strongly identified with females. That perverse magical powers were associated with womanhood in particular is apparent in the *Malleus Maleficarum*, a handbook on witchcraft written by two Dominican monks in 1484. According to that influential text, "[S]ince [women] are feebler in body and in mind, it is not surprising they should come under the spell of witchcraft." Furthermore, woman "is more carnal than man as is clear from her many carnal abominations." Thus all witchcraft is seen to stem from "the carnal lust which in women is insatiable" (quoted in Hays, 141). Significantly, historians have revealed that women accused of witchcraft were often midwives—hence female "magic" was associated with the issue of motherhood (Forbes).

What these few examples demonstrate is the flip side of the male magician–female subject paradigm. In the cases where women magicians exist, they are figures of dread. This makes clear the fact that woman is not always perceived as *powerless*, a passive prop. Rather, woman's power is often acknowledged, but it is viewed as perilous. Perhaps the male magician is not only performing tricks upon the female; he is preventing *her* from performing more dangerous tricks upon *him*.

But what precisely is the nature of these masculine fears, and what cultural/psychological evidence is there to support their existence? First of all, several texts have been written on the subject, including *The Fear of Women* by psychoanalyst Wolfgang Lederer, and *The Dangerous Sex* by H. R. Hays. Furthermore, various psychologists have produced essays on the topic, like Gregory Zilboorg's "Masculine and Feminine: Some Biological and Cultural Aspects," Karen Horney's "The Dread of Woman," and Frieda Fromm-Reichmann and Virginia Gunst's "On the Denial of Women's Sexual Pleasure." Freud himself spoke of male anxieties toward women in *Totem and Taboo*.

In most interpretations, this fear of woman centers on the female genitalia. According to Freud, in his essay "Medusa's Head," the female genitalia posit the threat of male castration and are thus viewed with terror. In other remarks in *Totem and Taboo*, Freud questions whether the male fear of woman might not stem from a fear of being "weakened" by her in the sexual act (Lederer, 3). In much of the writing on the subject, mythology has served as cultural evidence. For example, myths provide the suggestion that men may also fear *women's procreative powers* because they perceive them as entailing the *reverse power of death*. Fromm-Reichmann and Gunst cite the following Persian creation myth as proof of such an apprehension:

> In that myth a woman creates the world, and she creates it by the act of natural creativity which is hers and which cannot be duplicated by men. She gives birth to a great number of sons. The sons, greatly puzzled by this act which they cannot duplicate, become frightened. They think: "Who can tell us, that *if she can give life, she cannot also take life.*" And so, because of their fear of this *mysterious ability of woman, and of its reversible possibility*, they kill her. (88, my italics)

Thus once more woman's sexuality is linked to mutilation or death: if woman can conceive life, can she not also take it away? If the womb is a bearer of life, might it not also be a grave?

This irrational fear of female "magic" is apparent in many of the trick films. In *The Red Spectre*, it seems significant that the woman magician manages to kill the *male* devil, reducing him to a disembodied skeleton. In several other films, women are associated with death and skeletal symbolism. In Méliès's *The Vanishing Lady*, for example, when the woman disappears, she is replaced by a skeleton, an image that is replicated in Edison's *Mystic Swing*. Moreover, this fear of women may also explain why so many magic films involve tricks in which women are turned into *men*, such that their disturbing sexual difference is annihilated. In *A Delusion* (Biograph, 1902), a female model turns into a man each time the photographer looks into the camera lens. In *The Artist's Dilemma* (Edison, 1901), a woman turns into a male clown.

Given this basic fear of imagined female powers, it is not surprising to find the iconography of theatrical and cinematic magic plagued by a rampant *hostility* toward the female subject—an animosity that we might read as directed at motherhood. In fact, it is this very aggression that makes the theory of masculine fear most plausible. If the male magician only wished to "play" with the female subject, why has he devised for her such a chamber of horrors?

For instance, in many trick films women are symbolically dismembered. In Biograph's *A Mystic Reincarnation* (1902), a male magician conjures female body parts, then turns them into a woman. In *Extraordinary Illusions*, Méliès takes out mannequin limbs from a "magical box" and through stop-motion photography transforms them into a flesh-and-blood woman. As Linda Williams has perceptively noted, such dismemberment bespeaks not only a generalized antipathy to woman but a fear of female "lack" and "castration."[4]

In other films (like *Apparitions fugitives*, *L'Enchanteur Alcofrisbas*, and *The Red Spectre*), women are levitated, an action that can be seen to liken them to corpses in advanced states of rigor mortis. In such a posture they also impersonate the proper Victorian wife, whose sexuality was supposed to be dormant. According to Hays, women of the era often engaged in intercourse "in a sort of coma, apparently pretending that nothing was happening [since] the slightest sign of life on [their] part would have been a humiliating admission of depravity" (215).

In the canon of grandiose "stage illusions," we find a catalog of magical misogyny. Thus we have such tricks as "Rod through Body," in which a sword is placed through a woman's torso; "Dagger Chest," in which a series of knives are placed into a box around a woman's head;

---

[4] In Williams's article, she states that the male magician's power over women's bodies is no more important than that he wields over men's. Rather, she sees the dramas of dismemberment and reintegration (be the victims male or female) as reenactments of "the problem of difference, the threat of disunity and dismemberment posed by the woman's body" (31). Thus she finds the castration anxiety (and its attendant syndrome of fetishism) more central in the dynamics of magic than womb envy (a notion that I advance). Perhaps, however, these two interpretations are flip sides of the same coin. Both imply that the trick film dramatizes male fantasies regarding women, and that the magician's acts of prestidigitation are, symbolically, aimed at allaying fears of the female body—whether they attach to woman's "lack" of a penis, or to what she harbors inside "instead." In the practice of psychoanalysis, it is commonplace to observe that dream symbols are overdetermined—with one image serving to express a plethora of meanings. It would seem that the symbolization of the magic film (a discourse tied to the "collective unconscious") may operate in much the same way.

"Shooting a Woman out of a Canon"; "Sawing a Woman in Half"; "Shooting through a Woman"; and, finally, "The Electric Chair" (Doerflinger, Dunninger). Such tricks cannot simply be viewed as jovial and innocent demonstrations of imagined male powers, as a harmless flexing of the masculine ego. Rather, they must be regarded as symbolic acts of considerable violence.

Birth Envy: The Creative Mother

But certainly not *all* magical practice involves a thinly disguised hostility toward women. What about tricks producing rabbits from hats or flowers from cones? Though it is true that such stunts do not suggest male aggression toward women, they can, nonetheless, be seen as constituting a submerged discourse on male-female relations. For when one begins to examine those sleights of hand so characteristic of magic tradition, one is struck by how many of them center on the theme of *creation*: men pulling rabbits out of hats, making flowers grow from canes, bringing mechanical automata "to life." All of these acts seem like symbolic imitations of birth, and their occurrence at the hand of the male magician seems to speak an *envy* of what is, essentially, the *female procreative function*. Significantly, most of these magical births take place with the aid of a highly phallic object—a "mystic" cone or a cane, or perhaps an "enchanted candle."

In the canons of psychoanalytic literature, we are, of course, more familiar with a theory of the *reverse* situation, of the female's alleged jealousy of the male. According to Freud in his formulation of "penis envy," during a young girl's "phallic" phase (ages three to seven) she sees a naked boy or man and realizes that she "lacks" a penis. As Freud would have it, in his essay "Some Psychological Consequences of the Anatomical Distinction between the Sexes," the effects of the young girl's perception are devastating and far-reaching: "She develops, like a scar, a sense of inferiority. . . . she begins to share the contempt felt by men for a sex which is the lesser in so important a respect. . . . Even after penis-envy has abandoned its true object, it continues to exist . . . in the character trait of jealousy" (188). For Freud, even the baby that she will eventually bear is a mere "stand-in" for the missing and coveted penis: "[T]here is no other way of putting it—of the equation 'penis = child.' [The girl] gives up her wish for a penis and puts in place of it a wish for a child" (191). Thus in traditional psychoanalytic theory it is the female who is seen as biologically deficient and envious of the male. Within this framework, motherhood is a pathetic "substitution" trick.

Early in the history of psychology, voices were raised in protest against Freud's construal of sexual relations. And many of those who countered his claims did so by advancing an opposing notion: male envy of female life-giving powers. Thus, in the 1926 essay "The Flight from Womanhood," Karen Horney states:

> [F]rom the biological point of view woman has in motherhood, or in the capacity for motherhood, a quite physiological superiority. This is most clearly reflected in the unconscious of the male psyche in the boy's intense envy of motherhood. . . . When one begins . . . to analyze men . . . one receives a most surprising impression of the intensity of this envy of pregnancy, childbirth and motherhood, as well as of the breasts, and of the act of suckling. (60–61)

Similarly, psychoanalysts Fromm-Reichmann and Gunst state: "Men are not only unconsciously afraid of women as childbearers but many men are also envious of this ability of women. . . . We know it from our clinical practice. . . . We hear so much about penis envy but it is not fashionable in a patriarchal culture to talk about birth envy, although many of us know it exists" (91).

In discussing the issue of male envy, many psychoanalysts have felt the need to venture into the field of anthropology. Thus in the 1944 essay "Masculine and Feminine" psychoanalyst Gregory Zilboorg posited male envy as a determining force in the creation of primitive culture: "[T]he male who first overcame woman by means of rape was hostile and murderous toward the female. . . . But despite all his economic and sadistic and phallic superiority, man could not fail to discover that woman still possessed a unique power over mankind. She could produce children. . . . Thus man, who hated the woman-mother, must have envied her too" (124).

Zilboorg's assertions are clearly hypothetical, but many practicing anthropologists have documented concrete evidence of the male envy of the female. Margaret Mead, for example, in the chapter "Womb-Envying Patterns" in *Male and Female*, demonstrates how male initiation rituals of South Sea Island societies evince anxieties that are suppressed in Western culture:

> In our Occidental view of life, woman, fashioned from man's rib, can at most strive unsuccessfully to imitate man's superior powers and higher vocations. The basic theme of the initiatory cult, however, is that women, by virtue of their ability to make children, hold the secrets of life. Men's role is uncertain, undefined and perhaps unnecessary. By a great effort man has hit upon a method of compensating himself for his basic inferiority. Equipped with various mysterious noise-making instruments . . . they can get the male children away from the women, brand them as incomplete and themselves turn boys into men. Women, it is true, make human beings, but only men can make men. (102–3)

Thus Mead casts male initiatory rites as elaborate, compensatory "magic tricks."

Another researcher in the field of male envy is Bruno Bettelheim who, in his book *Symbolic Wounds*, describes the primitive ritual of *couvade*, wherein the husband of a parturient woman enacts a rite in which he mimics, and even appropriates, the childbearing act:

> The [pregnant] woman works as usual up until a few hours before birth; she goes to the forest with some women, and there, the birth takes place. In a few hours, she is up and at work . . . as soon as the child is born the father takes to his hammock and abstains from work, from all food but weak gruel . . . and is nursed and cared for by all the women of the place. This goes on for days, sometimes weeks. (109–10)

What these various quotations from psychologists and anthropologists demonstrate is that there exists a body of literature in which male envy of the female's procreative function is established and considered a crucial aspect of sexual dynamics. (One might also look toward the history of Western religion, in which a male god "preempts" the birthing powers of Eve [created from a man's rib] and Mary [birthing as a "virgin"].) Given that most cultures are patriarchal, however, it is clear that such feelings are not openly acknowledged and indeed are concealed and suppressed. In the "primitive" societies described by Mead and Bettelheim, this envy is released in the form of established cultural rituals. In modern culture, however, such sanctioned avenues of expression do not exist, and envy wears a more oblique disguise.

A propos of this issue, we might recall Freud's discussion in *Beyond the Pleasure Principle* of the child's first game of "fort" (gone) / "da" (there) in which he pulls a reel on a string within his field of vision, then pushes it away. For Freud, this game represents a therapeutic replay of anxieties toward maternal comings and goings, placing them within the child's imagined control. As Freud notes, the child has "compensated" for his mother's departure by "himself *staging* the disappearance and return of objects" (34, my italics). Thus, for each human being, the mother is the first "magician"—capable of appearing and disappearing mysteriously, at will.

Procreative Discourse

As stated earlier, the rhetoric of magic would appear to be a cultural artifact in which the male envy of female procreative powers is "disguised," yet manifest. But what is there about magical practice that supports such a reading?

I have already mentioned the general emphasis in conjuring tricks on the notion of creation or birth, be it rabbits from hats, women from umbrellas, or automata that move. But there are many standard magic tricks that evince a more overt symbolism. Within the canon of theatrical magic there is, for example, a whole series of tricks that involve the central prop of an *egg. Dunninger's Complete Encyclopedia of Magic* lists such tricks as "Eggs Extraordinary," in which a designated card is found within an egg; "Miraculous Eggs," in which a ring is produced from an egg; and "The Coin in Egg" routine (139, 262, 278). Doerflinger's *Magic Catalogue* notes tricks with even more tendentious implications. One entitled "Human Hen," for example, is described as follows:

> Egg after egg . . . are produced from magician's (or friend's) mouth. They are placed into a clear bowl or tray in plain view of everyone. You can make as many eggs as you wish appear. Mouth is seen as empty after each egg is removed. Eggs are real and can be cracked open to prove so. (123)

Shades of the feminized Professor Rath at his marriage feast in *The Blue Angel* (1930).

Other tricks, not specifically involving eggs, have similar birth implications. One entitled "Baby Trousseau Production" entails a male magician and a male subject:

> Performer shakes hands with person who helped him, notices a ravel on their collar. When he pulls it, it is really a tape, and as he continues to pull, audience sees that it is a long string of fluttering dolls' clothes in all colors. This causes a big laugh which gets bigger when a baby nursing bottle seemingly full of milk and complete with nipple, shows up on the end of the tape line. (Doerflinger, 113)

In a similar vein, one reads of a turn-of-the-century Mongolian conjurer, Chin Ling Foo, who was "noted for his production of large bowls of water or small children from an apparently empty cloth" (Doerflinger, 26).

While these tricks tend to mimic the procreative act, the canon of "escape tricks" evinces a male anxiety about the birth process itself. In *Houdini on Magic*, for example, the "Spanish Maiden" routine is described in terms that foreground those fears:

> [The Spanish Maiden] is shaped like a human body and the front is painted to resemble a maiden. The device hinges open at the side and both sections of the interior are lined with iron spikes. When you enter the device, you take a position between the spikes. The front is then closed, so that the spikes completely trap you within. Padlocks are attached to staples on the outside of

10. *The Brahmin and the Butterfly* (1906). A magician conjures a caterpillar from an egg-shaped cocoon. BFI

the Maiden to prevent you from opening the device. Nevertheless, soon after the cabinet is placed over the Spanish Maiden, you make your escape. (Houdini, 118)

The history of trick films evinces similar associations of magic and birth. *The Star Film Catalogue* lists such Méliès films as *Prolific Magical Egg* and *Marvelous Egg Producing with Surprising Developments*, both of 1902. And in *The Brahmin and the Butterfly* (1900), a male magician approaches an "egg-shaped cocoon" and conjures from it a caterpillar that turns into a beautiful princess.

Many other films, though devoid of overt egg symbolism, nonetheless display a submerged iconography of parturition. In *Pierrot's Problem*, for example, the clown-magician seems to give birth to two young ladies from the folds of his baggy pantaloons. (He eventually "combines" them into one huge "Great Mother" of a woman.) Similarly, it is telling that so many magic films, like *The Red Spectre* and *L'Enchanteur Alcofrisbas*, employ as their settings caves and grottoes. For according to historians of myth, like Mircea Eliade, these locales have commonly been associated with the world's womb in primitive Earth-Mother cults

(117). Finally, it is interesting to note that many magician's props seem to embody womb symbolism. One thinks of the classic "magic box," so nicely labeled as such in Méliès's *Extraordinary Illusions*. One notices as well the countless films (again, like *The Red Spectre* and *L'Enchanteur Alcofrisbas*) in which women are conjured from urns, as though to literalize the notion of womb as "magic vessel."

Thus in many magic films, the prestidigitation performed by the male magician seems to have relevance (among other things) to the issue of birth. It is as though through magical practice the male can symbolically imitate, or even appropriate, an aspect of female procreative powers.

Also noteworthy is a magic film that runs somewhat *counter* to the paradigm—one in which the role of female as procreator is not entirely suppressed. In *Transformation* (Pathé, ca. 1906), a *female* magician conjures live babies out of a series of flowers and vegetables, ending the film by bouncing the children blissfully on her knee. While, on one level, the film mocks the notion of children as generated from the "cabbage patch" (as they might be delivered by the "stork"), on another, the subtext of female procreation is brought to the surface.

In summary, then, the rhetoric of magic—in its theatrical and cinematic varieties—constitutes a complex drama of male-female relations. In the guise of the magician figure, Man enacts a series of symbolic rituals in which he expresses numerous, often contradictory attitudes toward Woman: his desire to control her, to employ her as decorative object, to cast her as sexual fantasy, to exorcise her imagined powers of death, and to appropriate her real powers of procreation.[5]

Cinematic Illusions

At various points, I have mentioned how the genre of the trick film owes its heritage to the legacy of theatrical magic. Yet the question arises as to *why* the conventions of stage magic were so easily translated onto the screen.

The very nature of the cinematic medium links it with magic, for the photographic process has always emanated a miraculous aura. Though grounded in physical realities, photography still strikes us as producing an image "conjured" (albeit "developed" in a wash of chemicals).

Historically, *motion* picture photography had even stronger ties to magic. One of the early predecessors of the film projector was the *magic* lantern, a device that projected painted, often hand-animated, slides.

[5] For the most complete discussion of the influence of magicians on movies, see Barnouw.

Clearly cinema, with its use of photography and its perfection of the illusion of movement, created an even more "magical" image of life. As Parker Tyler has written:

> Camera trickery is really camera magic, for illusion can be freely created by the movie camera with more mathematical accuracy and shock values than by sleight of hand or stage illusion. The very homogeneity of cinema illusion— the images of the actors themselves are illusive, their corporeal bodies absent—creates a throwback in the mood of the spectator to the vestiges . . . of ancient beliefs. (779)

It is interesting that among the trick films of the era are some whose iconography provides a commentary on the perceived magical qualities of the film medium. In *A Spiritualist Photographer* (Méliès, 1903), a male magician appears onstage with a huge empty picture frame. He fits blank paper into the frame and stands a woman before it. As a torch burns beneath her, she dissolves onto the photographic paper. The magician rolls up the print, and the flesh-and-blood woman reappears. The same play with conjuring the image of women appears in *The Red Spectre*. As part of the devil-magician's competition with his female counterpart, he produces not live women but the image of women on an ersatz movie screen. Having done this, he lies beneath it and peers lasciviously at his nubile creations.

Several conclusions can be drawn from the events portrayed in these two films. First, they establish that the photographic act is seen as a kind of conjuring: producing a cinematic image is viewed as a "magic trick" equivalent to those one might perform onstage. Second, they demonstrate how readily the magic of the film image was associated with the image of the *female*. As theatrical magicians had obsessively made live women appear onstage, so the film magicians might invoke their images on-screen.

Still another film of this era seems to enact the notion of the cinematic apparatus as a magical device for conjuring women. In Méliès's *The Magic Lantern* (1903), we find the characters of Pierrot and Harlequin in a children's playroom. They assemble a huge magic lantern and project its light upon the wall. After a while, however, they become curious about what is inside the lantern's cavity. They open it up and a stream of women swarm out. No other film so aptly literalizes the sense of the cinema as Man's device for procreating women.

Many later filmmakers were to draw on the instincts of Méliès. Ingmar Bergman (who made a film entitled *The Magician* in 1958), for example, admits that his own fascination with cinema began with the childhood gift of a magic lantern, complete with a set of colored glass fairy-tale slides. But it was the acquisition, a few years later, of a film

projector that had a profound effect upon the young director. And
Bergman's recollection of that experience makes clear his almost unconscious association of the powers of women, magic, and the movies as he
describes his own initial encounter with a "vanishing lady":

> When I was ten years old I received my first, rattling film projector, with its
> chimney and lamp. I found it both mystifying and fascinating. The first film
> I had was nine feet long and brown in color. It showed a girl lying asleep in
> a meadow, who woke up and stretched out her arms, then disappeared to the
> right. That was all there was to it. The film was a great success and was pro-
> jected every night until it broke and could not be mended anymore.
>
> This little rickety machine was my first conjuring set. And even today, I
> remind myself with childish excitement that I am really a conjurer. (xiv–xv)

Works Cited

Barnouw, Eric. "The Magician and the Movies." *American Film*, pt. 1, 4, no. 4
    (April 1978); pt. 2, 4, no. 5 (May 1978).
Beauvoir, Simone de. *The Second Sex*. Translated by H. M. Parshley. New York:
    Vintage, 1974.
Bergman, Ingmar. Introduction to *Four Screenplays of Bergman*. Edited by Lars
    Malstrom and David Kushner. New York: Simon and Schuster, 1960.
Bettelheim, Bruno. *Symbolic Wounds: Puberty Rites and the Envious Male*. New
    York: Collier, 1971.
Crafton, Donald. "Dream and Reality: Eugenics and Early French Cinema."
    Paper presented at the meeting of the Society for Cinema Studies, New York,
    March 1995.
Doerflinger, William. *The Magic Catalogue*. New York: Dutton, 1977.
Dunninger, Joseph. *Dunninger's Complete Encyclopedia of Magic*. New York:
    L. Stuart, 1967.
Eliade, Mircea. *Myths: Dreams and Mysteries*. Translated by Philip Mairet. New
    York: Harper, 1960.
Forbes, Thomas Roger. *The Midwife and the Witch*. New Haven and London:
    Yale University Press, 1966.
Freud, Sigmund. *Beyond the Pleasure Principle*. Translated by James Strachey.
    New York, Bantam, 1963.
———. "Medusa's Head." In *Sexuality and the Psychology of Love*, edited by
    Philip Rieff, 212–13. New York: Collier, 1963.
———. "Some Psychological Consequences of the Anatomical Distinction be-
    tween the Sexes." In *Sexuality and the Psychology of Love*, edited by Philip
    Rieff, 183–93. New York: Collier, 1963.
———. *Totem and Taboo: Resemblances of Savages and Neurotics*. Translated by
    James Strachey. New York: Norton, 1952.
Fromm-Reichmann, Frieda, and Gunst, Virginia. "On the Denial of Women's
    Sexual Pleasure." In *Psychoanalysis and Women*, edited by Jean Baker, 86–93.
    New York: Penguin, 1977.

Hammond, Paul. *Marvellous Méliès*. London: Gordon Fraser, 1974.

Hays, H. R. *The Dangerous Sex*. New York: G. P. Putnam, 1964.

Horney, Karen. "The Dread of Woman." 1932. Reprinted in *Feminine Psychology*, edited by Harold Kelman, 133–46. New York: Norton, 1967.

———. "The Flight From Womanhood." 1926. Reprinted in *Feminine Psychology*, edited by Harold Kelman, 54–70. New York: Norton, 1967.

Houdini, Harry. *Houdini on Magic*. Edited by Walter Gibson and Morris Young. New York: Dover, 1954.

Lederer, Wolfgang. *The Fear of Women*. New York: Harcourt, Brace, Jovanovich, 1968.

Mead, Margaret. *Male and Female*. New York: William Morrow, 1949.

Tyler, Parker. Preface to *Magic and Myth of the Movies*. In *Film Theory and Criticism*, edited by Gerald Mast and Marshall Cohen, 776–81. 3d ed. New York: Oxford University Press, 1979.

Williams, Linda. "Film Body: An Implantation of Perversions." *Cine-Tracts* 3, no. 4 (Winter 1981): 19–35.

Zilboorg, Gregory. "Masculine and Feminine: Some Biological and Cultural Aspects." In *Psychoanalysis and Women*, edited by Jean Baker, 96–131. New York: Penguin, 1977.

3

Silent Melodrama

WAY DOWN EAST: MELODRAMA, METAPHOR, AND THE MATERNAL BODY

Foreword

> With your milk, Mother, I swallowed ice. And here I am now,
> my insides frozen. . . . My blood no longer circulates to my
> feet or my hands, or as far as my head. It is immobilized,
> thickened by the cold. Obstructed by icy chunks which
> resist its flow.
>   (Luce Irigaray)

To state that *Way Down East* (1920) is a film about the maternal body seems an exercise in cliché. For it recounts the familiar story of Anna Moore (Lillian Gish), a country girl seduced (in a mock marriage) by an urbane playboy, then left to bear his illegitimate child. While the film's narrative connections to motherhood are abundantly clear, a maternal discourse reverberates on more submerged levels of the text, invoking its literary origins, its social context, its metaphoric structures, and its celluloid existence.

The Literary Body

> [P]ersonally it is always pleasing to recognize . . . the fact that
> our cinema is not altogether without parents and without
> pedigree, without a past.
>   (Sergei Eisenstein)

Like many works of the silent era, D. W. Griffith's *Way Down East* owes its creative "maternity" to literature. For Sergei Eisenstein, this " 'genetic' line of descent" is a positive feature, lending cinema a prestigious "birth-

place" (195). Other critics have found this artistic lineage more problematic, with film configured as an "illegitimate" offspring. As Judith
Mayne notes (in a passage reminiscent of *Way Down East*), "It has been
stated over and over again, in condemnations of the cinema as an inferior art form, that if the cinema is heir to the novel it is a *bastard child*"
(100, my italics). Retrospectively, even Eisenstein's phrasing abounds
with double meaning. His pride in a cinema "with a past" collides, in
Way Down East, with the shame of a woman "with a past"—a notion
that dogs the life of Anna Moore.

Way Down East was written in the mid-1890s by dramatist Lottie
Blair Parker. As he recounts in *Showman* (186–87), producer William A.
Brady found her original text promising but flawed, and commissioned
its "elaboration" by "play-doctor" Joseph R. Grismer. While the Manhattan premiere of the melodrama was financially disappointing, the play
succeeded on the road. When the production returned to New York, it
enjoyed a triumphant run (187–88). As Brady writes in "Drama in
Homespun," "The show was a repeater and it took twenty-one years to
wear it out" (100). Ultimately, Grismer published a novelization of the
play in 1900.

It is this literary property that Griffith claimed (for $175,000), not
from its "natural mother" (Parker), but from its "adoptive father"
(Brady), who had shrewdly acquired the rights (Brady, *Showman*, 185;
Henderson, 215). Many were shocked by Griffith's interest in this an-
tique, "by-gosh" melodrama. Lillian Gish recalled that Hollywood
"thought privately that [he] had lost his mind" (229).

Griffith was to make considerable changes in the literary material.
While Parker's play begins after Anna's tragic mistake (and slowly discloses the circumstances of her transgressive maternity), Griffith's narrative starts with her seduction. While Parker's play climaxes in the "sensation scene" of a winter snowstorm, Griffith concludes with Anna's
spectacular rescue from a waterfall and ice floe. Using a bodily (and
Frankensteinian) metaphor for cinematic paternity, Martin Williams
claims that "Griffith . . . breathe[d] new life into [the] old bones" of his
literary prototype. Arthur Lennig deems this process the "birth" of *Way
Down East* (105).

Griffith's faith in his source was well-founded. According to Gish,
Way Down East played for more than a year on Broadway and "made
more money than any other Griffith film except *The Birth of a Nation*."
Significantly, his "bastard" cinematic progeny played for "legitimate"
theater prices (236).

The Social Body

The "Fallen Woman"

> Against the background of history, too prominent to escape
> the observation from which it shrinks, stands a figure, mute,
> mournful, indescribably sad. It is a girl, holding in her arms
> the blessing and burden of motherhood, but in whose face
> one finds no traces of maternal joy and pride. There is scarcely
> a great writer of fiction who has not somewhere introduced
> this figure in the shifting panorama of romance. . . . Who is
> this woman so pitiable, yet so scorned? It is the mother of the
> illegitimate child.
>   (Albert Leffingwell)

Way Down East tells the story of Anna Moore, a fatherless young woman
who resides with her mother in rural Maine. When financial problems
plague the family, Mrs. Moore (Mrs. David Landau) suggests that Anna
visit her wealthy Boston relatives, the Tremonts, and seek their assistance. While at a party, Anna meets Lennox Sanderson (Lowell Sherman), a notorious womanizer. He courts her and disingenuously proposes a secret marriage. Anna falls for Sanderson's ruse and participates
in a mock nuptial. Later, Anna returns home (without revealing the
truth to her mother). Sanderson visits her periodically, while conducting
adulterous affairs in the city. When Anna reveals to him that she is pregnant, he confesses his marital deception but abandons her. Anna's
mother supports her through her travail, but when Mrs. Moore dies,
Anna and her infant son move to a nearby town. The baby expires from
a sudden illness, and the landlady, Maria Poole (Emily Fitzroy), sends
Anna away, suspecting that she has no husband. Anna finds work on the
Bartlett farm, where she is cherished by Squire and Mrs. Bartlett (Burr
McIntosh and Kate Bruce) and loved by their son David (Richard
Barthelmess). Eventually, Sanderson reenters the picture, when visiting
a nearby family estate. He demands that Anna leave the area to save him
embarrassment, but she refuses. A crisis ensues when Maria Poole visits
the farm and, recognizing Anna, tells the town gossip, Martha Perkins
(Vivia Ogden), about her past. When Squire Bartlett learns that Anna is
an unwed mother, he turns her out. She delivers an impassioned speech,
disclosing Sanderson's paternity and decrying Bartlett's selective punishment of her. Distraught, she wanders off into a raging late-winter
snowstorm. David conducts an all-night search, discovering her on a
breaking ice floe. He saves her as she is about to succumb to the water-

fall, and brings her home. His family begs for forgiveness, and the couple soon wed.

It takes no sophisticated decoding to comprehend how thoroughly the narrative of *Way Down East* is imbricated with the maternal. The tale begins with a hermetic mother-daughter dyad, and after Sanderson's desertion, it is Mrs. Moore who saves Anna from despondency. Here is how Joseph Grismer represents Anna's bond with her mother and grief at her parent's demise:

> She realized after her mother's death what the gentle companionship had been to her, what a prop the frail mother had become in her hour of need . . . never by look or word did she chide her daughter, or make her affliction anything but easier to bear by her gentle presence. (79)

The remaining narrative is populated with a series of good and bad surrogate mothers for Anna. Clearly, Maria Poole and Martha Perkins are pernicious, but Mrs. Bartlett is nurturing. A religious woman, she convinces the squire to hire Anna and, at the end of the film, to take her back, appealing to his Christian charity.

But the focus of maternal melodrama in *Way Down East* is upon Anna, an unwed mother, a figure that Victorian Albert Leffingwell found "mute, mournful, [and] indescribably sad." While the concept of mutism seems extraordinarily apt for the heroine of a silent film, we shall see that Anna "speaks" to us in a variety of social, historical, and figurative discourses.

Skeletons in the Closet

> Purity was as essential as piety to a young woman, its absence
> as unnatural and unfeminine. Without it she was, in fact, no
> woman at all, but a member of some lower order.
>   (Barbara Welter)

The play *Way Down East* was written in the late nineteenth century, but it was not adapted for the screen until 1920. The tumultuous thirty years that span these events leave their trace upon the text and are relevant to Anna's fictional plight.

At one end of the historical spectrum is the Victorian period, whose views on women, maternity, and sexuality inflect the film. According to Walter E. Houghton, sex was not openly discussed in the bourgeois home of this era. "It was the skeleton in the parental chamber" (353). Particularly shielded were females, regarded as ethereal angels: "an image wonderfully calculated . . . to dissociate love from sex" (355). For

Houghton, female eroticism "was kept under wraps": "To employ it, except obliquely, was to run the risk of being considered 'fast'" (353). While premarital continence was an ideal for men, it was often violated. (As Sanderson tells Anna, a man is "supposed to sow his wild oats.") For "respectable" women, chastity was de rigueur (354).

Given this ethic, it is clear why the narrative casts Anna as *convinced* of her marriage to Sanderson. Had she had intercourse without such an "assurance," she would have been an unsympathetic heroine. Griffith chooses, rather, to give us "a fallen woman who is not really fallen" (Sochen, 9). In truth, there were many sexually active, unmarried females in Victorian England and America. Houghton claims that, in 1851, one out of every twelve girls in England and Wales "strayed from the path of virtue" (366). Most unfortunate were those who bore one of the 42,000 illegitimate children delivered that year. Obviously, such women could not hide their sexual transgression, which was stamped on their bodies with the mark of pregnancy. Hence they, like Anna Moore, were punished for the sin of physical visibility and plenitude (an ironic twist on women's frequent chastisement for genital invisibility and lack). Clearly, to pun on Anna's name, "more was less," in this regard. These females were further ostracized if they turned to prostitution, one of the few vocations available to them. In *Way Down East*, this probable occupational choice is masked by Anna's wholesome job as a farmhand.

By the turn of the century, attitudes toward the unwed mother began to change. In *Illegitimacy* (1892), Leffingwell finds "questionable" the "sentiment which affixes upon illegitimate motherhood . . . the stigma of irreparable infamy" (82). He condemns those (like Maria Poole or Martha Perkins) who banish such females, pushing them toward solicitation: "That Christian woman who, deaf to all entreaty, turns her maid into the streets because about to become a mother, may fancy she is only upholding the dignity of virtue; but she is also opening to her sister woman the gates of hell" (83). More radically, Leffingwell attacks the value system that blames the mother but vindicates the father: "[M]ight it not be possible to suggest . . . that paternity, even outside the law, creates duties which no honourable man will ever seek to evade?" (81). Similarly, in 1914, Ellen Key regrets that society divorces man's sexual morality from "his 'honour' and 'virtue'" (30–31).

It is precisely this struggle against a gendered "double standard" that animates *Way Down East*, a dynamic verbalized in its opening titles:

> Today woman brought up from childhood to expect ONE CONSTANT MATE possibly suffers more than at any point in the history of mankind because not yet has the man-animal reached this high standard—except perhaps in theory.

While these words address one problematic of the film's narrative (Sanderson's polygamy in light of Anna's monogamy), they avoid the true dilemma: her degradation as "fallen woman" in the face of his initial exculpation. This issue, however, is not entirely silenced but returns toward the close of the film when Anna (hardly "mute") challenges Squire Bartlett's persecution: "You found out so much. Why don't you find out the whole truth? That I was an ignorant girl betrayed through a mock marriage. Why don't you find out what [Sanderson's] life has been?" Clearly, by 1920, these words evince a growing social defense of the unwed mother.

The Care of the Unmarried Mother (1929) notes that by this time nearly all American states punish seduction (having intercourse with a virginal minor). While this crime may not apply to Anna, whose age is indeterminate, another transgression definitely does: "Betrayal After Promise of Marriage" (Barrett, 37). Studies of the era call for the enforcement of penalties against this act, as well as for the guarantee of paternal support when a child is involved.

While the drama of *Way Down East* hinges on Anna's status as an unwed mother, she inhabits that role very briefly. Her infant dies and, for the remainder of the story, her child is a "skeleton in the parental chamber." Thus we seem to have a drama of "mock motherhood" as much as one of mock marriage. We might ask why, given the logic of melodrama, this death "must" happen (as filmmaker Sally Potter inquires in *Thriller* [1979] why the heroine of *La Bohème* "must" die).

Several explanations propose themselves—from aesthetic and political registers. Clearly, pathos is essential to the genre, and the passing of Anna's baby raises its quotient. (Interestingly, as Mary Ann Doane has noted, from the perspective of the reader "[p]athos . . . is a kind of textual rape" [95]; hence the aesthetic strategy employed by *Way Down East* relates to the crime that Anna suffers.) Following tender scenes in which Anna plays with her son, the child sickens. As she rushes to baptize him, heart-wrenching intertitles proclaim: "Alone in the dreadful hours of the night and stricken with this terrible fear of her baby's soul—she performs the sacred rite." Infant mortality was high at this time, and a death in early childhood was not uncommon. Hence the passing of Anna's son lends the fiction a "documentary" note.

However, the literature on unwed motherhood is consumed with *another* kind of childhood fate: murder. In 1892, Leffingwell writes that far "more serious than disgrace [for the unmarried mother] is that saddest crime of humanity, the infanticide to which it so often leads" (69–70). And in 1918, Percy Gamble Kammerer predicts that "[t]he mortality of [illegitimate] children will remain high" (18). His forecast would seem to have been well-founded. An article from a May 1990 Pittsburgh newspaper reports the umbilical strangulation of an infant by his seventeen-year-old unwed mother (Fuocco). Another, in November 1991, documents the disposal of an illegitimate newborn by its distraught postpartum parent (Ackerman). Yet another appears in July of 1993 with the headline "Death of Newborn at Home Draws Inquiry. . . ." As the article notes, "The mother of the baby is unmarried and lives with her parents." This horrific image has also surfaced in fiction. In *The Joy Luck Club*, a Chinese-born mother primes her American-born daughter for urban danger with the following warning: "A man can grab you off the streets . . . make you have a baby. Then you'll kill the baby. And when they find this baby in a garbage can, then what can be done?" (Tan, 106). Does it seem possible that the morose death of Anna's baby in *Way Down East* "stands in for" (and sanitizes) the heinous act of infanticide committed by so many women in her position?

There is a final reason why the baby's loss seems "necessary" within the narrative system. While woman's experience of premarital sex remains hidden, motherhood "writes" that fact across her body and her universe—like a scarlet *M*. As Robert Lang has noted, in melodrama "[t]he suffering body of the hero(ine) becomes a privileged site for the inscription of the Law" (62). Since the genre favors an innocent heroine, the death of Anna's son "erases" sexuality from her corpus and her realm—making her more "suitable" for David Bartlett. Indeed, Leffingwell called for a more significant "erasure": that of such "distinction[s] of birth" that deem some children illegitimate (43). The double oppression of the unwed mother led Leffingwell to question, "Is it maternity that destroys the purity of womanhood, or the lapse which precedes [it]?" (82).

The social space surrounding *Way Down East* is populated by other female figures. The mid–nineteenth century saw the rise of the "New Woman"—middle-class, educated females (like the Tremonts) with interests in career and/or civic duties. They were less inclined toward traditional motherhood and sought to limit the size of their families. As Key notes in 1914, motherhood has "ceased to be the sweet secret dream of the maiden, the glad hope of the wife" (110). According to Carroll Smith-Rosenberg, the New Woman's presence triggered an anti-abortion backlash, spearheaded by the American Medical Association. As she notes: "The urbane married woman constituted the dangerous actor. An A.M.A.-created caricature of the declining middle-class birth rate and the new wealth and customs of the cities, she sought to please herself in the public and urban arena, not to serve others in the cloistered home" (105).

Counterposed to the New Woman was the conventional "True Woman," who "accepted her biological destiny and gloried in her reproductive sexuality" (106). Given these two competing female paradigms, the unwed mother might have been somewhat "redeemed," bound, as she was, to her maternal fate—a True Woman by default.

The Metaphoric Body

> Narrative is [the] acting out of the implications of metaphor.
>   (Peter Brooks)

The question of motherhood not only animates the diegetic level of *Way Down East*; it drives its rhetorical machinery. In *Reading for the Plot*, Peter Brooks argues for the inherent ties between dramatic and figurative discourse: "Plot . . . must *use* metaphor as the trope of its achieved interrelations, and it must *be* metaphor insofar as it is totalizing" (91). If one is to employ such a theory, it is imperative to identify the semantic heart of a text. Following Brooks's lead, we might start with the conclusion of the tale, for him always a privileged site: "The sense of a beginning . . . must in some important way be determined by the sense of an ending" (94). For Brooks, the metonymies of the unfolding narrative literally "give birth" to its metaphorical denouement (29).

It seems significant that one of the major ways in which Griffith transformed his theatrical source is by hyperbolizing its final scenes. While the play's denouement has Anna lost in a snowstorm, the cinematic version finds her adrift upon a river's ice floe, headed for a waterfall. On one level, such a revision can be read as a commercial move: outdoing theater at its own game, giving the film audience something novel for its entertainment dollar. But on another plane, it must be read for its semiotic contribution to the text—its power to shift, retrospectively, all that has preceded it.

Critics have analyzed the import of water imagery in *Way Down East*. Virginia Wright Wexman finds the romantic axis inflected by this symbolism. David first encounters Anna beside a well and later courts her by the river (remarking, suggestively, how its tributaries merge [5]). In Grismer's novelization, when Anna first encounters David, her voice sounds to him like "the far-off droning of a river" (93). For Wexman, Anna's flight toward the raging rapids doubles the "torrential powers of her own sexual urges" (11). Wexman's point seems validated by an ambiguous intertitle in the sequence: "Frenzied, tortured—the calling river." Curiously, we do not know to what the adjectives refer—Anna or the river.

But this figurative linkage of femininity and water can be pursued much further. It seems important that Griffith focuses more on the *river* for his sensational finale than he does on the blizzard. For aquatic metaphors have long been associated with female sexuality. As Luce Irigaray remarks, "[H]istorically the properties of fluids have been abandoned to the feminine" (*This Sex Which Is Not One*, 116). Hence Anna's perilous placement on a river has implications beyond the literal. She is positioned on the water for the sin of having "broken" maternal "waters." That she is near a water*fall* resounds with the biblical notion of woman's spiritual descent. As Nina Auerbach notes, the fallen woman's moral "lapse" is figured in her bodily pose; hence her "prone form" is a staple of illustrative tradition (154). With *Way Down East* that pantheon expands to include the supine Anna Moore.

But Anna is not simply adrift on the river; she is positioned on an *ice floe* that is breaking at winter's end. For Luce Irigaray, ice imagery is always pernicious. In describing the Western male subject (whom she identifies with "solids"), she stresses his rejection of woman's "mechanic of fluids":

> Woman never speaks the same way [as he]. What she emits is flowing. . . . And she is not listened to. . . . Whence the resistances to that voice that *overflows* the [masculine] "subject." Which the "subject" . . . *congeals, freezes*, in its categories until it paralyzes the *voice in its flow*. (*This Sex Which Is Not One*, 112, my italics)

Hence the fact that ice thaws under Anna's body—following a scene in which she challenges patriarchal categories of "good" and "bad" girls—seems suggestive of a certain power in woman to render solids fluid. Significantly, Auerbach sees the novelistic fallen woman as emanating a "hidden potency": she embodies "the defiant powers of all womanhood in the face of little men who would disown them" (163).

The splitting ice resonates with other valences as well. Anna's sin has been that, in a milieu which instructs girls to guard their chastity, she has not. (A Victorian poem waxes lyrical about women "as pure as *snow* on the mount" [Welter, 120, my italics].) In contrast, Anna has been overwhelmed by her attraction to a man. Here is how Grismer describes Anna and Sanderson's initial physical contact: "Their lips met in a first long kiss. *The man was to have his way*" (36, my italics). Similarly, in the film version, an intertitle tells us that Anna's heart has been "caught in a tide of infatuation." Hence she has dared to be erotic in an age that trains women for romantic restraint.

In "Civilized Sexual Morality and Modern Nervous Illness," Freud characterized woman as having a "weaker sexual instinct" (192), and Houghton found that intercourse "was associated by many [Victorian] wives only with a duty" (353). If we were to push this dubious theory of female asexuality further, we might say that Anna was passionate in an age that preferred women "frigid." In the essay entitled "On the Universal Tendency to Debasement in the Sphere of Love," Freud posited direct links between this condition and social repression: "[Women's] long holding back from sexuality . . . has [an] important consequence for them. They are subsequently often unable to undo the connection

11. *Way Down East* (1920). Griffith's denouement finds the heroine (Lillian Gish) on an ice floe. MOMA

between sensual activity and the prohibition and prove to be . . . frigid when such activity is at last allowed them" (186). The vision of Anna, unconscious on the ice, literalizes Freud's notion of sexual "anesthesia." That she is almost killed by such "frigidity" underscores his sense of its psychosocial peril.

In this regard, it is intriguing to query why female sexual dysfunction is associated with a trope for temperature (the cold) while male "impotence" is associated with levels of power. Thomas Laqueur reminds us that in Victorian times human menstruation (and hence normal female sexuality) was equated with mammalian "heat" (estrus) (27), lending new meaning to Anna's meltdown of the frozen river.

The image of Anna insentient on the ice invokes yet another debate of the nineteenth century that intersects the film's narrative line. According to Mary Poovey, midwives and obstetricians of this era debated the efficacy of anesthesia for childbirth. One of their primary reservations involved its alleged excitation of woman's erotic impulses. Here is how W. Tyler Smith describes such a phenomenon in 1848:

> [I]n women, to whom either ether-vapour had been administered during parturition, the signal orgasm had been substituted for their natural pains. . . . Under the chloroform, too, I have been informed of instances in which the lying-in room has been defiled by the most painful and obscene conversation. There appears, therefore . . . to be a moral objection to the administration of the anesthetic agents now in use. (Quoted in Poovey, 147)

Hence Anna's insensibility figures as a trope for the tension between sexual repression (frigidity) and its liberation through anesthetic promiscuity.

It also seems significant that Anna must keep her sexual liaison with Sanderson secret. Though there is a narrative rationale for her act (his alleged desire to hide their "betrothal" from his snobbish father), her gesture evokes Freud's characterization of the bourgeois married woman who needs an adulterous affair to assure her sexual pleasure. Thus the perennially frigid wife is restored to "normal sensation as soon as the condition of prohibition is reestablished by a secret love affair" ("On the Universal Tendency," 186).

Anna posed on the breaking river urges yet another interpretation. *Way Down East* is a work about female erotic transgression, defloration, and illegitimate birth. As such, it is a film structured by the specter of the hymen. According to Sidonie Smith: 'The material and symbolic boundary of the female body . . . [is] the hymen—that physical screen whose presence or absence signals so much. . . . Gender ideologies assign so much meaning to that rupture because they identify that thin skin signed by blood as the irreducible material core of woman's selfhood" (12). For Jane Gallop, this membrane is not only a body part but an "emblematic wall partitioning . . . two realms." It marks an opposition between "innocence/ignorance/virginity" on the one side, and "experience/knowledge/sexuality" on the other; it divides womanly existence into "a before and an after" (52). Clearly, such a dichotomy marks the narrative line of *Way Down East*, with seduction as its temporal midpoint. When Anna realizes that she adores David, an intertitle warns us that her newfound love will be "halted by the past." (Previously, an intertitle informed us, he imagined her his "virginal white flower.") Later, when David trudges along the ice floe, the movement of the river pulls him backward, as though to the past and the moment of Anna's tragedy.

Specifically, that drama turns on the puncturing of her hymen, the act by which a woman passes over the corporeo-symbolic line. Given metaphoric associations between water and female sexuality, it is not difficult to read the ice break as mimetic of the membrane's rupture. That the ice floe is the site of Anna's greatest trial seems fitting, in view of the traumatic role of defloration in her life. In a sense, she relives the trauma through the fragmentation of the river's surface, this time being rescued by the "proper" male: David Bartlett.

There is yet another way in which *Way Down East* is haunted by repetition, and it circles back to Freud. In "The Taboo of Virginity" (1917–1918), he discusses the practice in "primitive" cultures of having a bride deflowered by a surrogate for the groom. Often this process is divided into two stages: "perforation and intercourse" (195): "after the hymen has been ruptured (by hand or with some instrument) there follows a ceremonial act of coitus or mock-intercourse with representatives of the husband" (202). The purpose of this ritual is to spare the husband "the woman's reaction to the painful injury" (202), to shield him from her "unleash[ing] an archaic reaction of hostility towards him" (208).

In an uncanny fashion, the narrative of *Way Down East* replays this scenario. Anna's sexual initiation involves no "mock-intercourse" but entails "mock-marriage intercourse," and she ends up enraged at her partner. Her legitimate bridegroom, David, then steps in to marry her and, as her second mate, avoids her feminine wrath. As Freud notes: "I think it must strike the observer in how uncommonly large a number of cases the woman remains frigid and feels unhappy in a first marriage, whereas after it has been dissolved she becomes a tender wife, able to make her second husband happy. The archaic reaction has, so to speak, exhausted itself on the first object" (206).

If *Way Down East* makes the physical world a trope for woman's body, it also treats her corpus in a figurative mode. In *The Flesh Made Word*, Helena Michie suggests that, in Victorian literature, "dead metaphor" "shrouds" the heroine's body in trite description, accomplishing a murder of both language and subject. Sometimes this operates through the trope of "physiognomy," a catalog of belabored phrases delineating the heroine's appearance. Significantly, in *Way Down East* Anna is identified (through both intertitle and score) with "Those Endearing Young Charms." But Michie finds that metaphor also does vio-

lence to the female protagonist through synechdochal dismemberment—denying her full sexuality by fetishizing privileged body parts
(like arms and hair). This fragmentation announces itself in *Way Down
East* when, in the rescue scene (a melodramatic cliché), Anna trails her
hand in the icy, killing waters. (In her memoir, Gish states that to this
day her limb "aches if [she is] out in the cold for very long" [233–34].)
But Anna's unruly tresses also drift in the water, reminding us that "the
hair of a whole series of Victorian heroines comes . . . to represent their
wantonness, their unnameable body parts" (Michie, 99–100). While,
for Michie, these tired tropes "entrap" women's novelistic bodies, they
ultimately "dissolve"—like the ice upon which Anna struggles.[1]

Clearly, the figure of Anna Moore is not a triumphant one, and
Wexman is correct to suggest that Griffith uses Gish's "frail body to
demonstrate how desperately women need men to rescue them from the
travails of independence" (11). Yet, on another level, Anna seems subversive—in her refusal of double standards, in her resistance to frigidity,
in her heated female liquefaction of the solid masculine world.

The Actress-Body

All that winter, whenever Mr. Griffith saw an ice cake, he
wasn't satisfied till he had me on it.
  (Lillian Gish)

Miss Gish was the gamest little woman in the world. It was
really pathetic to see the forlorn little creature huddled on a
block of ice and the men pushing it off into the stream. . . .
But the cold was bitter and Miss Gish was bare-headed and
bare-handed and without a heavy outer coat so it was necessary at intervals to bring her in and get her warm. Sometimes
when the ice wouldn't behave she was almost helpless from
the cold.
  (Lee Smith)

It is not surprising that, in discussing Anna's plight, Wexman makes
reference to "Gish's frail body," for the production of *Way Down East*
has become notorious in film history for its demands on its performers. Shooting the rescue sequence on location (at White River Junc-
tion, Vermont; Farmington, Connecticut; and Mamaroneck, New

---

[1] It was pointed out to me by an audience member at an MLA session in which I gave a
short version of this paper that Anna's dousing in the water at the end of the film is also a
kind of "baptism" which erases her prior status as a fallen woman. Clearly, if this is so, it
resonates with the earlier scene in which she baptizes her dying illegitimate child.

York), the cast and crew were subjected to harrowing winter conditions. Gish recalls:

> Again and again, I struggled through the storm. Once I fainted—and it wasn't in the script. I was hauled to the studio on a sled; thawed out with hot tea, then brought back to the blizzard. . . . At one time my face was caked with a crust of ice and snow, and icicles like spikes formed on my eyelashes, making it difficult to keep my eyes open. (233)

Above the howling storm, she heard a calculating Griffith shouting to the cameraman: "Billy, move in! Get that face! that face—*get that face!*" (233). Commenting on this extradiegetic melodrama, Robert Henderson wryly notes, "It must have seemed as though Griffith had turned into a Simon Legree with Lillian Gish . . . being pursued across the ice" (213).

Griffith was all but obsessed with his snowstorm. A technical director remembers his eternally yelling, "More ice, more ice." The crew produced some floes by dynamiting the frozen river or by cutting it with a saw (Lennig, 110). For others, he used wooden platforms or blocks of paraffin (112). When his synthetic ice was lost down the falls, he would shout, "How long would it take to build more ice?" (110–12). In addition to artificial ice, Griffith occasionally employed "simulacra" for his actors: either dummies or "doubles" for his principle players.

Significantly, while Griffith was freezing Gish on the river's ice, he was also (like Lennox Sanderson) giving her the "cold shoulder," looking for her amorous "double." As Wexman notes, Griffith's condemnation of male inconstancy in the film "was especially ironic given the director's personal situation, for he was then in the process of transferring his own affections from Lillian Gish . . . to Carol Dempster, whom he would star in future productions. Thus, if Gish had cause to suffer at that moment in history, it was Griffith himself who was to blame" (3).[2]

The Film Body

> The writer is someone who plays with his mother's body . . .
> in order to glorify it, embellish it, or in order to dismember it,
> to take it to the limit of what can be known about the body.
>   (Roland Barthes)

Wexman argues that at the conclusion of *Way Down East*, Anna suffers a "figurative death" from which she is resuscitated by David. In reviving her he thus "appropriates her procreative power" (12).

---

[2] This information concerning Griffith's private life is also discussed in Henderson, 219–20.

If a maternal metaphor animates David's narrative actions, it also informs the discourse around the film's celluloid existence. Following its 1920 release, Griffith continued to edit it (in an act of "glorification" and "dismemberment"), and by 1921 he had "aborted" some thirty minutes of footage (Gunning, 18). In subsequent years, several versions circulated, without any clarity regarding their relative "legitimacy." Aware of this, the Museum of Modern Art decided to preserve *Way Down East* and to restore it to its original length. Tom Gunning deems this process (begun in 1979 and completed in 1984) the "Rebirth of a Movie."

As I have demonstrated, tropes of parturition have long dominated the cinema. For Eisenstein, the image is "birthed" through decoupage, then is "born again" within the viewer's consciousness: "[E]very spectator . . . out of the *womb* of his fantasy . . . creates an image" (33, my italics). Filmic elements not only fabricate an image; they "give birth to a dynamically emerging emotion" (44).

Clearly, the histrionic rescue scene of *Way Down East* is a masterful instance of "birthing" viewer affect through decoupage, and one that Eisenstein especially admired (253). Hence, in a sequence laced with the theme of motherhood, Griffith employs a style that comes to be placed within a maternal discourse. Like the cracking of the river's surface, or the rupturing of Anna's hymen, the fragmenting of the celluloid signals narrative trauma. Like Anna, the text is ultimately saved and "reborn"— this time through the reproductive technologies of archival regeneration.

Works Cited

Ackerman, Jan. "Woman to Be Tried in Her Baby's Death." *Pittsburgh Post-Gazette*, 28 November 1991, C4.

Auerbach, Nina. *Woman and the Demon: The Life of a Victorian Myth.* Cambridge, MA, and London: Harvard University Press, 1982.

Barrett, Robert South. *The Care of the Unmarried Mother.* Alexandria, VA, 1929. Reprint, New York and London: Garland, 1987.

Barthes, Roland. *Pleasure of the Text.* Translated by Richard Miller. New York: Hill & Wang, 1975.

Brady, William A. "Drama in Homespun." *Stage*, January 1937, 98–100.

———. *Showman.* New York: Dutton, 1937.

Brooks, Peter. *Reading for the Plot: Design and Intention in Narrative.* New York: Knopf, 1984.

"Death of Newborn at Home Draws Inquiry in Armstrong." *Pittsburgh Post-Gazette*, 23 July 1993, B5.

Doane, Mary Ann. *The Desire to Desire: The Woman's Film of the 1940s.* Bloomington and Indianapolis: Indiana University Press, 1987.

Eisenstein, Sergei. *Film Form*. Edited and translated by Jay Leyda. New York: Harcourt, Brace and World, 1949.

Freud, Sigmund. "Civilized Sexual Morality and Modern Nervous Illness." 1908. In *The Standard Edition of the Complete Psychological Works of Sigmund Freud*, edited by James Strachey, 9:177–204. London: Hogarth Press, 1959.

———. "On the Universal Tendency to Debasement in the Sphere of Love." 1912. In *The Standard Edition of the Complete Psychological Works of Sigmund Freud*, edited by James Strachey, 11:177–90. London: Hogarth Press, 1957.

———. "The Taboo of Virginity."1917–1918. In *The Standard Edition of the Complete Psychological Works of Sigmund Freud*, edited by James Strachey, 11:193–208. London: Hogarth Press, 1957.

Fuocco, Michael A. "Umbilical Cord Used to Kill Baby, Police Say." *Pittsburgh Post-Gazette*, 4 May 1990, 1, 5.

Gallop, Jane. *Thinking through the Body*. New York: Columbia University Press, 1988.

Gish, Lillian (with Ann Pinchot). *Lillian Gish: The Movies, Mr. Griffith and Me*. Englewood Cliffs, NJ: Prentice-Hall, 1969.

Grismer, Joseph. *Way Down East: A Romance of New England Life*. New York: J. S. Ogilvie, 1900.

Gunning, Tom. "Rebirth of a Movie." *American Film* 10, no. 1 (October 1984): 18–19, 93.

Henderson, Robert M. *D. W. Griffith*. New York: Oxford University Press, 1979.

Houghton, Walter E. *The Victorian Frame of Mind 1830–1870*. 1957. New Haven and London: Yale University Press, 1966.

Irigaray, Luce. "And the One Does Not Stir without the Other." *Signs* 7, no. 1 (Autumn 1981): 60–67.

———. *This Sex Which Is Not One*. Translated by Catherine Porter. Ithaca, NY: Cornell University Press, 1985.

Kammerer, Percy Gamble. *The Unmarried Mother: A Study of Five Hundred Cases*. Boston: Little, Brown, 1918.

Key, Ellen. *The Renaissance of Motherhood*. Translated by Ann E. B. Fries. New York and London: Putnam, 1914.

Lacqueur, Thomas. "Orgasm, Generation, and the Politics of Reproductive Biology." In *The Making of the Modern Body: Sexuality and Society in the Nineteenth Century*, edited by Catherine Gallagher and Thomas Lacqueur, 1–41. Berkeley, Los Angeles and London: University of California Press, 1987.

Lang, Robert. *American Film Melodrama: Griffith, Vidor, Minnelli*. Princeton, NJ: Princeton University Press, 1989.

Leffingwell, Albert. *Illegitimacy and the Influence of Seasons upon Conduct: Two Studies in Demography*. New York: Charles Scribners' Sons, 1892.

Lennig, Arthur. "The Birth of *Way Down East*." *Quarterly Review of Film Studies* 6, no. 1 (Winter 1981): 105–16.

Mayne, Judith. *Private Novels, Public Films*. Athens, GA, and London: University of Georgia Press, 1988.

Michie, Helena. *The Flesh Made Word: Female Figures and Women's Bodies*. New York: Oxford University Press, 1987.

O'Dell, Paul. *Griffith and the Rise of Hollywood*. New York: A. S. Barnes, 1970.

Poovey, Mary. " 'Scenes of an Indelicate Character': The Medical 'Treatment' of Victorian Women." In *The Making of the Modern Body: Sexuality and Society in the Nineteenth Century*, edited by Catherine Gallagher and Thomas Laquer, 137–68. Berkeley, Los Angeles, and London: University of California Press, 1987.

Smith, Lee. "How Griffith Shot the Ice Stuff." *American Cinematographer*, 1 December 1921, 4–5.

Smith, Sidonie. *Subjectivity, Identity, and the Body*. Bloomington and Indianapolis: Indiana University Press, 1993.

Smith-Rosenberg, Carroll. "The Body Politic." In *Coming to Terms: Feminism, Theory, Politics*, edited by Elizabeth Weed, 101–21. New York and London: Routledge, 1989.

Sochen, June. "The New Woman and Twenties America." In *American History/American Film: Interpreting the Hollywood Image*, edited by John E. O'Connor and Martin A. Jackson, 1–15. New York: Ungar, 1979.

Tan, Amy. *The Joy Luck Club*. New York: Putnam, 1989.

Welter, Barbara. "The Cult of True Womanhood: 1820–1860." In *The American Family in Social-Historical Perspective*, edited by Michael Gordon, 224–50. New York: St. Martin's Press, 1973.

Wexman, Virginia Wright. "Birth, Power and Women's Choices in Griffith's *Way Down East*." Paper delivered at the Society for Cinema Studies Conference, 1990. Republished in another form in *Creating the Couple: Love, Marriage, and Hollywood Performance*, 49–63. Princeton, NJ: Princeton University Press, 1993.

Williams, Martin. *Griffith: First Artist of the Movies*. New York: Oxford University Press, 1980.

4

The Horror Film

BIRTH TRAUMAS: PARTURITION AND HORROR IN
ROSEMARY'S BABY

Multiple Births

Before you were born darling
I carried you on my lap the prince
 of whales and I huffed and I puffed
through the great acline making our own
 mountain from testaments of wet love
Love's labor to skin to blood
to cellular surprise
 (Summer Brenner, "Blissed Raga")

nausea, vomit, muscle strain . . .
afraid of what it will/won't be.
anxious. it's got to look like him
it's got to look like me. be healthy. be live. be all right
 (Wanda Coleman, "Giving Birth")

Contemporary popular culture has delivered us multiple embodiments of childbirth.[1] In the supermarket, the slick cover of *Working Mother* presents a radiant television personality who is "Pretty and Pregnant." *Newsweek* flaunts a responsible expectant couple purchasing Mass Mutual Insurance. *Parents* pictures a postpartum madonna gazing raptly at her infant—nursing now, but planning to use Gerber Baby Formula.[2] In the local video store, the self-help aisle is stocked with reassuring instructional tapes: *Your First Baby* and *Childbirth Preparation*. The neighborhood bookshop features *Pregnant and Lovin' It*, a guide to "one of the greatest, most pleasurable events of . . . life" (Curtis, Caroles, and Beard, 4).

---

[1] Throughout this chapter I will use terms like "childbirth" and "parturition" to signify a series of events associated with the process of pregnancy, delivery, and postpartum experience.

[2] I am referring to material in *Newsweek* (14 May 1990) and *Working Mother* (June 1989). The precise issue of *Parents* is not known.

12. *Rosemary's Baby* (1968). Rosemary (Mia Farrow) and Guy (John Cassavetes) anticipating the arrival of their child. MOMA

The popular cinema of past decades, however, has proffered alternative views of maternity. *It's Alive* (1974) opens with a woman in labor, trying to quell a premonition that something is dreadfully wrong. The sequence ends with bloodied doctors evacuating a delivery room where they have inadvertently birthed her murderous monster. This eerie scenario is extended in the film's two sequels: *It Lives Again* (1978) and *It's Alive III* (1987). In *The Brood* (1979) a female mental patient incubates heinous fetuses in external belly sacs; *Embryo* (1976) and *Eraserhead* (1978) pursue the theme of malevolent extrauterine conception.[3]

Our reflex is to keep these diverse impressions of childbirth separate: to deem some idyllic and others grotesque, some accurate and others apocryphal, some objective and others subjective, some natural and others perverse. But work on horror suspects such binary oppositions, recognizing realism in the bizarre. Caryn James sees the genre as evoking "universal" terrors (15); Dennis L. White notes its roots in "the common fears of everyday life" (16).

Some scholars have claimed veracity for horror in the *psychological* domain, seeing its diegetic dementia as but a transmutation of "normal" consciousness. Thus the doppelgänger is viewed not only as a supernatural fiction, but as a metaphor for the perennially divided human self.[4] Other critics have found horror's "validity" in the *political* sphere: it is claimed that Robert Weine created a harbinger of Nazi Germany (Kracauer); that George Romero crafted a bourgeois American Nightmare (Wood, *Hollywood*, 70–134); that Don Siegel created a parable of the red menace (Biskind, 140). For some writers, horror articulates cultural tensions. Dana Polan finds domestic strife in *The Howling* (202–8), and Serafina Bathrick decodes sexual fears in *Carrie* (9–10). Andrew Tudor locates a "trend toward family-oriented horror" that he sees as "part of a larger pattern . . . reflecting . . . the increasing *proximity* (physical, psychic and social) of the fictional threat" (128). Hence in psychic or in social registers horror constitutes an expressionistic "allegory of the real."[5]

It is from this perspective that we will view Roman Polanski's *Rosemary's Baby* (1968)—a movie that heralds both the birth of horror and the horror of birth in the modern cinema (Carroll, *The Philosophy of Horror*, 2, 107). Though the film is certainly an odious fable of parturition, it is also a skewed "documentary" of the societal and personal turmoil that has regularly attended female reproduction. While for Rhona

---

[3] For further discussion of some of these films see also Paul, 354–80; and Creed, *The Monstrous Feminine*, 43–58.

[4] See Keppler.

[5] Dana Polan coined this term for me in a discussion of the paper, but let me elaborate on its use. Allegory is commonly understood to be an extended narrative that carries a second meaning along with the surface story. As Gay Clifford points out, "[A]llegorical action often takes the form of a . . . quest, or a pursuit" exposing a "credible and realistic hero to a journey through an extraordinary allegorical world" (11, 25). Often, as in the case of *Frankenstein* or *The Trial* (both cited by Clifford), though the diegetic universe is fantastic, it invokes a real social order (moribund and irrational bureaucracy in *The Trial*; the perils of technological invention in *Frankenstein*). It is in this sense that I apply the term to *Rosemary's Baby*. While on one level Rosemary's journey proceeds as a hyperbolic

Berenstein the film reflects the "horrifying status of motherhood in American patriarchal culture" (55), I will read the film against that grain, for its utterance of women's private experience of pregnancy.

As Brenda O. Daly and Maureen T. Reddy have noted, "Any effort at redefining motherhood must include some consideration of childbirth's meaning" (4).

The "Gynecological Gothic"[6]

> Last night I dreamed I gave birth to a monster. Are you that menacing creature I saw in my dream? My monster, my-self. . . . *Maybe it's Rosemary's baby in there.*
> (Phyllis Chesler, my italics)

Rosemary's Baby is the story of Rosemary and Guy Woodhouse (Mia Farrow and John Cassavetes), newlyweds who rent an apartment in the Bramford, a Victorian high-rise reputed to have been haunted by witches. Guy, an actor, is consumed with his career. Rosemary, a traditional homemaker, wants to start a family. Once the Woodhouses move in, their eccentric, elderly neighbors, Roman and Minnie Castevet (Sidney Blackmer and Ruth Gordon), insinuate themselves into the couple's life. At first, Guy resists them, while Rosemary urges him to socialize. But after a dinner party during which Roman claims a certain influence in the theater world, Guy seems bent on befriending the Castevets. Soon, he expresses his willingness to have a child. Gradually, Rosemary becomes wary of the Castevets: she wonders why the previous tenant barricaded a door leading to their apartment; she hears strange chants emanating through their adjoining wall; a young female guest of the Castevets suddenly commits suicide; Minnie gives Rosemary a foul-smelling amulet to wear.

Rosemary becomes pregnant and, despite her reservations, allows Minnie to advise her—to administer herbal medicines and to enlist the medical attentions of Dr. Abraham Sapirstein (Ralph Bellamy). Rather than thrive, Rosemary sickens and fears that something is amiss. When her friend Hutch (Maurice Evans) warns her that the Castevets are demons, he mysteriously dies, willing her a volume on witchcraft through

---

fiction, on another it charts the psychological and historical "realities" of quotidian pregnancy. According to theorists, allegory can apply either to the process by which an author creates a fiction or to the strategy by which a critic reads it. It is this latter sense that I invoke, and I make no claims for allegorical intentionality on the part of Ira Levin (the film is based on Ira Levin's 1967 novel of the same title) or Roman Polanski.

[6] This term was used by Penelope Gilliatt in her review of *Rosemary's Baby*.

which she learns the terrible facts. She tries, frantically, to escape the clutches of the Castevets, who have ensnared Guy with the promise of stage stardom. When Rosemary seeks refuge with her own obstetrician, Dr. Hill (Charles Grodin), he thinks she is crazed and calls Dr. Sapirstein and Guy to retrieve her. Rosemary flees and gives birth to a baby in her home, but the infant is taken from her and she is told it is dead. As the film ends, she follows the sound of a baby's cry to the Castevets' apartment where a coven is celebrating the arrival of the devil-child. Though at first repulsed, Rosemary soon approaches the cradle to comfort the infant.

Significantly, Rosemary gains access to her child through a door that conjoins the Woodhouse and Castevet abodes—a geographic proximity that has doomed her pregnancy. This trope of *contiguity* will also inform our methodology, as we read the film in the "space" of various neighboring cultural discourses on childbirth: the sacred, the mythic, the obstetrical, the psychiatric, the therapeautic, and the artistic. Through the juxtaposition of such diverse textual "locales," their complex boundaries will be outlined. For as Stuart Hall has noted, the study of popular culture "yields most when it is seen in relation to a more general, a wider history" (230).

False Labor

> One might say that the true subject of the horror genre is the struggle for recognition of all that our civilization *re*presses or *op*presses.
> (Robin Wood)

As multifarious visions of childbirth have proliferated, so have competing discourses, each seeking to explain and contain it. Despite this vocality, the dialogue has disempowered woman or relegated her to virtual silence. Religious thought elides her from the birth act (as in Eve's appearance from Adam's rib, Athena's creation from the forehead of Zeus, or Aphrodite's formation from the phallus of Uranus). Traditional obstetrics denies the parturient woman agency, configuring her as passive patient. Psychiatry damns her with faint praise for successfully achieving maternal maturity by sublimating her penis envy.

No wonder that in this plethora of voices many sense a mutism. Iris Marion Young is not "surprised to learn that discourse on pregnancy omits subjectivity," and that "the specific experience of women has been absent from most of our culture's discourse about human experience" (45). Myra Leifer corroborates this insight: "Although for many years researchers have been interested in the effect of the trauma of birth on the newborn . . . strikingly less attention has been given to its impact upon the mother" (117). It is important that Leifer (writing in 1980) uses the term "trauma"; for in the decades immediately preceding, voluntary, middle-class pregnancy was regarded more romantically. As E. Zajicek remarks, "In the 1930s and 1940s, when views of women were more obviously stereotyped . . . it was considered important for them to experience only the rewarding, fulfilling aspects of pregnancy and motherhood." Any deviance from this was regarded as "a sign of maladjustment" (Wolkind and Zajicek, 32, 35). Even a current manual promises expectant women a purely "joyful" pregnancy, urging them to "be free of fear and full of confidence" (Curtis, Caroles, and Beard, 4).

The feminist movement of the 1970s spurred a reconsideration of parturition in two contradictory ways. On the one hand, reproduction was further glorified by the proponents of woman-centered, natural childbirth. Suzanne Arms deems this the "most profound, personal experience a woman can have" and claims that if woman finds it "dangerous, risky, painful and terrifying," it is only because the male medical system has made it so (xiii, 23). On the other hand, the era saw a lifting of taboos concerning childbirth. In a satiric attack on the Lamaze method, Nora Ephron complains that it "never crossed [her] mind that [she] would live through the late 60's and early 70's in America only to discover that in the end what was expected of [her] was a brave, albeit vigorous squat in the fields like the heroine of *The Good Earth*" (88). On a darker note, Adrienne Rich admits that pregnancy is not only an exquisite phenomenon but one characterized by "[a]nxiety, depression, [and] the sense of being a sacrificial victim" (153). While the bleak side of parturition represents just another rival discourse, its admission stands as a corrective to more ubiquitous and sanguine views.[7] Released in 1968, *Rosemary's Baby* announces this discursive disturbance, and the film's malign mise-en-scène bespeaks a return of the repressed.

In considering the film, we might first examine the work's chilling atmosphere (the threatening Bramford, its repugnant tenants, the rumors of savagery, the nightmare imagery). As Diane Waldman has noted, the narrative has all the earmarks of the Gothic mode (the naive young heroine, her opaque husband, the awesome mansion, the supernatural events [308–25]). As such, it might well be dismissed as mere phantasmagoria, but it is more challenging to query the film's relevance to childbirth lore. In so doing, we follow the lead of James Twitchell, who finds all horror related to themes of "sex and reproduction" (66).

[7] Marcia Landy helped focus the discussion on the issue of discourse and suggested the usefulness of Michel Foucault's *The History of Sexuality*, vol. 1.

In 1945, Freudian psychiatrist Helene Deutsch acknowledged maternity's disquieting aspects, despite her conviction that it was woman's sublime calling. In one passage, she spoke of pregnancy as having an "abnormal psychic charge," and employed the term "horror" to characterize delivery. She resorted to the same phrasing to describe women with postpartum problems: "Something has happened during childbirth to disappoint [them] and fill them with *horror*" (135, 251). More recently, in Leifer's interviews with primiparous women, subjects related the "horror stories" they had heard (45).

Such tales are not entirely fictional. As Ann Dally has stated, "[T]hroughout history, until recent times, motherhood was always close to death." Death stalked the newborn in periods of high infant mortality; in England and Wales of 1885, for example, 14–16 percent of babies died during their first year. But childbirth was also "one of the greatest hazards that adult women had to face" (26, 31). One specter in the chamber of maternal horrors was puerperal fever, which reached epidemic proportions between the seventeenth and nineteenth centuries. Most ghoulish was its transmission by doctors, who, unaware of sepsis, went directly from dissecting cadavers to delivering babies. As Julia Kristeva remarks, "[H]ere is a fever where what bears life passes over to the side of the dead body" (159).[8] Another potential medical crisis was obstructed labor, for which physicians used torturous tools—reminiscent of those in *Dead Ringers* (1988)—to extract (or decapitate) the baby. Sheila Kitzinger describes such a delivery scene, evocative of a sequence in the film *Alien* (1979): "[A] long . . . labour may be terminated by rupture of the uterus and death of the baby and mother, and to those helping it must look really *as if the baby has burst up out of the womb*" (85–86, my italics).

Beyond such parallels between the macabre and childbirth, what else can we read from the supernatural aura of *Rosemary's Baby*? Rich speaks of female reproduction as conventionally assigned "malign occult influences," as being "vulnerable to or emanating evil" (163–64). Kitzinger talks of parturition as a "ritual state" necessitating the intervention of shamans, priests, and priestesses (71). Both associate pregnancy with "possession." For Kitzinger, this means "being taken over by an unknown and even hostile stranger" (78); for Rich, it connotes domination by labor's painful contractions. Both remark on the uncanny sense of "doubling" and "splitting" in reproduction—the former at conception; the latter at delivery.[9] Hence pregnancy is a "liminal" or "marginal" state (Kitzinger, 67). Kristeva extends this discussion, noting the link between maternity and sacred defilement: "Because of her parturition and

---

[8] On this issue, see also Creed, "Horror and the Monstrous Feminine," 44–71.

[9] See also Young, 46.

the blood that goes with it, *she* will be 'impure'" (99). While such characterizations are, clearly, pernicious, Grete Bibring wonders whether, by banishing "magical and superstitious customs surrounding pregnancy," science has "removed certain concepts and activities which . . . help in organizing and channeling the intense emotional reactions of the pregnant woman" (113–21).

But what of *Rosemary's Baby*'s specific references to witchcraft? What social or psychic echoes reverberate here? It is necessary to recall the history of childbirth, prior to the ascendancy of the male physician, when care of the pregnant woman was entrusted to a midwife—often a poor, older peasant woman with little standing in the community. Frequently, such individuals were thought to bear evil spirits, capable of inducing female fertility or male impotence (Deutsch, 206; Rich, 135ff.). Consequently, midwives were often accused of sorcery and were cited in the *Malleus Maleficarum*, the primary reference volume on witchcraft of its era. As Thomas Rogers Forbes writes, "Because midwives so often were in bad repute, even an innocent practitioner might be accused of witchcraft if the delivery had an unhappy outcome" (Forbes, 5; Ehrenreich, 13). When the birth was successful, midwives might still be charged with selling an infant's soul to the devil. In the *Compendium Maleficarum* of 1626, Guaccius writes: "[W]hen [witches] do not kill the babies, they offer them (horrible to relate) to the demons in this execrable manner. After the child is born the witch-midwife . . . pretends that something should be done to restore the strength of the baby, carries it outside the bedroom, and elevating it on high [offers] it to the Prince of Devils" (quoted in Forbes, 128).

In recent years, feminists have challenged liturgical discourse, reclaiming the figure of the midwife/witch. By rereading it, they have seen her as the repository of patriarchal fears of female strength, and as a scapegoat for the emergent obstetrical profession. As Rich notes, "[M]en gradually annexed the role of birth-attendant and thus assumed authority over the very sphere which had originally been one source of female power and charisma" (129).

In this light, it is tempting to recast Minnie Castevet as an ersatz modern midwife, shrouded in misogyny. From her first entrance into the Woodhouse apartment (when she asks if Rosemary will have children), she is concerned with her neighbor's reproductive life, and when Rosemary becomes pregnant, it is Minnie who administers homeopathic potions (filled with "snails and puppy dog tails"). Like the ancient midwife, she must transfer her power to a male physician (Abe Sapirstein), who, nonetheless, relies on her expertise. Significantly, rumors of the Bramford's haunting center on the Trench sisters' cannibalism—they are said to have fed upon babies. The historical roots of the midwife/

witch are consonant with Minnie's naturalistic presentation, a touch that caught critics off guard. Robert Chapetta complains that the demons in Polanski's film are "not frightening, but an absurd lot, rather like a small far-out California religious sect" (38).

Hysterical Pregnancy

> The key to monster movies . . . is the theme of horrible and mysterious psychological and physical change . . . which is directly associated with secondary sexual characteristics . . . and with . . . erotic behavior.
>   (Walter Evans)

Although some unsettling elements of the film are explained by the actual linkage of witchcraft and childbirth, it is equally fruitful to place them within a *psychological* frame. For much of what passes for Rosemary's demented musings echoes representations of women's *ordinary experience of parturition.* The birth process starts with conception and, in *Rosemary's Baby*, the primal scene is overlaid with terror. One night, Guy reveals his sudden desire to father a baby, whereupon he choreographs a candlelight dinner. The meal is interrupted by the arrival of Minnie, who brings her special "chocolate mouse [her pronunciation]." Though Rosemary dislikes its "chalky undertaste," Guy urges her to eat it. (Significantly, Kristeva finds a link between culinary and maternal defilement: "Dietary abomination" has "a parallel . . . in the abomination provoked by the fertilizable or fertile feminine body" [100].)

Within moments of eating, Rosemary collapses and Guy carries her to bed. Rosemary suffers a distraught delirium: she sails on a ship; Guy rips off her clothing; Rosemary gazes up at religious paintings; she walks through flames; a monster's hand maims her; hags tie her down and paint her body; she begs the pope for forgiveness. "This is not a dream," she shouts; "this is really happening!" The next morning, when Rosemary notices scratches on her skin, she asks Guy what has transpired. He says that, despite her faint, he had not wanted to "miss baby night," and confesses that sex had been fun in a "necrophilic sort of way."

This warped rape fantasy reverberates with cultural clichés of woman's sexual position. With female eroticism conceived as "the embodiment of guilt," it is logical that Rosemary seeks the Holy Father's blessing (Rich, 164). That she is semiconscious during intercourse mocks woman's "designated" coital stance: passive and undemanding. That Guy is uninvolved with her impregnation evokes primitive beliefs that human males are removed from procreation. Finally, the devious denouement of Rosemary's pregnancy assigns her blame. It is *she* who has most wanted a child: even in her drugged stupor, she pleads to "make a baby." It is *she* who has arranged to live in the Bramford, despite its chilling reputation. It is *she* who has pushed intimacy with the Castevets; Guy had originally warned, "If we get friendly with an old couple . . . we'll never get rid of them." Thus the New Eve is charged with Original Sin.

Louise Sweeney found viewing *Rosemary's Baby* "like having someone else's nightmare" (6). In truth, dreams have long been linked to the horror genre, and Noël Carroll sees the form as fraught with "nightmare imagery" ("Nightmare," 16). Significantly, researchers have also noted the importance of dreams to pregnancy. Deutsch deems the nine-month period a quasi-oneiric state, since women must imagine an abstract being. She also finds women prone to reverie in this condition and records some patient dreams that are reminiscent of Rosemary's. Certain fantasies occur involving water, conjuring the amniotic fluid; others offer scenarios of harassment: "In such dreams wild beasts chase the dreamer, or a sharp claw or tooth is plunged into some part of her body. She tries to flee, but her persecutors run after her from behind while she faces another danger in front" (233).

As Rosemary's pregnancy progresses, its baroque narrative constructs a distorted projection of quotidian experience. Almost immediately, she is consumed with angst: she is uneasy when Dr. Hill requests a second blood sample; she develops insomnia upon hearing the Castevets' voices next door. When Rosemary visits Dr. Sapirstein, she reveals that she fears an ectopic complication. Though, within the diegesis, there is an unearthly rationale for Rosemary's concerns, her state of mind is not unusual. Leifer notes a "growing sense of anxiety" accompanying pregnancy, along with a feeling of "emotional liability" (31). In the past, such nervousness was often regarded as hysterical, and its admission was discouraged. Recently, however, clinicians have seen such tension in a positive light as "a significant reflection of the developing maternal bond" (47). That Rosemary's fearfulness borders on paranoia is understandable, given the assumptions of the plot. Yet pregnant women unburdened by diabolical interference can approach this state. As Leifer notes: "Women commonly beg[in] to view the outside world as potentially threatening. They bec[ome] more cautious in their activities, fear[ing] that they might be harmed or attacked" (49). For Leifer, this is not a pathological symptom but a protective stance that reflects "realistic concerns" for safety.

The premise of *Rosemary's Baby* is that the heroine gestates a devil-child; but worries of an abnormal fetus are common. Deutsch mentions the "painful idea that [the baby] will be a monster, an idiot, a cripple"

(151). And Leifer reports that "[w]omen typically . . . vividly imagine a variety of deformities that they had either read about or seen" (47). Some women perceive the fetus as a foreign being: Deutsch admits that it can be seen as a "parasite" which "exploits" the maternal host (131). Interestingly, an upbeat 1968 pregnancy manual uses this precise language, characterizing the "tiny parasite of a fetus" as appropriating the body of its "mother-host" for "his own purposes" (Liley and Day). Even the cool discourse of modern science casts the fetus in an eerie light. Three years before the release of *Rosemary's Baby*, Lennart Nilsson published his shocking, groundbreaking photographs of embryos in *Life* magazine. As ontogeny repeats phylogeny, the embryo is seen to resemble an aquatic being—what poet Brenner calls "the prince of whales." Genetics catalogs the fetus's sequential organ development, informing us when it acquires what; in Carroll's words, "categorical incompleteness" is an attribute of the monster (*The Philosophy of Horror*, 33).

While women have been told to purge such disturbing thoughts (to deny pregnancy's "chalky undertaste"), Leifer argues for their validity: "These concerns often represen[t] realistic apprehensions about a variety of unknown events" (47). Patriarchy has its own reasons for eliding female ambivalence. While man has traditionally imagined the *mother* as "abject"—associated as she is with menstrual blood and infantile excrement (115–16, 99–100)—he rejects the thought that she might find abjection in *him* (the beloved child). Such inversion constitutes a narcissistic wound to one who refuses to see the "Other" in himself.

Along with a case of the "nerves," Rosemary suffers illness, a fact that surfaces cultural confusion about the status of pregnancy. On the one hand, history has amassed a compendium of medical disorders that collectively mark the state a "disease"—from eclampsia, to toxemia, to varicose veins, to morning sickness. Yet with the threat of physiological harm abated, women have challenged institutionalized paternalism, claiming recognition for the pregnant woman's health, strength, and fortitude.

Ironically, while physicians have made the parturient woman an Imaginary Invalid, they have often disregarded her justified complaints. In *Rosemary's Baby*, the heroine's discomforts are consistently minimized, as though "pain, like love, [were] embedded in the ideology of motherhood" (Rich, 157). Guy ignores her ailments, and Dr. Sapirstein implies that they are psychosomatic. In 1939, a study showed nausea in pregnancy to entail the repudiation of femininity; in 1943, another found queasiness prevalent in women "who had an unconscious desire not to be pregnant" (Wolkind and Zajicek, 77, 76). Though Guy and Dr. Sapirstein have devious reasons for slighting Rosemary's grievances, most doctors and husbands ostensibly do not.

Following the trajectory of documented pregnancies, Rosemary's discomfort and fear temporarily lessen at the moment of "quickening." As Leifer notes, "The almost universal reactions to this event [are] immense relief . . . and a new feeling of confidence" (78). However, when Rosemary shouts "It's alive!," the contemporary audience is struck by the intertextual irony of her words.

As Rosemary's term continues, she becomes appalled by her pallid and wasted appearance. While her condition results from demonic poisoning and stands in *inverse* relation to the usual plenitude of pregnancy, some ordinary expectant women dread their corporeal transformation. Leifer claims that many regard their swelling bodies as "ego-alien" and view them in fantastic terms: "The rapidly growing abdomen continued to evoke anxiety, and women reported feeling like Alice in Wonderland, upon taking the magic pills: growing and growing, with no end in sight . . . losing control over their bodies" (35). For Walter Evans such "mysterious" metamorphosis of secondary sex characteristics is central to horror (54).

Consumed by her fears of possession, Rosemary refuses to see friends, tracing the pregnant woman's alleged "increased self-preoccupation and . . . decline of emotional investment in the external world" (Leifer, 43). Virginia Wright Wexman and Diane Waldman see Rosemary not only as carrying a child, but as becoming infantilized (Wexman, 34; Waldman, 310).

As Rosemary's worries multiply, she grows leery of Guy's involvement with the Castevets: She is puzzled by the scratches he has made on her body; she searches for cult markings on his shoulder; she is perplexed that he can no longer return her gaze; she wonders why he is suddenly a popular actor, whose "break" comes at the expense of another's welfare. While Rosemary's doubts are induced by supernatural causes, such behavior can occur in ordinary circumstances. "Anxiety about losing one's husband . . . was expressed by more than half of the women [questioned]" (Leifer, 49–50).

For these myriad reasons, expectant women may feel a loss of control, a challenge to their physical and spiritual autonomy. For Zajicek, pregnancy is "a period of emotional stress" with a "high potential for psychiatric breakdown." Women seek external support out of a desire "to be cared for and protected"—a fact mirrored in Rosemary's unwise turn to Minnie Castevet (Wolkind and Zajicek, 60; Leifer, 54). The film chronicles this dependency, as Rosemary passively "transfers" stewardship of her pregnancy to others. Though she has wanted a child, it is Guy who orchestrates conception. One friend sends Rosemary to Dr. Hill; then Minnie reroutes her to Dr. Sapirstein. Since the latter is a "front," Minnie engineers Rosemary's care behind the scenes. Both Guy and

Sapirstein attempt to keep Rosemary ignorant, cautioning her against reading. In a drugged delivery fraught with childbirth "amnesia," Rosemary's baby is stolen from her in fulfillment of Guy's Faustian pact.

An alternative title for the film might read: *Whose Baby Is It Anyway?*

Postpartum Document

> I cannot remember the birth. Cold white rooms, cleanliness
> the color of nothing. Sometimes a woman dreams that she's
> given birth to a litter of piglets attached to her breasts like
> pink balloons. When I look in the crib there is no baby.
> (Maxine Chernoff, "A Birth")

The arrival of Rosemary's child is one of the most ghastly scenes in the film. Taken by Guy and Abe Sapirstein from Dr. Hill's office, she returns to her apartment, where she falls on the floor in the throes of labor. A hallucinatory sequence unfolds in which a coven of witches gag her, tie her down, sedate her, and deliver her of a male child whom they spirit away. On one level (divested of the occult), the scene can be read as a dramatization of old-fashioned home birth, with a female midwife present. The feigned death of Rosemary's child stands in for the infant mortality that obtained until the modern era. (In justifying his evil sacrifice to the Castevets, Guy even asks Rosemary, "Suppose you had had the baby and lost it—wouldn't it have been the same?") On another tier, the birth scene superimposes upon that historical site the malevolent mythology of witchcraft: the notion of midwives as satanic, as stealing babies for the devil. On a final plateau, the vignette subjectively replicates woman's experience of traditional hospital birth—of being physically restrained, anesthetized, and summarily separated from her baby. Here is how poet Diana Di Prima portrays such an event in "Nativity":

> Dark timbers of lost forests falling into my bed.
> My hairs stirring, not asleep. Did they fetter me
> with cat's paw, rock root, the beard
> (o shame) of woman? They fettered me
> w/ leather straps, on delivery table. I cd not
> cry out. Forced gas mask over mouth,
> slave. I cd not
> turn head. Did they fetter me
> w/ breath of a fish? These poison airs? I cd not
> turn head, move hand, or leg
> thus forced. They tore child from me. Whose?
>
> (Chester, 107)

A woman interviewed by Leifer recalls postpartum stress that is also comparable to Rosemary's:

> The next day . . . all my fears came to the fore. I was so tired, and in a very strange state. . . [E]very time I heard a baby crying, I thought it was mine and that nobody was responding to his screaming . . . I began to feel really paranoid, very persecuted, that maybe they didn't bring him in because something was wrong with him. Then I began to think that maybe the baby had died that night, and I got into a whole fantasy about that. (Leifer, 59)

Though Rosemary suspects that her "dead" child is living—not that a live one is dead—her sense of disorientation approaches this. She becomes alarmed when she hears a muffled infant's wail next door, and when one of Minnie's friends saves the milk expressed from the maternal breast.

Even Rosemary's response to her demon-child suggests a new mother's contradictory emotions. Bibring finds frequent "disturbances in the earliest attitudes of the young mother toward her newborn baby," and Deutsch remarks that many women first view their newborn as a "rejected alien object" (Deutsch, 251; Bibring, 117). Rosemary's vacillation between love and hate should not surprise us in a genre structured by the "conflict between attraction and repulsion" (Carroll, "Nightmare," 17). Such a magnetic field sustains the tension of *Rosemary's Baby*, which acknowledges parturition as a bliss and a blight.

Like most social groups, the Castevets' coven harnesses guilt to prod Rosemary toward parental bonding. "Aren't you his mother?" they ask; "Be a mother to your baby." Maternal "instinct" triumphs; ambivalence is quashed. On the one hand, this ending can be seen as oppressive. Even in the hands of the devil, the dominant (Christian) ideology of mothering obtains (Waldman, 314–15). From another perspective, the denouement is progressive. Rather than reject the devil child (the virtual anti-Christ), Rosemary accepts it—distancing herself from the Catholic madonna (Berenstein, 68–69). This ending so displeased Ray Bradbury that he authored another: "I went back to see *Rosemary's Baby* the other night. I had to go back. . . . Sitting there in the dark watching, I felt the same sense of dissatisfaction. The truth is I simply do not believe or accept the ending of *Rosemary's Baby*" (Bradbury, 149). In his script, Rosemary carries her newborn to a church, confronting the Almighty with his "son"— harking back to the biblical connection between Lucifer and God.

It seems significant that as Rosemary rocks the cradle, we never fully glimpse her infamous baby, who remains forever offscreen.[10] On one level, this scopic denial foregrounds Carroll's notion that monsters are

---

[10] Though we do not see the baby in this sequence, there is an earlier moment (after Rosemary has first approached the cradle) when she is horrified by the child's appearance and asks, "What have you done to his eyes?" Later, when she learns that her son is the

"inconceivable" (*The Philosophy of Horror*, 21). But on another, it addresses horror's appropriation of the quotidian. In accepting her loathsome progeny, Rosemary acknowledges her *own* demons—the fears of motherhood that society wants hushed. Thus, in some respects, Rosemary's baby is her double, reminding us of Marcia Landy's observation that "the monster's transformation is associated with reproduction, like a woman" (411). In her diary, Phyllis Chesler calls her own fetus "my monster, myself," querying, "What if [it's] born . . . with my anger, my excesses?" (101). Polan notes an introspective trend in contemporary Grand Guignol, which now "suggest[s] that the horror is not merely among us, but rather part of us" (202). But there is another reason that the monster comes, ultimately, to be identified with Rosemary. As Marie-Hélène Huet points out, historically the deformation of babies was tied to the agency of the *female* parent. As she notes: "Instead of reproducing the father's image, as nature commands, the monstrous child bore witness to the violent desires that moved the mother at the time of conception or during pregnancy. . . . The monster thus erased paternity and proclaimed the dangerous power of the female imagination" (1).

If *Rosemary's Baby* assumes a certain "banality" to horror, it replays that thesis on the level of style. With the exception of the dream/hallucination sequences, the work is crafted with conventional cinematic verisimilitude: long-shot/long-take format, standard lenses, location shooting, continuity editing, credible costume and decor. For Beverle Houston and Marsha Kinder, *Rosemary's Baby* "create[s] the impression that never . . . were things so clearly seen, so concrete, so 'real'" (18).

This dialectic aspect of pregnancy is evident in Margaret Atwood's short story "Giving Birth," where a parturient woman (Jeannie) is "shadowed" by an invisible lady who accompanies her to the hospital. While Jeannie takes an optimistic view of pregnancy, her alter ego voices reservations:

> [T]here is another woman in the car. She's sitting in the front seat, and she hasn't turned or acknowledged Jeannie in any way. She, like Jeannie, is going to the hospital. She too is pregnant. She is not going to the hospital to *give* birth, however, because the word, the words, are too alien to her experience. . . . Jeannie has seen her before, but she knows little about her except that she is a woman who did not wish to become pregnant, who did not choose to divide herself like this, who did not choose any of these ordeals, these initiations. *It would be no use telling her that everything is going to be fine.* (139, my italics)

---

devil's child, she shouts, "It's not true," and her image is superimposed with a shot of a creature's eyes. These eyes may be her child's eyes or they may be those of the devil; it is unclear.

Afterbirth

> A pointing finger always accompanies the classic text: the
> truth is thereby long desired and avoided, kept in a kind of
> *pregnancy* for its full term, a *pregnancy* whose end, both liber-
> ating and catastrophic, will bring about the utter end of the
> discourse.
>
>   (Roland Barthes, my italics)

Early on in *Rosemary's Baby* we learn that the Woodhouse and Castevet
apartments were once a single residence, which was later subdivided.
The Woodhouses now live in the "back rooms" of the original lodging.
Significantly, at the film's conclusion, Rosemary opens the barricaded
door that conjoins the two habitations. Sensing that her attendants are
sequestering her child, she goes to her hall closet and removes the rear
shelves. Like Lewis Carroll's Alice, she peers through a hole into her
neighbors' cultic abode (Wexman, 41). Grasping a knife, she traverses
the space, leaving home for a satanic Wonderland. (As Julia Kristeva has
noted, abjection involves an ambiguity of "borders" [67].)

Clearly, Rosemary's trajectory has implications beyond the physical,
for it replays (in navigational terms) the thematic project of the film.
While contemporary discourse, be it patriarchal or feminist, has often
idealized childbirth and suppressed its disturbing terrain, the film nego-
tiates the geography that connects these ideological quarters. In jour-
neying to the Castevets' suite, Rosemary links woman's conscious and
unconscious pregnancies, her ecstatic and despondent views, modern
and ancient medical practices, scientific and mystical beliefs, realistic and
supernatural portrayals. In unleashing the horrific, Rosemary has un-
"shelved" the Maternal Macabre, has reclaimed its "back rooms," has
forced it out of the cultural and cinematic "closet."

In 1968, many middle-class expectant mothers were enrolled in uplifting Lamaze classes where they dutifully viewed graphic movies of
labor and delivery. (On the same page as Andrew Sarris's *Village Voice*
critique of *Rosemary's Baby* is a notice for a screening of an instructional
childbirth film.) Here is how Margaret Atwood depicts such a session in
"Giving Birth":

> They have seen the film made by the hospital, a full-colour film of a woman
> giving birth to, can it be a baby? "Not all babies will be this large at birth," the
> Australian nurse who introduces the movie says. Still, the audience, half of
> which is pregnant, doesn't look very relaxed when the lights go on. ("If you
> don't like the visuals," a friend of Jeannie's has told her, "you can always close
> your eyes.") (139)

Such Lamaze devotees may well have avoided Polanski's thriller, fearing the distress it could engender. Retrospectively, however, one wonders *which* women were most "prepared" for parturition: Which saw the horror film and which the documentary?

Works Cited

Arms, Suzanne. *Immaculate Deception: A New Look at Women and Childbirth in America*. Boston: Houghton Mifflin, 1975.

Atwood, Margaret. "Giving Birth." In *We Are the Stories We Tell*, edited by Wendy Martin, 134–49. New York: Pantheon, 1990.

Barthes, Roland. *S/Z: An Essay*. Translated by Richard Miller. New York: Hill and Wang, 1974.

Bathrick, Serafina Kent. "Ragtime: The Horror of Growing Up Female." *Jump Cut*, no. 14 (March 1977): 9–10.

Berenstein, Rhona. "Mommie Dearest: *Aliens*, *Rosemary's Baby* and Mothering." *Journal of Popular Culture* 24, no. 2 (Fall 1990): 55–73.

Bibring, Grete L. "Some Considerations of the Psychological Process in Pregnancy." *Psychoanalytic Study of the Child* 14 (1959): 113–21.

Biskind, Peter. *Seeing Is Believing: How Hollywood Taught Us to Stop Worrying and Love the Fifties*. New York: Pantheon, 1983.

Bradbury, Ray. "A New Ending to *Rosemary's Baby*." In *Focus on the Horror Film*, edited by Roy Huss and T. J. Ross, 149–51. Englewood Cliffs, NJ: Prentice-Hall, 1972.

Carroll, Noël. "Nightmare and the Horror Film: The Symbolic Biology of Fantastic Beings." *Film Quarterly* 34, no. 3 (Spring 1981): 16–25.

———. *The Philosophy of Horror or Paradoxes of the Heart*. New York and London: Routledge, 1990.

Chapetta, Robert. "*Rosemary's Baby*." *Film Quarterly* 22 (Spring 1969): 35–38.

Chesler, Phyllis. *With Child: A Diary of Motherhood*. New York: Thomas V. Crowell, 1979.

Chester, Laura, ed. *Cradle and All: Women Writers on Pregnancy and Childbirth*. Boston and London: Faber and Faber, 1989.

Clifford, Gay. *The Transformations of Allegory*. London and Boston: Routledge & Kegan Paul, 1974.

Creed, Barbara. "Horror and the Monstrous Feminine—an Imaginary Abjection." *Screen* 27, no. 1 (January–February 1986): 44–71.

———. *The Monstrous Feminine: Film, Feminism, Psychoanalysis*. London and New York: Routledge, 1993.

Curtis, Lindsay R., Yvonne Caroles, and Mark K. Beard. *Pregnant and Lovin' It*. New York: Berkley Publishing Group, 1992.

Dally, Ann. *Inventing Motherhood: The Consequences of an Ideal*. New York: Schocken, 1983.

Daly, Brenda O., and Maureen T. Reddy, eds. *Narrating Mothers: Theorizing Maternal Subjectivities*. Knoxville: University of Tennessee Press, 1991.

Deutsch, Helene. *The Psychology of Woman.* Vol. 3. New York: Grune and Stratton, 1945.

Ehrenreich, Barbara. *Witches, Midwives, and Nurses: A History of Woman Healers.* Old Westbury, NY: The Feminist Press, 1973.

Ephron, Nora. "Having a Baby after Thirty-Five." *New York Times Magazine,* 26 November 1978, 28–29, 86, 88–89.

Evans, Walter. "Monster Movies: A Sexual Theory." In Grant, 53–64.

Forbes, Thomas Rogers. *The Midwife and the Witch.* New Haven and London: Yale University Press, 1966.

Foucault, Michel. *The History of Sexuality,* Vol. 1. Translated by Robert Hurley. 1978. New York: Random House, 1990.

Gilliatt, Penelope. "Anguish under the Skin." *New Yorker,* 15 June 1968, 87–89.

Grant, Barry, ed. *Planks of Reason: Essays on the Horror Film.* Metuchen, NJ, and London: Scarecrow Press, 1984.

Hall, Stuart. "Notes on Deconstructing 'The Popular.'" In *People's History and Socialist Theory,* edited by Raphael Samuel, 227–40. London, Boston, and Henley: Routledge & Kegan Paul, 1981.

Houston, Beverle, and Marsha Kinder. "*Rosemary's Baby.*" *Sight and Sound* 38, no. 1 (Winter 1968–1969): 17–19.

Huet, Marie-Hélène. *Monstrous Imagination.* Cambridge, MA, and London: Harvard University Press, 1993.

James, Caryn. "The High Art of Horror Films Can Cut Deep into the Psyche." *New York Times,* 27 May 1990, sec. 2, pp. 1, 15.

Keppler, C. F. *The Literature of the Second Self.* Tucson: University of Arizona Press, 1972.

Kitzinger, Sheila. *Women as Mothers.* New York: Random House, 1978.

Kracauer, Siegfried. *From Caligari to Hitler: A Psychological History of the German Film.* Princeton, NJ: Princeton University Press, 1947. Reprint, 1974.

Kristeva, Julia. *The Powers of Horror: An Essay on Abjection.* Translated by Leon S. Roudiez. New York: Columbia University Press, 1982.

Landy, Marcia. *British Genres: Cinema and Society, 1930–1960.* Princeton, NJ: Princeton University Press, 1991.

Leifer, Myra. *Psychological Effects of Motherhood: A Study of First Pregnancy.* New York: Praeger, 1980.

Levin, Ira. *Rosemary's Baby.* New York: Random House, 1967.

Liley, H. M., and Beth Day. "The Inside Story of Your Baby's Life before Birth." *Expecting.* A guide for expectant mothers published by *Parents Magazine,* Fall 1968.

Nilsson, Lennart. "Drama of Life before Birth." *Life* 58, no. 17 (30 April 1965).

Paul, William. *Laughing Screaming: Modern Hollywood Horror and Comedy.* New York: Columbia University Press, 1994.

Polan, Dana. "Eros and Syphilization: The Contemporary Horror Film." In Grant, 201–11.

Rich, Adrienne. *Of Woman Born: Motherhood as Experience and Institution.* New York and London: Norton, 1986.

Sarris, Andrew. Review of *Rosemary's Baby*. *Village Voice*, 25 July 1968, 37.

Sweeney, Louise. "Polanski's Satanic Parody." *Christian Science Monitor* (Western edition), 22 June 1968, 6.

Tudor, Andrew. *Monsters and Mad Scientists: A Cultural History of the Horror Movie*. Oxford and Cambridge: Basil Blackwell, 1989.

Twitchell, James B. *Dreadful Pleasures: An Anatomy of Modern Horror*. New York and Oxford: Oxford University Press, 1985.

Waldman, Diane. "Horror and Domesticity: The Modern Romance Film of the 1940s." Ph.D. diss., University of Wisconsin–Madison, 1981.

Wexman, Virginia Wright. "The Trauma of Infancy in Roman Polanski's *Rosemary's Baby*." In *American Horrors: Essays on the Modern American Horror Film*, edited by Gregory Waller, 30–43. Urbana and Chicago: University of Illinois Press, 1987.

White, Dennis L. "The Poetics of Horror: More Than Meets the Eye." *Cinema Journal* 10, no. 2 (Spring 1987): 1–18.

Wolkind, S., and E. Zajicek. *Pregnancy: A Psychological and Social Study*. London: Academic Press, 1981.

Wood, Robin. *Hollywood from Vietnam to Reagan*. New York: Columbia University Press, 1986.

———. "An Introduction to the American Horror Film." In Grant, 164–200.

Young, Iris Marion. "Pregnant Embodiment: Subjectivity and Alienation." *Journal of Medicine and Philosophy* 9 (1984): 45–62.

The Crime Film

MAMA'S BOY: FILIAL HYSTERIA IN *WHITE HEAT*

Foreword: A Womb of One's Own

> Acting as a woman . . . is not necessarily a tribute to the feminine.
>   (Elaine Showalter)

Feminist film criticism of the 1970s and 1980s has been haunted by the theme of hysteria. This should not surprise us, as the etymological root for the ailment is tied to the female body—to "a suffering in the womb." Initially, such writing focused on the screen heroine, revealing how in the mainstream cinema she is plagued by the syndrome—configured as mute, neurotic, unstable, hormonal, or out of control. Writing on American film of the 1940s, Mary Ann Doane finds the mark of psychosis in the treatment of *all* female illness: "In *Beyond the Forest* (1949) Bette Davis ostensibly dies of peritonitis . . . but her death is really caused by an irrepressible and feverish desire to leave her small town life behind and take the train to Chicago" (39). No such deflection obtains in *The Dark Mirror* (1946), where a woman is openly diagnosed as a demented murderess (Fischer, 172–94).

Over the decades, the discourse on hysteria has manifested ideological change (or political "conversion," as it were). While the female sufferer was originally seen as an embarrassing cultural stereotype, she was later valorized by some as a martyred rebel. In *The Newly Born Woman*, Hélène Cixous and Catherine Clément deem the hysteric an "anti-establishment" figure "because [her] symptoms . . . revolt and shake up the public, the group, the men" (5). In the film *Sigmund Freud's Dora* (1979), a brazen female patient is applauded for terminating her treatment with Doctor Freud.

While at first critics associated hysteria with woman, later some ascribed it to man. In analyzing *Letter from an Unknown Woman* (1948), Tania Modleski shifts the site of psychological suspicion from the masochistic Lisa Berndle to the womanizing Stefan Brand ("Time and De-

13. *White Heat* (1949). Ma (Margaret Wycherly) gives Cody (James Cagney) medicine for his headache. MOMA

sire").[1] More recently, controversy has arisen over the "status" of the newly hystericized male (who now claims a womb of his own). While Constance Penley celebrates the regressive deconstruction of patriarchal postures in the stance of Pee-wee Herman, Modleski cautions against such a move: "Despite . . . the celebrated 'oscillation' . . . between femininity and masculinity, *both* modes entail a certain degree of misogyny" ("Incredible," 66).

A particularly resonant work through which to extend the debate on male hysteria is *White Heat* (1949), notorious for its crazed and volatile hero, Cody Jarrett (James Cagney). (*Variety* called him a "trigger-happy paranoiac.") Beyond its hero, the very text has been scanned for its neurotic tics: Dana Polan finds it constructed on a "perverse register" (165). Albeit hysteria has been classically linked to the female, it is ubiquitous

[1] See also my chapter on *Letter from an Unknown Woman* in *Shot/Countershot* (89–131), in which I pursue the theme of hysteria in Stefan Brand by focusing on his symptoms of Don Juanism and amnesia.

in this macho gangster film. Yet woman is not entirely erased from the scene. She is present, as requisite, in Verna (Virginia Mayo), Cody's gun-moll wife. And she is present, as excess, in Ma Jarrett (Margaret Wycherly), Cody's pistol-packin' Mama.

In *White Heat*, rather than dismantle patriarchy, male hysteria secures it. For while exiting the position of the insane *subject*, woman reenters as insanity's *cause*—embodied in the figure of Mother. Hence male hysteria seems to evacuate the uterus only to return there with a vengeance, assigning guilt to the maternal womb.

Juvenile Delinquency

> We do not know what went wrong with [Cody] Jarrett but
> we know he loved his mother.
>   (Neil Hurley)

But what does it mean to call Cody Jarrett a hysteric? And how does such an appellation intersect norms of "masculinity" and "femininity"?

Clearly, Cody is to be seen as unbalanced and suffering from "frequent neurotic fits" (review, *Rotarian*). But his dementia takes a particular form—that of migraine headaches.[2] In the 1940s, psychosomatic medical theories were in vogue. As Stanley Cobb states: "A new word has come into medicine. It is quite the rage. One must know about 'psychosomatics' to be up with the times" (149). In 1947, Flanders Dunbar quotes P. S. Graven on the subject of Cody's specific affliction: "One of the most baffling problems in medical therapeutics is that dealing with the treatment of *headaches*. The main reasons for this lies in the failure to detect . . . the causal factor, the *psychic*" (74, my italics). Even recently, migraines have been seen as psychologically motivated. Oliver Sacks compares them to "dreams, hysterical formations, and neurotic symptoms" (207–8). In *White Heat*, we are told that Cody's headaches arose in childhood, as an attempt to garner attention. (As Philip Hartung remarks, they "were fancied at first and later became real" [560].) Thus Cody exhibits the hysteric's "conversion" of unconscious tensions into concrete physical symptoms.

If hysteria is coded feminine, so are migraines. As Joseph Patrick Perry notes, "[F]emales are more likely to experience [them] than

---

[2] In my discussion of Cody Jarrett's migraine headaches and of the medical research on the subject, I am not arguing for the accuracy of those portrayals. I am simply reporting their depiction, allowing for the possibility that they are shaped by ideological factors.

males" (12). That Cody's illness is psychogenic doubly feminizes him. With mind associated with the male, and body with the female, his mental pain (and its translation into *corporeal* spasms) challenges his masculinity. Cobb argues that a patient's "choice" of psychosomatic symptom has semantic overtones: "The psychological situation, through its symbolic meaning, can enter the pathological functioning upon one or another organ" (158).

Cody bears another mark of hysteria: the tendency to hallucinate. After his mother's death, he roams the woods just "talkin' to Ma." The fact that Jarrett's delusions are maternal is crucial. For the root of his hysteria is, clearly, his *uncommon attachment to his mother*—something that would have interested an audience of the 1940s, witnessing the ascendancy of psychoanalysis. Polan calls Cody's syndrome a "perverse mother fixation" (165); Bosley Crowther and Dwight C. Smith Jr. call Jarrett a "mama's boy"; Hurley deems his problem an "Oedipal complex" and labels the text a "Freudian gangster film" (11); a *Time* review calls Jarrett a "mother-dependent killer" ("The New Pictures"). More recently, Russell Baker joked that "nobody who remembers *White Heat* can hear the words 'family values' without shuddering." Hence Cody's infantile regression seems the cause of both his neurosis and his criminality, making him a middle-aged "juvenile" delinquent. He eventually loses his gang leadership to a man named *Big* Ed who, though younger than Cody, seems more developmentally mature.

As the only child of a widowed mother, Cody has had Ma to himself. Though he is married, his spouse two-times him, and it is Ma who reveals Verna's treachery. (Later on, Cody witnesses Verna and Big Ed in an adulterous embrace—a sequence that resonates with overtones of the parental Primal Scene.) Tom Conley sees Cody as romantically trapped within the "double bind of subservience to mother and wife" (144). When Cody is imprisoned and separated from his mother, he transfers his affections to Hank Fallon (Edmund O'Brien), a Treasury Department agent posing as an inmate. Patrick McGilligan calls Fallon Cody's "surrogate Ma" (30). Fallon's association with the maternal is amplified when we learn that the last time he was stationed undercover in a jail, his police contact was a woman who posed as his mother on visiting days. Remembering the woman's lack of skill, Fallon tells his supervisor: "I had awful trouble with 'Mother' in San Quentin" (McGilligan, 96).

Significantly, Cody's hysterical episodes are tied to his mother. His first headache occurs after the gang has pulled a train heist and has fled to a cabin hideaway. It is Ma who nurses Cody, retreating with him from the public space of the living room to the private sphere of the boudoir, massaging his temples, and cradling him upon her lap. As Mary Ann

Doane once noted, in speaking of the forties cinema, "[E]ven criminality is confounded and subdued by the maternal" (93). Cody's next seizure (which takes place in the prison machine shop), follows Ma's visit; and the last comes in the mess hall when he learns of Ma's death. Like this film, research on migraines sought to link the disease to motherhood. John Pearce describes a 1935 study in which "[a] psychic mechanism of the migraine attack was tentatively postulated . . . as a conflict between the desire to escape from the mother's influence and a compulsion not to leave her" (52). Thus patients were seen as caught in a "maternal attachment" (Pearce, 52). More recently, Sacks has tied aggressive migraines to family dynamics. Such headaches "are implicit assaults or vengeful attacks, and tend to occur in situations of intense emotional ambivalence, that is, in relation to *individuals who are both loved and hated . . . with parents, [or] children*" (205, my italics).

Cody's final hysterical symptom is his excessive violence, a trait that shocked critics of the time. Crowther found the film "cruelly vicious," while the *Saturday Review* called it "tough, bloodstained . . . corpse-strewn" and "callous" (28). Cody's aggression is encapsulated in the refinery explosion that ends the film and his life. It is then that he utters the famous lines "Made it Ma! Top of the world!" Some have seen the maternal metaphor imprinted on the segment's very mise-en-scène. McGilligan remarks that the "swirling pipes, retorts, Hortonspheres, coils, and tubes of [the] sprawling oil refinery suggested [to the screenwriters] 'mother earth in metal'" (18). Yet despite the setting's "gynecological" associations, it is the quintessential space of science, technology, and industry—the very adult male terrain from which Cody seems banned.

If Cody is "emasculated" through his hysteria, traditional gender roles are disrupted at other levels of the text. First of all, there is the fact that his illness inscribes a melodramatic scenario onto the script of the crime film. Furthermore, though feminine enough to indict Motherhood, Ma Jarrett is also highly "masculine." (The *Saturday Review* called her Cody's "*tough* old Ma" [28].) She is an arch-criminal, a leader of the Jarrett gang, the inheritor of her deceased husband's mob mantle. Almost all research on criminality supports its prevalence in males. As Michael R. Gottfredson and Travis Hirschi state, "Men are always and everywhere more likely than women to commit criminal acts" (145). As enacted by Margaret Wycherly (with her broad-shouldered suits and stern, punchy delivery), Ma is rather camp and even "butch."

In actuality, the Jarrett story is based on the historic Barker gang—a family of outlaws who terrorized America in the 1930s. It consisted of Ma (Arizona Clark) Barker and her four sons, as well as several others.

A controversy reigns about Ma's status as gangster. While legend paints her a hardened criminal, gang member Alvin Karpis begs to differ: "She was just an old-fashioned homebody from the Ozarks. . . . Her spare time was spent working jigsaw puzzles and listening to the radio—the way any mother would whose family had grown up" (81). A hint of condescension taints Karpis's refusal to see Ma as a mastermind: "With her personality, brains and style it was impossible" (91). Clearly, Ma Jarrett is modeled on the mythic Barker—a fearsome female who may or may not have existed as such.

In *White Heat*'s scrambling of sex roles, Fallon also figures. Though he is a he-man T-man, his undercover operation requires that he assume the female position to win Cody's confidence. Hence during Jarrett's machine-shop migraine, Fallon (or *Phall*-on) protects and nurtures Cody, standing in his mother's place. Gender confusion also dominates the details of Ma's murder. While Cody believes at first that the perpetrator is Big Ed, he later learns that it is Verna.

The polymorphous world of *White Heat* is imbued with no sense of naive abandon; rather, it is overlaid with perverse control. "Fair is foul and foul fair" when men act like women and women like men. Indeed, it is not hard to envision Ma Jarrett as a film noir Lady Macbeth, incestuously manipulating her son instead of her husband, transferring her infamous hysteria to her child. ("Out damned headache!")

The Cagney Persona: Real Men Don't Sing and Dance

Made it, Ma! Top of the world!
   (Cody Jarrett)

[I]n our mother we always had somebody we could show off for. Whatever impressive things we did, we were saying in effect, "Look, Ma, I'm dancin."
   (James Cagney)

It is inviting to place the narrative of Cody Jarrett within the context of the life of the actor who portrayed him. Having grown up on the tough West Side of New York City, James Cagney might have met a fate similar to Cody's. What saved him (by his own testimony) was his mother: "A question people have asked me through the years is why the Cagney boys didn't get involved with guns and crime the way my old Sing Sing pals did. The answer is simple: there wasn't a chance. We had a mother to answer to" (25). Mrs. Cagney was evidently no Betty Crocker; in fact, at times her son's descriptions make her sound like Ma Jarrett. As

Cagney recalls, "If any of us got out of line, she just belted us and belted us emphatically" (25). He recounts how Mrs. Cagney once sent his brother back to fight a battle he had avoided. "My mother . . . knew that . . . running away did no one any good" (8). On another occasion she retaliated against a boy who had attacked her son Harry: "My mother at the time possessed two handy items: a thick, six-foot-long horsewhip and a blazing temper. When she heard of the injustice done to Harry, she put on her little jacket, ran downstairs . . . and whipped [the bully] up and down the street" (4). Despite "the great staunchness of her" (25), James loved his parent: "Without hesitating I can say my mother was the key to the Cagneys" (2).

Critics have remarked on how the issue of maternity permeates Cagney's movie image. As McGilligan notes, "[H]aving a 'mother' who roots for him was an essential part of Cagney's screen persona" (26). And Hurley sees in Cagney the mark of a "child-within-[a]-man" (11). The case for *White Heat*'s focus on motherhood is already clear. But the film was preceded by another crime film—*The Public Enemy* (1931)—in which a maternal discourse is central. The film concerns two brothers: Mike (Donald Cook) and Tom (Cagney) Powers. Growing up in a tough neighborhood, Mike (like the real Cagney) takes the straight and narrow path, gaining an education and succeeding legally. Tom, on the other hand, becomes a criminal. Loving both of them equally is Ma Powers (Beryl Mercer), who—unlike Ma Jarrett—is an Angel in the House. At the end of the drama, Tom, who has been shot, medicated, and bandaged, is kidnapped from a hospital by a rival gang and left on his mother's doorstep, deceased. A virtual "mummy" comes home to "mommy" in a regression synonymous with death.

Although Cagney began his career as a vaudevillian, his movie fame was tied to the gangster genre: not only to *Public Enemy*, but to *G-Men* (1935), *Angels with Dirty Faces* (1938), and *The Roaring Twenties* (1939). In the 1940s he resisted stereotyping and won an Oscar for his performance in the musical *Yankee Doodle Dandy* (1942). Following that triumph, he left Warner Brothers and formed a production company, seeking less violent roles. He released three films in six years (*Johnny Come Lately* [1943], *Blood on the Sun* [1935], *The Time of Your Life* [1948]), but none were financially remunerative.

Defeated, Cagney returned to Warner's in 1949, reviving his macho persona, and critics embraced him for it. John McCarten finds it "unfortunate" that in the intervening years "Mr. Cagney mellowed, became almost lovable, and moved to the side of the angels." He applauds him for returning to the "fold" (55). *Life* shouts "Cagney Kills Again" and assures us that "[t]he old Jimmy is back" (83). *Time* celebrates his reprise of "the kind of thug role that made him famous" ("The New Pictures"). A film poster brags, "Jimmy's in action again!" (Halliwell, 122).

For Cagney, however, *White Heat* was just "another cheapjack job," a "formula" picture (125). His preference lay in the more benign role of hoofer:

> In just about every interview, in most conversations, one question emerges unfailingly: what is my favorite picture? Many people assume that one of those knock-down-drag-'em-outs would be my choice. A discerning critic . . . can't understand why I choose *Yankee Doodle Dandy* over *White Heat* and *The Public Enemy*. The answer is simple . . . once a song-and-dance-man, always a song-and-dance-man. In that brief statement you have my life story. (104)

McGilligan comments on the irony of Cagney's situation, placing it within a biographical frame: "[He] spent a lifetime resisting his 'tough guy' image by rising above the 'hell's kitchen' of his childhood and later by fighting the gangster typecasting that dogged him. . . . A sensitive artist . . . he preferred to think of himself as a song-and-dance man" (21).

Veiled in this discussion of opposing roles for Cagney is a discourse on "masculinity" and "femininity." Crime films are linked to the male, while musicals are tied to the female (Schatz, 35). While this gender association pertains to the narrative and to the audience, it also relates to the male star. Steve Neale claims that musicals allow for "feminisation" and are the only mainstream genre "in which the male body has been unabashedly put on display" (15). While the paradigm gangster (e.g., Edward G. Robinson) is macho, the archetypal dancer (e.g. Fred Astaire) "risks" effeminacy. Though Astaire remains heterosexually "viable," one need only think of the cultural clichés attached to the male ballet dancer to see the end point on the continuum. Notice the language McCarten uses to describe Cagney's shift away from gangster roles. He regrets that Cagney has "mellowed," that he has become "lovable," that he has turned into an "angel"—all "soft" words associated with the feminine. Similarly, McGilligan refers to Cagney as a "sensitive artist." Hence when Cagney says that he prefers to be "a song-and-dance-man," perhaps he seeks to be relieved of monolithic gender dictates: to be a "male-and-female-man." One is reminded of Tom Powers's line in *The Public Enemy* as he succumbs to a volley of bullets: "I ain't so tough." But the audience (another public enemy?) rejected the image of Cagney Power-less.

Even in *White Heat*, however—that "cauldron of violent masculine passion" ("Big Shots,"18)—Cagney is responsible for courting "effeminacy." In his autobiography, he claims authorship for the idea of having Cody sit on Ma's lap as she nurses his headache:[3] "I thought we would try something, take a little *gamble*. . . . I wondered if we *dare* have him

---

[3] Raoul Walsh also claims authorship for the idea of having Cagney sit on Wycherly's lap, but McGilligan favors Cagney's claim (26).

sit in her lap once for comfort. I said to the director, Raoul Walsh, 'Let's see if we can *get away with this.*' He said, 'Let's try it.' We did and it worked" (126, my italics). Screenwriter Ben Roberts (who collaborated with Ivan Goff) recalls how excited Cagney was on the day of the shoot: "Jimmy stopped by the office one day and said, 'I just did something *startling.* I don't know if it will work.' . . . We said, 'What did you do?' He said, 'I sat on Mama's lap'" (McGilligan, 26, my italics). Goff recalls that when the picture was released, "[t]he audience was startled but they knew they were looking at something *awfully personal*" (McGilligan, 26, my italics).

Again, the descriptive phrasing seems revealing. The act of having a grown man sit on his mother's lap is a "gamble," "startling," "daring," something to "get away with." Raoul Walsh also uses the latter term (348), as does the *Time* review ("The New Pictures"). Thomas Schatz varies the pattern, noting that only Cagney could "pull [this] off" (108). It would seem that it is not only the regression of this act that is shocking, but its *femininity*. While most grown-ups do not sit on other adults' laps, women can—but men cannot.

Significantly, Goff sensed in Cagney's gesture "something *awfully* personal." Given what we know of the song-and-dance man who adored his mother, this might well have been true. But why is it the *awful* truth?

White Heat and Cold Sweats

> Certain illnesses seem so closely related to the culture of an
> era that it's as though they sprang from the dark side of the
> collective imagination.
>   (Michael Vincent Miller)

Having surfaced both maternal and hysterical discourses in *White Heat*, we might ask how the film is a product of its times. Conley has called it a "scenario" for the "unconscious of the post-war years" (138). What cultural trends in forties America help us to decode the film's aberrant, yet powerful, address?

Clearly, we must examine the impact of World War II, ended barely four years before the movie premiered. Some critics have mentioned *White Heat*'s apocalyptic ending, citing parallels between the refinery explosion and the atomic bomb.[4] Similarly, McCarten compares the film's high-tech police pursuit to "the invasion of Normandy" (55). Other writers have noted the movie's rampant cynicism, seen as indicative of the era's disillusionment. McGilligan claims that the screenwrit-

---

[4] Clark (62) compares the end of the film to the destruction of Germany and Japan.

ers symbolized "everything that had gone wrong with the world. . . . the United States had emerged a victor . . . but crippled veterans returning home found a changed spirit in the land" (9). While the postwar angst of *White Heat* is noted, no one draws a specific parallel between Cody Jarrett and the returning GI—this despite McGilligan's reference to "crippled veterans." Yet once we imagine the comparison, it becomes unavoidable.

Weighing upon the American mind were the myriad men declared "psychoneurotic" during enlistment or in the war itself. Speaking of the draft, Benjamin C. Bowker states that "approximately fourteen per cent of all men examined for service were rejected for psychoneurotic reasons" (33). Commenting on shell shock, Willard Waller remarks that "the armed services were discharging psychoneurotic veterans at the rate of 10,000 cases a month in late 1943 and in early 1944" (166). Hence the topic of male hysteria was in the air, and it is understandable that it should drift into *White Heat*. But why, specifically, might we compare Cody Jarrett to a psychoneurotic vet?

Primary among the concerns for the returning soldier was his potential *violence*. It was understood that he had been trained as a murder machine and that he might fail to override his "education" in a civilian context. Waller calls the vet a "threat to society" (13) and a "connoisseur of death" (247): "The soldier's business . . . is killing, and the army does a good job of conditioning him for it. The soldier learns to kill in a cold-blooded, professional way. . . . On occasion, however, the sadistic-aggressive tendencies of men in uniform get out of control" (45–46). It is not a great leap to apply this description to Cody Jarrett, a "cold-blooded," "professional" "connoisseur of death," who shoots a cohort in the trunk of a car. Waller also lends the term "explosive" to the returning GI (167), and Bowker tells us that society is consequently "sitting on an atomic bomb" (30). Again, one is reminded of the denouement of *White Heat*, with Jarrett straddling a detonating oil storage tank.

But there are even stronger parallels between Cody and the returned vet: their mutual association with *crime*. Bowker catalogs the menacing headlines that inundate the American public:

VETERAN BEHEADS WIFE WITH JUNGLE MACHETE

EX-MARINE HELD IN RAPE MURDER

FATHER SHOT TO DEATH BY YEOMAN SON

TWO VETERANS HELD AS HOLDUP SUSPECTS (25–26)

And Waller claims that "the veteran has been so completely alienated from the attitudes and controls of civilian life that he becomes a criminal" (124). Elsewhere, Waller's description of the military evokes a gang. He talks of the soldier following the "will of the leader" (19), and of the institution's "crushing out every resurgence of . . . private will against it" (21). He also compares the returned vet to a released prisoner: "Like the orphan and the prisoner, the soldier has been institutionalized and thereby to some extent incapacitated for any life but the soldier's" (119). (Jarrett is, of course, both orphaned and imprisoned.) Finally, Waller cites statistics that link war and sociopathology. Based on the experience of World War I, "we should expect at least 60,000 of the mobilized men [from World War II] to be sent to prison for serious crimes" (127). According to Bowker, in "San Quentin alone, 25% of convicts consist of veterans of World War II" (28).[5] For Ernest Mandel, the source of postwar crime is the "vast scale of black market operations by GIs in occupied Germany and France" (91).

While one fear of the returning GI involved his inordinate violence, another anticipated the inverse: his weakness and nervousness. The first problem might be culturally imagined as an excess of masculinity; the other might be conceived as its paucity. As Waller notes, "Where men of previously stable personality break under the strain of combat, their condition may be diagnosed as traumatic war neurosis" (167). Erik Erikson describes a soldier who (like Cody Jarrett) suffered "incapacitating headaches" (38). Intriguingly, they first occurred in a mess hall, the site of one of Cody's monumental attacks:

> The metallic noise of the mess utensils went through his head like a salvo of shots. It was as if he had no defense whatsoever against these noises, which were so unbearable that he crawled under a cover while the others ate.
>
> From then on his life was made miserable by raging headaches . . . his headaches and jumpiness made it necessary for him to be returned to the States and to be discharged. (40)

Similarly, Dixon Wecter speaks of a soldier whose "association of terror with the sound of planes [made] even the noise of a passing truck intolerable" (546). Here, we are reminded of the scene of Cody, Ma, and Verna at a drive-in movie that is playing a war film, *Task Force* (1949). As the noise of battle echoes, it annoys Cody, who shuts the sound track off.

Let There Be Light, directed by John Huston in 1946, is an extraordinarily interesting artifact to examine intertextually with *White Heat*. For, in this documentary, rather than see the soldier as conquering hero, we view him as patient, wreck, "human salvage" (Bowker, 28), as "casualty of the spirit." In vignettes represented as unstaged, we witness physicians treating men for a variety of war-related nervous disorders: amnesia, hysterical paralysis, stuttering, depression, insomnia, tics, and head-

---

[5] Bowker is quoting a July 1945 issue of the *Technocrat*.

aches. Submitting themselves to hypnosis, truth serum, art therapy, and psychoanalysis, they are subject to the "medical gaze" that normally attends the female (Doane, 38–69). The film's narrative proposes a series of optimistic cures, moving the GIs from illness to health, from hospitalization to release.

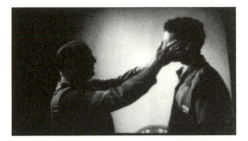

14. *Let There Be Light* (1946). A physician lays hands on a soldier suffering from postwar trauma. MOMA

Describing one of the privileged histrionic moments of *White Heat* (when Cody sits on Ma's lap), Hurley, interestingly, uses the word "disarming" (11). Given the demilitarization of the era, this term has a resonant double meaning, highlighting the linkage of war, shock, and hysteria.

"Their Mothers' Sons"

> The first thing I remember hearing about mothers and sons
> . . . was the story of the "brave Spartan mothers" who sent
> their sons forth to battle with the adjuration: *with your shield*
> *or on it*, meaning that the young man was to return victorious
> or dead. Over and over a picture played in my mind: the
> young man, wounded, without his shield, finds his way back
> to his mother's door. Would she really refuse to open it?
> *Vous travaillez pour l'armée, Madame?*
> *(Adrienne Rich)*
>
> What a monstrous old witch was she. And yet—yes, friends—
> was she not also a mother? A mother, too, who adored her
> only son, Cody Jarrett, murderous psychopath though he
> was.
> (Russell Baker)

With mounting concern for the mental health of the American male came a search for causal agents, and it landed at mother's doorstep (much as Tom Powers does in *The Public Enemy*). When he falls to the ground, bound, bandaged, and wrapped in a blanket, he looks more like an overgrown papoose, or a babe in swaddling, than he does a mature criminal. At the end of the film, a title reads: "'The Public Enemy' is not a man, nor is it a character—it is a problem that sooner or later WE . . . must solve." The homily correctly predicts that the public enemy is "not a man," for (by the forties) it is Mother, reconfigured as heinous "Mom." As Edward Strecker states, "No nation is in greater danger of failing to solve the mother-child dilemma than our own" (24).

The charge that American culture was warped by "Momism" reverberated everywhere.[6] One of the first to register alarm was Philip Wylie in *Generation of Vipers* (1942), a text that reflects its wartime milieu: "I cannot think, offhand, of any civilization except ours in which an entire division of men has been used, during wartime . . . to spell out the word 'mom' on a drill field" (184). On one level, Wylie seems to find Mom the driving force behind *all* combat: "Mom . . . has patriotism. If a war comes, . . . the departure of her son may be her means to grace in old age. Often, however, the going of her son is . . . an occasion for more show. . . . She does not miss him" (192). Elsewhere, he likens her to a "Hitler" who masters "a new slave population continually go[ing] to work at making more munitions for momism" (193).

But Mom's major link to the military comes through her ruination of the American child. Strecker describes her progeny "paddling about in a kind of psychological amniotic fluid" (31). Wylie sees her as a "female devouring her young" (185), keeping them close at the expense of their normal development: "Our land, subjectively mapped, would have more silver cords and apron strings crisscrossing it than railroads and telephone wires" (185).

Wylie's use of the term "silver" is important, as he especially disdains the middle-aged mother with her "menopausal nature" (186). At one point he implies that such women should simply have expired: "Usually, until very recently, mom folded up and died of hard work somewhere in the middle of her life. . . . Nowadays, with nothing to do . . . [she] survives for an incredible number of years" (186).

Though Moms have children of both sexes, it is the *male* to whom these writers attend. Without openly acknowledging their bias, they slip into references to mothers and sons. Even in 1976 Hans Sebald talks of the special "vulnerability of the boy": "Why is [it] the mother-son relationship . . . that appears to be the most frequent setting of Momism? . . . If a girl is exposed to a Mom, she will rarely suffer the harm that befalls her brother because she can escape from being a stifled personality by imitating the mother's ways." Boys, on the other hand, "may not imitate their mother. Not being allowed to identify with his mother ren-

---

[6] In addition to the texts discussed below, see the work of David Levy.

ders the boy helpless against her guiding powers" (105). Thus he suffers from a failure of mimesis.

In *Their Mothers' Sons* (1946), Strecker argues that rampant Momism caused the rejection or discharge of men from the armed services. He concludes that while not all traumatized soldiers had Moms, "very often they did. A psychoneurosis serves the same purpose mom served." Hence Mom is not only a social problem but a psychiatric disease.

In *Let There Be Light*, when doctors examine patients, they raise questions about the soldiers' mothers, even when the men have not mentioned them. When one soldier says he felt uncomfortable as a youngster being restricted to playing with select children, the physician tells him that his *mother* must have felt inferior to people. When another admits that he fails to confide problems to his parents, a doctor remarks how his *mother* must have hidden family troubles. When a veteran (under Pentothal) mentions arguing with his mother, the doctor queries leadingly, "Have you *always* tried to please her?"

In *Modern Woman: The Lost Sex* (1947), Ferdinand Lundberg and Marynia Farnham state as the central thesis of their book that "contemporary women . . . are psychologically disordered and . . . their disorder is having terrible social and personal effects involving men in all departments" (v). In particular, the authors blame the feminists for "turning their backs" on a traditional life, and for expressing "penis-envy" (303–4). Thus Moms are overly masculine women who "castrate" their sons, "stripp[ing] them of their male powers," turning them into "passive echoes" (317–19). Through a taxonomy of malign maternal paradigms, they attack "rejecting," "oversolicitous," and "dominating" mothers—all of whom "slaughter the innocents" (298). Here is how they describe one of these parental types: "The dominating mother . . . obtains release for her misdirected ego drives at the expense of the child . . . she makes her children her pawns, usually requires of them stellar performances in all their undertakings" (304). All three Moms are blamed for the rise of crime. They "produce delinquents" and "some substantial percentage of criminals" (305).

Erik Erikson is a lone voice in defense of maternity, wondering if such mass condemnation masks some "revengeful triumph": "Who is this 'Mom'? How did she lose her good, her simple name? How could she become an excuse for all that is rotten in the state of the nation and a subject of literary temper and tantrums? *Is* Mom really to blame?" (289).

It is intriguing to read *White Heat* against these contemporaneous debates on Momism. Of all the critics who covered the film, only one made this connection. The writer for *Saturday Review* comments on how Cody feels "an affection [for Ma] which would startle Philip Wylie.

Momism has seldom found a less likely victim or produced a more incredible mother's boy (28)."

Like the male child mourned in the literature, Cody is neurotic and tied to his aging mother's silver apron strings. Hence the furor around his sitting on her lap—the site at which this "psychic umbilicus" is most clear (Wylie, 195). Though Cody is hardly passive, he can be seen as sexually "castrated," loving Ma more than Verna. As Wylie warned us, "Mom steals from the generation of women behind her . . . that part of her boy's personality which should have become the love of a female contemporary" (196). Significantly, at one moment of the film Verna mocks Ma Jarrett for making a special trip to get strawberries "for her boy." When Fallon enters the picture, he stands in triangular relation to Cody and Verna as well as to Ma. In Wylie's 1953 revision of *A Generation of Vipers*, he condemns Mom for her "mass affaire [*sic*] with Liberace," raising the specter of homosexuality.

Ma Jarrett is portrayed as a masculine woman (a godmother in the land of godfathers), confirming Lundberg and Farnham's worst fears. We might even imagine her as a cartoon "feminist"—an "ego-driven," widowed career woman who runs the family business while her son is in jail. In many respects, her perverse representation smacks not only of Momism but of the hostility felt by the discharged soldier for the working woman who had taken his job. As Strecker notes, "The returning veteran feels perhaps that his wife has gained entirely too much independence during his absence" (144).

Ma fits clearly into Farnham and Lundberg's "dominating" category, requiring of her son "stellar" feats. Hence the taunt in Cody's self-destructive cheer: "Made it Ma! Top of the world!" As Wylie tells us, "Men live for [Mom] and die for her . . . and whisper her name as they pass away" (185–86). Like the sons of all Moms, Cody comes to an ignominious end: here, criminality and suicide.

Epilogue: When the Woman Looks

[Horror] films offer yet another form of the look of recognition between the woman and the monster. The monster who attacks both looks like and, in some sense, *is* a woman.
  (Linda Williams)

I think I see it now; they chase me
because I'm mad, and I'm mad because
they chase me. So said the doctor
when I told him I was kidnapped

from my secret island by movie men
and a tiny blond in love with screaming,
that I was a God and may still be,
that I'm immune to bombs and bullets.
He said it would be years before
I'm cured, that Mother is behind it all.
   (William Trowbridge, "The Madness of Kong")

Despite *White Heat*'s denouement, Tom Conley imagines that Cody Jarrett has achieved a degree of health before the film's climax:

> [Q]uite plainly, the death of Cody's mother constitutes his *final cure.* . . . After "Ma" is reported dead, Cody becomes a wise crook; he turns Verna around and gets rid of Big Ed, and finally has communion with a different collective mother "on top o' the world." Now the oedipal role is generally cast to bind the American male in the paradigm . . . of the nuclear family. . . . But this too is what *White Heat* finally rebukes. Bereft of a mother with a proper name, Cody wrests free . . . and reinscribes the letters A.M. into the more effective political and historical figure of Mother Nature . . . communing with an etherealized "Ma." (144, my italics)

While Strecker equates mother love with psychoneurosis, Conley likens maternal death to psychiatric cure. Only through the eradication of mother is man able to achieve his "career" potential, to be liberated from the chains of the nuclear family. In place of an embodied mother, Conley prefers a spiritual Ma, coequal with Nature.

The impulse to blame mother is also manifest in a previously cited quotation from Neil Hurley: "We do not know what went wrong with Jarrett, but we know he loved his mother. This is the source of the film's complexity and its impenetrable fascination, comparable . . . to the unexpected humanity of King Kong" (12).

Presumably, what Hurley finds "impenetrable" in the film is not only "what went wrong" with Cody Jarrett, but the character of his crime. In classic Hollywood fashion, the narrative provides a convenient answer: robbery, perjury, murder. But we suspect that it evades the point.

Hurley's language implies that Cody's neurosis and his love for his mother are *separate* issues: "We do not know what went wrong with Jarrett, *but* we know he loved his mother." Yet mother-love is precisely the transgression—not simply incestuous desire, but any affection at all. With the American Mom a "Hitler" and the maternal bond a "danger" to the state, what legitimate affection could remain? If the crime is filial sentiment, it is also the institution of motherhood. On some level, "what went wrong" with Cody Jarrett is that he was "of woman born": that he loved his mother and that she loved him.

That Hurley (and, perhaps, poet Trowbridge) compare Cody to King Kong is also telling, in that the comparison likens Jarrett to a monster, an analogy also made by Thomas Clark. But, as Linda Williams notes, in the horror film the Creature (though perceived as masculine) is often feminized, reflecting the image of the terrorized heroine. If Cody is *White Heat*'s monster, Ma is its damsel-in-distress, a conclusion consonant with Erikson's sense that Mom, in the forties, "is a victim, not a victor" (291).

By this logic, the monstrous in *White Heat* is not only the hysterical man but Womanhood, as viewed by a male Generation of Vipers.

Works Cited

Baker, Russell. "That Ma's a Killer." *New York Times*, 2 June 1992, A21.

"Big Shots." *Movietone News* 45, no. 11 (1975): 14–21.

Blanpied, John W., ed. *Movieworks*. Rochester, NY: The Little Theatre Press, 1990.

Bowker, Benjamin C. *Out of Uniform*. New York: W. W. Norton & Co., 1946.

Cagney, James. *Cagney by Cagney*. Garden City, NY: Doubleday, 1976.

"Cagney Kills Again." *Life* 27 (26 September 1949): 83–84.

Cixous, Hélène, and Catherine Clément. *The Newly Born Woman*. Translated by Betsy Wing. Minneapolis: University of Minnesota Press, 1986.

Clark, Thomas. "*White Heat*: The Old and the New." *Wide Angle* 1, no. 1 (Spring 1976): 60–65.

Cobb, Stanley. *Borderlands of Psychiatry*. Cambridge: Harvard University Press, 1943.

Conley, Tom. "Apocalypse Yesterday." *Enclitic* 5/6, nos. 1–2 (1981–1982): 137–46.

Crowther, Bosley. "James Cagney Back as Gangster in *White Heat*, Thriller New at the Strand." *New York Times*, 3 September 1949, 7.

Doane, Mary Ann. *The Desire to Desire: The Woman's Film of the 1940s*. Bloomington and Indianapolis: Indiana University Press, 1987.

Dunbar, Flanders. *Emotions and Bodily Changes: A Survey of Literature on Psychosomatic Interrelationship 1910–45*. 3d ed. New York: Columbia University Press, 1947.

Erikson, Erik H. *Childhood and Society*. 1950. 2d ed. New York: W. W. Norton, 1963.

Fischer, Lucy. *Shot/Countershot: Film Tradition and Women's Cinema*. Princeton, NJ: Princeton University Press, 1989.

Gottfredson, Michael R., and Travis Hirschi. *A General Theory of Crime*. Stanford: Stanford University Press, 1990.

Halliwell, Leslie. *The Filmgoer's Companion*. 6th ed. New York: Hill and Wang, 1977.

Hartung, Philip T. "The Screen." *Commonweal* 50, no. 23 (16 September 1949): 560.

Hurley, Neil, S.J. "James Cagney: The Quintessential Rebel." *New Orleans Review* 14, no. 2 (Summer 1987): 5–15.

Karpis, Alvin (with Bill Trent). *The Alvin Karpis Story.* New York: Coward, McCann and Geoghan, 1971.

Levy, David. *Maternal Overprotection.* New York: Columbia, 1943.

Lundberg, Ferdinand, and Marynia Farnham. *Modern Woman: The Lost Sex.* New York and London: Harper, 1947.

Mandel, Ernest. *Delightful Murder: A Social History of the Crime Story.* London and Sydney: Pluto Press, 1984.

McCarten, John. "The Current Cinema." *New Yorker* 25 (9 September 1949): 55.

McGilligan, Patrick, ed. *White Heat.* Madison: University of Wisconsin Press, 1984.

Miller, Michael Vincent. "Anybody Who Was Anybody Was Neurasthenic." *New York Times Book Review,* 7 July 1991, 1, 24–25.

Modleski, Tania. "The Incredible Shrinking He(r)man: Male Regression, the Male Body and Film." *Differences* 2, no. 2 (1990): 55–75.

———. "Time and Desire in the Woman's Film." *Cinema Journal* 23, no. 3 (Spring 1984): 19–30.

Neale, Steve. "Masculinity as Spectacle: Reflections on Men and Mainstream Cinema." *Screen* 24, no. 6 (November–December 1983): 2–16.

"The New Pictures." *Time* 54 (19 September 1949): 100.

Pearce, John. *Modern Topics in Migraine.* London: William Heinemann Medical Books, 1975.

Penley, Constance. "The Cabinet of Dr. Pee-wee: Consumerism and Sexual Terror." In *The Future of an Illusion: Film, Feminism and Psychoanalysis,* 141–62. Minneapolis: University of Minnesota Press, 1989.

Perry, Joseph Patrick. "A Descriptive Study of the Subjective Experience of Migraine Headache." Ph.D. diss., University of Pittsburgh, 1981.

Polan, Dana. *Power and Paranoia: History, Narrative and the American Cinema, 1940–1950.* New York: Columbia University Press, 1986.

Review of *White Heat. Rotarian* 76 (January 1950): 41.

Rich, Adrienne. *Of Woman Born: Motherhood as Experience and Institution.* 10th ed. New York and London: W. W. Norton, 1986.

Sacks, Oliver. *Migraine: Understanding a Common Disorder.* Berkeley: University of California Press, 1985.

Saturday Review 32 (1 October 1949): 28–29.

Schatz, Thomas. *Hollywood Genres: Formulas, Filmmaking, and the Studio System.* New York: Random House, 1981.

Sebald, Hans. *Momism: The Silent Disease of America.* Chicago: Nelson-Hall, 1976.

Showalter, Elaine. "Critical Cross-Dressing and The Woman of the Year." *Raritan* 3, no. 2 (Fall 1983): 130–49.

Smith, Dwight C., Jr. *The Mafia Mystique.* New York: Basic Books, 1975.

Strecker, Edward. *Their Mothers' Sons: The Psychiatrist Examines an American Problem*. Philadelphia and New York: J. B. Lippincott, 1946.

Trowbridge, William. "The Madness of Kong." In *Movieworks*, edited by John W. Blanpied, 77. Rochester, NY: The Little Theatre Press, 1990.

Variety 175, no. 13 (31 August 1949): 18.

Waller, Willard. *The Veteran Comes Back*. New York: Dryden Press, 1944.

Walsh, Raoul. *Each Man in His Time: The Life Story of a Director*. New York: Farrar, Straus & Giroux, 1974.

Wecter, Dixon. *When Johnny Comes Marching Home*. Boston: Houghton Mifflin, 1944.

Williams, Linda. "When the Woman Looks." In *Re-Vision: Essays in Feminist Criticism*, edited by Mary Ann Doane, Patricia Mellencamp, and Linda Williams, 83–99. Frederick, MD: University Publications of America, 1984.

Wylie, Philip. *Generation of Vipers*. New York and Toronto: Rinehart and Co., 1942, 1946, 1953.

Film Comedy

"SOMETIMES I FEEL LIKE A MOTHERLESS CHILD": COMEDY AND MATRICIDE

> Impatience kicks and thrashes inside the clown, like a violent
> baby in the womb that cannot bring itself to term.
> (Walter Kerr)

The Incredible Shrinking Woman

In the 1981 comedy *The Incredible Shrinking Woman*, Lily Tomlin plays
Pat Kramer, a housewife and mother who inexplicably begins to diminish in size. In the beginning of the story, she is of average height; by the
middle, a Lilliputian (living in an Ibsenesque doll's house); near the end,
invisible. Her corporeal reduction is ascribed to industrial pollution—
contamination by the combined ingredients of myriad consumer products: cleaning aids, cosmetics, synthetic foods, and the like. Within the
film, a standard sociological explanation is advanced for Pat's tragedy:
one newscaster speculates that she is a "metaphor for the modern
woman," and notes that "the role of the . . . housewife has become in-
creasingly less significant." Another inquires, "Did she begin to shrink
because her role as homemaker was belittling?" Pat's surname seems to
validate this reading, with its reference to *Kramer vs. Kramer* (1979)—a
film about the male absorption of woman's domestic function. I, however, would like to offer another interpretation of Pat's plight: that it
represents not only the position of woman in bourgeois culture but the
fate of woman in traditional comedy.

The notion of female absence has been a commonplace of contemporary film criticism. Woman has been seen to suffer a narrative lack in the
patriarchal cinema equivalent to her alleged physiological omission. Canonical modes, like the western or action picture, either ban women
from centrality in the scenario or include them in pernicious incarnations
(the femme fatale of film noir). Where women do populate the screen,
in musical or melodrama, they are frequently fashioned as a patriarchal

construct—the mere "pseudocenter" of the filmic discourse (Johnston, Kaplan, Mulvey, Dozoretz).

While these perceptions have illuminated numerous cinematic genres, they have rarely spotlighted comedy, as though the topic of misogyny were too grave to consider within a jocular light (Doane, "Film and the Masquerade" and "The Film's Time"; Leibman; Mellencamp; Modleski, 'Three Men" and *The Women Who Knew Too Much*). I wish to add some levity to the subject (or, at least, some gallows humor) by approaching comedy with the lessons of feminist film theory in mind.

To pursue this, we must temporarily avert our eyes from the comic image, attending, rather, to the theoretical offscreen space that structures and frames it—a discourse honed on literature, drama, and verbal anecdote. In the critical milieu that surrounds the genre, we will detect the masculine biases familiar to us from other branches of narratology.

Central to this discussion is the work of Northrop Frye, who, in *The Anatomy of Criticism*, constructs a paradigm for the classic comic form. In so doing, he configures a story told from the male perspective, in which the female is present only as subsidiary, as object of the hero's quest: "What normally happens is that a young man wants a young woman, that his desire is resisted by some opposition . . . and that near the end of the play some twist in the plot enables the hero to have his will" (163). Equal to the male youth in comedy is the patriarch, who usually poses some hindrance to the protagonist's romantic pursuits. This generational dynamic invokes another scenario: the Freudian Oedipal conflict—a struggle enacted between men.

While Frye's theory favors the youth of this archetypal narrative, others have foregrounded the elder. Ludwig Jekels sees comedy as opposing tragedy by displacing guilt onto the father, enacting a vindictive drama in which the son takes revenge on his precursor (174). Similarly, Martin Grotjahn views the comic form as choreographing a degradation of the patriarch. "The clown," he writes "is a one-man comedy; he represents a depreciated father" (91).

Clearly, in the formulations of Frye, Jekels, and Grotjahn, there lurks an obsession with the male personae of the comic diegesis. But even in considerations of nondramatic humor, woman is erased from the theoretical decor. When Freud executes his brilliant analysis of jokes, he consistently configures woman as the object (not the agent) of their production. On numerous occasions, in his typology of wit, Freud's examples cast woman as humor's butt. For the category of double meaning, he relates the following jest, one worthy of Henny Youngman: "A doctor, as he came away from a lady's bedside, said to her husband with a shake of his head: 'I don't like her looks.' 'I've not liked her looks for a long time,' the husband hastened to agree" (37).

But it is with Freud's delineation of dirty jokes that the elision of woman is truly accomplished. For here, he initially imagines the female as indispensable to the comic process—as the locus of the male joke teller's desires. "Smut," he writes, "is directed to a particular person, by whom one is sexually excited and who, on hearing it, is expected to become aware of the speaker's excitement and as a result to become sexually excited in turn. . . . Smut is originally directed [by men] towards women and may be equated with attempts at seduction" (97). According to Freud, this scenario obtains quite literally for lower-class males who make off-color remarks in the presence of the opposite sex. At higher societal levels, where women are imagined more "proper," this dynamic is significantly revised. The men save up this kind of entertainment, which "originally presupposed the presence of a woman . . . till they are '*alone together*.' So that gradually, in place of the woman, the onlooker, now the listener becomes the person to whom the smut is addressed" (99, my italics). Hence woman, once the core of the joke structure (as the target of sexual desire), is, eventually, eliminated from the scene entirely—replaced by the male auditor. If her specter rematerializes, it embodies psychic opposition. As Freud remarks, the obstacle to seduction "is . . . nothing other than women's incapacity to tolerate undisguised sexuality." Hence the female is an emblem of repression: an intransigency that fuels the artistic evolution of smut into joke (Doane, "Film and the Masquerade").

The circumvention of woman can also be seen in the theory and practice of female impersonation, a form of theatrical, sexual burlesque (to be discussed further in chapter 8). As critics have noted, this direction of cross-dressing prevails over the obverse, in which women are costumed as men. In favoring this mode, comedy once more privileges the male—claiming his dominance, even when woman is apparently there. Annette Kuhn perceives deep psychological motives for this practice: "It is possible that such a spectacle . . . fulfills the primal fantasy of the fetishistic look, a fantasy which 'real' women must always frustrate; it banishes the castration threat by gratifying a masculine desire for a woman to be . . . more like a man" (73).

Finding women "like men" is precisely what typifies Grotjahn's view of the comedienne. For he extends the association of transvestism and comedy by seeing the male specter inhabiting the bodies of *all* comic women. "The comedienne of modern times," he writes, "seems to play the strange role of a woman impersonating a man" (98–99). According to Grotjahn, man laughs at such a woman because of her pathetic penis envy. She "confirms his superiority" and demonstrates that "what she wants to be" is him. For Grotjahn, the unconscious male response is to think: "She may try hard, she may be witty and aggressive and even exhibitionistic like a man, but she still is not a man. She tries to be what I am. It is really funny" (99).

The excision of woman in formulations of comedy is particularly bizarre, given the origins of the mode in female fertility rites. Frye speaks of the comic narrative as enacting a "return to the womb" (186), and Walter Kerr sees it as "derived from that portion of Greek ritual which sang 'the *hymen*eal hymn'" (64, my italics).

The theorist who most privileges this view, however, is Mikhail Bakhtin, in his influential work on Rabelais and the carnivalesque. For in characterizing the medieval grotesque, he stresses the centrality of female birth imagery, a system counterposed to an iconography of death. Both poles express comedy's downward thrust—toward the earth, and the lower bodily region. As Bakhtin writes: "Degradation . . . means . . . the contact with earth as an element that swallows up and gives birth at the same time. . . . To degrade also means to concern oneself with the lower stratum of the body, the life of the belly and the reproductive organs" (21). As Mary Russo notes, Bakhtin finds this aesthetic emblematized in certain terra-cotta figurines of women: "senile pregnant hags" who embody "a death that gives birth" (Bakhtin, 25; Russo, 219).

Given this perspective on comedy's roots, the most shocking elision of a female character is that of *the mother*. Grotjahn explains this phenomenon by noting her saturation in taboo. As he writes, "It is difficult to distort the relationship to the mother in a way which makes us laugh" (102).

Frye's discussion of the comic family—of male generational angst—reveals little sustained consideration of the maternal dimension. At one point he notes that female *alazons* (impostors of a parental cast) are "rare" (172). And he mentions, only in passing, that comedy involves an Oedipal replacement of the mother by the hero's young lover: "The fact that the son and father are so often in conflict means that they are frequently rivals for the same girl, and the psychological alliance of the hero's bride and the mother is often expressed or implied" (180). Thus the maternal is reduced to a spirit in comedy that haunts the hero's paramour—her diegetic stand-in.

While Frye notes the erasure of the *hero*'s mother, Stanley Cavell examines the obliteration of the *heroine*'s. In the comedy of remarriage, he finds that "the price of the woman's happiness . . . is the absence of her mother" (Cavell, "Psychoanalysis," 16). He also notices a "strict absence of children for [the heroine]"—"the denial of her *as a mother*— as if the woman has been *abandoned. . .to the world of men*" (17, my italics).

If these filmic heroines have been "abandoned to the world of men," the same might be said of the comic genre. Though female sexuality underlies comedy's ancient rites, in the Greek elaboration of the form it is obscured and appropriated by the masculine erotic. It is well known that the costumes of comic actors were replete with oversized male genitalia. As Plutarch remarked, in delineating standard comic types, "One carried an amphora of wine and a bough; another dragged along a goat; a third followed carrying a basket of dried figs; and, *to crown all, the phallus*" (Kerr, 155). It is not only man's organ, however, that is enlarged in comedy, but his ego, which has executed an elaborate "substitution trick" on the figure of the mother. As the male role has stretched, so the female position has shrunk—as incredibly as the body of Pat Kramer.

Adam's Rib

When we turn from the abstract frame of comic theory to the films themselves, we find a world shaped by the critical offscreen space. The figure of the mother is largely absent, suppressed, violated, or replaced. Thus the genre urges us to "throw Momma from the train."

Woman's disappearance strikes us most obviously in the cinema's fraternity of comic stars: Charles Chaplin, Buster Keaton, Harry Langdon, Harold Lloyd, Max Linder, John Bunny, the Marx Brothers, Laurel and Hardy, W. C. Fields, Martin and Lewis, Eddie Murphy, Pee-wee Herman, Jim Carrey. While comediennes appear on-screen, few are invested with the consistent comic persona identified with the male pantheon—a feature that allows such men to anchor a series of films. Mae West is the notable exception in the American cinema during the period encompassing the teens through the thirties. Even today, when comediennes star in films, they seem stripped of the personality that defined them as stage performers. In that respect, Lily Tomlin shrinks as much as her alter ego, Pat Kramer.

Where comedies are thematically "domestic," the maternal woman does appear, but she is often pernicious and peripheral to the male comic focus. In *It's a Gift* (1934) and *The Man on the Flying Trapeze* (1935), W. C. Fields plays a henpecked husband who is saddled with a castrating wife. In *Their First Mistake* (1932), Oliver Hardy plays a married man who is nagged by his spouse.

But it is those comic works which are *not* specifically domestic that assist us most to uncover the real fate of the maternal. What happens to the mother when the humorous text does *not* mandate her presence

through the exigencies of plot? In some films, the nuclear family exists
as a shadow thrown upon the dramatic mise-en-scène. In Chaplin's *The
Pawnshop* (1916), the Tramp works for a small business run by a father
and daughter: the mother is nowhere in sight. In flirting with Edna
(Edna Purviance), his boss's child, the Tramp is seeking not only a lover
but a parent. At one point, when he mischievously fights with a co-
worker, Edna enters the scene. The Tramp suddenly and willfully drops
to the floor, playing the role of passive victim, relishing Edna's nurturing, protective response. As he puts his finger to his lips, rolls his eyes
upward, and leans on her breast, he is more infantile than amorous. Perhaps if the maternal figure were scripted into the narrative, this psychic
doubling of lover and mother would be jammed: after all, moms cannot
be in two places at the same time.

In this superimposition of lover and mother, one is reminded of Jacqueline Rose's insights concerning *Peter Pan*. She foregrounds a scene
in which the seductive moves of Tiger Lily, Wendy, and Tinkerbell are
frustrated by Peter's misprision of their nature (37). When the females
state that they each wish to be Peter's wife, he responds, "Very well—
that's really wishing to be my mother." This slippage between lover and
parent continues in *Throw Momma from the Train* (1988), in which two
men trade murder assignments. That Larry (Billy Crystal) detests his ex-
wife and Owen (Danny DeVito) loathes his mother places the women in
a symmetrical relation. As though recognizing this, Owen decides that
they should "crisscross" slaughters and eliminate each other's nemeses.
Clearly, the men are alter egos, and their mothers and paramours are
doubled as well.

A suppression of the maternal is also apparent in the films of Buster
Keaton. In *Steamboat Bill, Jr.* (1928), the hero, who has been raised by
his now-deceased mother, visits the father from whom he has been separated since birth. (Ironically, as he arrives in town, the local florist shop
advertises bouquets for Mother's Day.) The narrative that follows is devoted to his father's attempts to divest him of maternal influence—to
change him from a mama's to a papa's boy. Even the family of the heroine is motherless; she resides with her father alone.[1]

This elimination of the maternal occurs in screwball comedies as
well—even those which avoid a domestic setting. In *His Girl Friday*
(1940), though neither of the romantic couple's mothers appears on-
screen, comments gratuitously circulate that malign motherhood.
When Walter Burns (Cary Grant) wants to convince Hildy Johnson

---

[1] A similar absence of the heroine's mother is found in Keaton's *The General* (1926),
while her father is depicted.

(Rosalind Russell) that his false sincerity is genuine, he swears on his mother's grave. It is she who reminds him that his mother is still alive, unmasking his tendentious wish. When Hildy refers to her own "mother" (meaning her prospective in-law), Walter cruelly comments that her mother "kicked the bucket." When a columnist writes a sentimental poem about a criminal, Walter singles out the line about his "white-haired mother" to mock. And when Hildy wishes to criticize the mayor's sense of justice, she claims he would "hang [his] own mother." Finally, when Hildy's future mother-in-law appears on the scene, Walter orders his cronies to cart the lady away, at which point she is bodily carried from the room. These images of kidnapping, sudden death, and hanging are resonant metaphors for the fate of the mother in comedy itself.

But maternal exclusion goes deeper in Howard Hawks's film. Hildy's decision to divorce Walter and marry Bruce Baldwin (Ralph Bellamy) is a clear response to her desire to have children—a possibility foreclosed with Burns—a workaholic. Yet within the terms of the film, this aspiration is ridiculed. When Hildy says she wants to "have babies" and "give them cod-liver oil," the audience is positioned to find her remark retrograde. Similarly, its point of view is aligned with that of the male reporters who travesty the vision of her "singin' lullabies and hanging out didies." The complete erasure of her project is summarized in Walter's burlesque of her plans for "a home with mother in Albany, too."

Though contemporary feminist criticism has applauded Hildy for her professionalism (Haskell, 135), this victory is garnered at a cost: the devaluation of the maternal so ubiquitous in comedy. But if Hildy is denied parenthood, Walter is not, for it is he who is credited with, symbolically, re-creating his ex-wife, with reviving her sagging joie de vivre, with educating her. Cavell has surfaced this pattern in the genre, relating it to the birth process, but has ignored its implicit sexism:

> [T]he demand for [the woman's] education in the comedies presents itself as a matter of becoming created [by man], as if the women's lives heretofore have been nonexistent . . . as if their materialization will constitute a creation of the new woman. . . . Theologically, it alludes to the creation of the woman from Adam in *Genesis*. ("Psychoanalysis," 17)

So while Hildy's generative possibilities are contained, Walter's are liberated.

Ironically, in the film's crime subplot, much is made of Earl Williams's hearing the radical political phrase "Production for use," which he misreads as signifying that all things fabricated must be utilized. It is ostensibly this statement that has caused him to fire a gun he has had in hand. When it comes to the case of the female body, however, this motto is powerless. Hildy rejects female "re-production for use"—turning the job over to a man.[2]

Bachelor Father

To pursue this issue further, it is useful to turn our attention to those comic films that sustain female absence, while positioning maternity at center stage. Among the most curious of these are the movies of Laurel and Hardy. While in many shorts, the teammates fluctuate between postures of parent and child, in others, they constitute an adult couple—and this status is given a parental twist. In *Brats* (1930), the men play double roles, cast both as themselves and as their own offspring. The film concerns an evening of game playing at what appears to be Laurel and Hardy's collective home. The comedy unrolls as Baby Stan and Baby Ollie, who share an upstairs bedroom, continually fight and misbehave. In this ambiguous domestic setup, wives are rarely mentioned; it is as though (as Freud would have it), the men are simply "alone together." Beyond comedic implications of procreative homosexuality, it is never explained how the Laurel and Hardy "clones" have been produced. At one point, Ollie complains to the uncooperative kids that when *mother* is home, they always go to bed. Baby Ollie replies that she always sings *them* to sleep—implying that the children share one female parent. Precisely what, we may wonder, is the nature of this domestic and genetic arrangement?

Their First Mistake presents an equally nontraditional portrait of familial life. The film begins with Mrs. Hardy enraged at her husband for spending time with Stan. Ollie goes across the hall to his friend's apartment to discuss the matter. As the two loll around on the bed, Stan suggests that Hardy adopt a baby to keep his wife occupied, thus allowing the men time together. In the next shot, the men approach the rooming house, babe in arms, as though they had ordered the child from the Sears catalog. When Ollie returns to his apartment, he finds that his wife has gone. That evening, the two men retire to a comfortable double bed and try to put the newborn to sleep. Various comic bits ensue: Stan provocatively produces a bottle of milk from inside the bib of his nightshirt and sucks on it as frequently as he offers it to the child.

---

[2] It is worth mentioning that in another screwball comedy of the forties, *The Miracle of Morgan's Creek* (1944) directed by Preston Sturges, we would seem to have a counterexample of a very present mother (played by Betty Hutton) and an absent father (played by Eddie Bracken). It seems significant, however, that this comic "reversal" comes during World War II when women were achieving power on the home front, displacing the male.

15. *Brats* (1930). Baby Stan (Laurel) and Baby Ollie (Hardy) play with blocks.
MOMA

Ollie attempts to pull out the tip of an inverted rubber nipple, which repeatedly snaps back—simulating the bodily pain of S & M pornography. In so doing, he invokes a discourse of the convex and the concave that evokes the contrast between male and female bodies.

While Laurel and Hardy's films are the most eccentric of this type, other comedies more tamely substitute the clown for mother. In Chaplin's *The Kid* (1921) an unwed woman abandons her infant son. The Tramp finds him, and with him a note that reads, "Please love and care for this orphan child." He proceeds to do this for the next five years, naming the boy John. Meanwhile, the boy's mother has become a successful actress who does volunteer work in impoverished neighborhoods, secretly atoning for her parental sins. She routinely passes her own child without knowing it. When John falls ill, the Tramp calls in a physician, who learns that the urchin is not the vagrant's natural or adopted son. The doctor alerts the authorities, who take the child away. The actress realizes that the boy is her own, and the two are reunited.

16. *The Kid* (1921). The Tramp (Charles Chaplin) with his "adopted" son (Jackie Coogan). MOMA

The film closes abruptly with a shot of the woman's home, as a police-man ushers the Tramp to the door. John and the actress open it, smile, and invite the Tramp in. But what compromise they will strike we cannot imagine.

What Chaplin initiated in the 1920s, others have continued. It is crucial to recall that *The Kid* was both comic and tragic: "A picture with a smile and perhaps a tear," as Chaplin deemed it. Bearing out Chaplin's insight, the specter of male motherhood first appeared in contemporary *melodrama* before propagating in the comic realm: *Kramer vs. Kramer*, *Ordinary People* (1980), and *Table for Five* (1983) were notorious cases in point.

Subsequently, a slew of comedies were spawned in which men supplant the female parent—a virtual "baby boom." In the American cinema, one thinks of *Mr. Mom* (1983), *Three Men and a Baby* (1987);[3] on television, of *Who's the Boss?*, *Full House*, and *My Two Dads*. Eventually, in a film like *Baby Boom* (1987), woman herself comes to be configured as the incompetent mom—as though, to reclaim her maternal/cinematic role, she must now mimic a genre determined by men.

Though the male comic hero repeatedly elects a Tiresian passage—placing himself in the woman's position—he denies that the feminine impulse issues from him. In *All of Me* (1984), Roger Cobb (Steve Martin) imagines himself haunted by a female phantom, Edwina Cutwater (Lily Tomlin), who appropriates his body; thus he disavows that he may have invited the possession himself. But *All of Me* is also provocative for a particular image that recurs throughout the diegesis. Whenever Roger looks at himself in a mirror, his own reflection is replaced by that of Edwina. In this trope, we sense a relapse to the state of the Imaginary in which the infant cannot distinguish between itself and others. Hence the mother is perceived not only as a continuation of the self, but as a "mirror" in which one's being is reflected back. Kaja Silverman, in fact, likens the Lacanian mirror phase to an experience "in which the subject identifies with the mother's breast, voice, gaze" (158). In envisioning a female doppelgänger in the mirror, the male comic hero reveals a wish to return to a time of maternal union, when "all of him" was "all of her." Interestingly, French theorist Charles Mauron finds all "comic art . . . founded on a triumphal game—originally the restoration of the lost mother" (quoted in Holland, 58). Perhaps that is why the comic hero tries to *be* her, in his madcap mimicry of the maternal mode. At one moment during Roger's bewitchment, he asks the $64,000 question: "What if I got pregnant?"

In this equation of comic hero and mother, we are reminded of an essay by René Girard in which he characterizes passion as essentially imitative. "Metaphysical desire is mimetic," he writes (192). What he means is that a person does not directly desire another but rather desires *to be an individual who is prized by the coveted other*. He uses the example of comedy to illustrate his point—specifically *A Midsummer Night's Dream*, in which "Helena would like to be translated . . . into Hermia,

---

[3] After this essay was originally written, Tania Modleski published an excellent article on *Three Men and a Baby*, "Three Men and Baby M." Though Modleski's focus is not on comic theory, per se, many of her insights extend, complement, and/or coincide with my own thoughts on *Three Men and a Cradle*.

because Hermia enjoys the love of Demetrius" (191). If we apply this notion to the comedy of male parenting, we can chart desire's circuitous route. Though the comic hero may think he seeks the love of a baby, he truly wants to be transformed into the one whom the baby loves: the primary caregiver, mother. Girard sees this passion as involving "the copy of a model," a model configured as rival.

Bringing Up Baby

Now that we have traced the broad configurations of this mimetic trend, it is useful to sketch its trajectory within the confines of a single text. The French film *Three Men and a Cradle* (1985) seems a more than likely candidate. For in this work, written and directed by Coline Serreau, we will see the feminine reduced or repressed in both its erotic and maternal manifestations. As woman shrinks (incredibly) in our estimation, so man expands—to prove that he is truly the nurturant gender.

The movie concerns three friends and roommates: Jacques, an airplane steward; Michel, a cartoonist; and Pierre, an office manager. One night, during a party, an acquaintance of Jacques's asks him to receive a delivery and hold the package for several days. Jacques agrees but forgets to tell his roommates. He recalls only moments before he boards a flight for Japan and telephones Pierre at work.

On the specified day, the doorbell rings, and when Michel opens the door, he finds a baby. A note accompanying the child, addressed to Jacques from Sylvia, informs him that Marie is the "fruit of their passion." Sylvia will be modeling in the United States for six months and intends to leave the child with him. Thinking that Jacques has agreed to Marie's arrival without informing them, the roommates are furious. They realize, however, that they must tend the girl until the "package" is retrieved. Myriad comic scenes ensue that delineate the men's incapacities in mothering: they do not know how to comfort a crying baby, or what formula to buy; they do not know how to feed Marie, or to change her clothes.

The roommates are soon stressed and depressed, suffering from sleep deprivation. When the real package arrives, Michel is so distracted that he does not realize that it is the delivery to which Jacques had referred. It turns out to be a packet of illegal drugs—a fact that eventually turns this feminized domestic comedy into a male caper film. When Jacques returns from Asia and learns of his daughter's existence, he faces his friends' ire. He tries to pawn the baby off on his mother and is enraged when she leaves on vacation. He returns to his flat, and the men resign themselves to a period of joint custody. Their social life is entirely eclipsed.

When Sylvia comes back from the States and collects Marie, the men find themselves surprisingly despondent, suffering from a postpartum depression of a nonbiological sort. (Interestingly, in the American version, one of the roommates refers to a "post-party depression" in the opening scene.) One day, Michel finds Marie unattended, as her mother works a modeling job. Another time, Jacques visits Sylvia's apartment and discovers a callous baby-sitter minding the girl. Ultimately, Sylvia appears at the men's flat and confesses her incompetence as a mother: "I'm freaking out," she admits; "I'm cracking . . . I can't handle it alone." She explains that she must model to make money but cannot do so looking a maternal wreck. "How can I pose like this?" she inquires. The men gleefully offer to watch Marie until Sylvia recuperates, and they wander off to feed the child. When they next encounter Sylvia, she is asleep in her daughter's cradle (in a fetal position, sucking her thumb). On that regressive note, the film comes to an end.

In some respects *Three Men* conspicuously replicates the structure of recent paternal melodrama. Like *Kramer vs. Kramer*, it begins with a woman's abandoning her child and domestic duties, leaving them to a reluctant man. As the film progresses, however, the man rises to the occasion and is deemed superior to the woman at the job she has vacated.

Northrop Frye has noted how comedies often duplicate the structure of legal confrontations. In the genre's valorization of a new society, a "case" is made for the failure of the old: "The action of comedy," he writes, "is not unlike the action of a lawsuit, in which plaintiff and defendant construct different versions of the same situation, one finally being judged as real and the other as illusory" (166). From this perspective, the male maternal comedy enacts a symbolic court case—a custody battle—in which responsibility for the child is eventually awarded to the man. Woman is judged the "illusory" parent: real men do change diapers.

Beyond finding in favor of the masculine, *Three Men* performs a series of eradications of the feminine—be it configured as maternal or sexual. When Pierre and Michel first find Marie, one of them suggests contacting Jacques's mother; the other rejects the idea, labeling the woman an "old harpy." When one of them thinks of telephoning his own mother, the other urges him to "[l]eave the moms out." Later, in desperation, the men call the "Second Mommy Agency" and hire a nanny. By the time Nurse Rapons arrives, they have become so proprietary about child care that they vilify the woman until she resigns. At another point, when Jacques and a paramour are in bed, he interrupts their lovemaking to check on the child. The unsympathetic woman makes a hasty and irritated exit, stating, "I'm no wallflower." Later, a female dinner guest is equally intolerant when her meal is interrupted by Marie's cries. "It's just a whim," she claims, "put her in bed." Clearly, in all these cases, the women are conceived as nonmaternal. Though Nurse Rapons is "certified," Father knows best.

But, we should inquire, might we not see the men as merely *fatherly* parents, rather than as necessarily subsuming the female position? Might we not see the comedy as delineating a progressive expansion of the paternal, rather than a problematic contraction of the maternal? Within the logic of the film, this option is disallowed. The men never consider calling their dads for advice on child rearing, and Marie's father, Jacques, is the least devoted of the three. Furthermore, though Pierre and Michel are devastated when Marie leaves, they never pursue the option of becoming parents themselves. The women in their lives continue to function only as potential lovers—not as potential mothers of their children. Finally, when the need arises for Pierre to cut back his work hours, the men suggest he request a "maternity leave." Hence man is not a father but a "second *mommy*," and the nurturant role he fills is seen in feminine terms.

Beyond these instances of literal banishment, woman is extracted from the film in more subtle ways. For if she is denigrated in her maternal role, she is equally humiliated in her status as spectacle. In the opening party scene, the camera pans over a picture of a female nude on the apartment wall. Jacques then tells his friends of his sexual exploits with Clementine. In this dramatization of a smutty exchange, we recognize the Freudian scenario: the woman is no longer necessary within the dynamic, entirely bypassed in the system of male relays. We also perceive the connection between the defamation of the maternal and of the female erotic; as Erma Bombeck has noted, motherhood is the "second oldest profession."

Though the men are romantically obsessed with women, they seem to detest them. They have, in fact, made a "deal" with each other that forbids cohabitation with the opposite sex. "If a woman stays here more than a night," Pierre declaims, "I move out." The men's submerged hostility erupts at several points, when women are given such appellations as "hags," "whores," and "plagues." When Jacques returns from Japan, he telephones Sylvia in New York and is enraged when she hangs up on him. "Bitch," he yells, "Women, . . . I'd slap them back into place."

It is significant that much of the comedy in the film is of the "low" variety—focused on the body. Thus most of the gags center on Marie's eating, sleeping, urinating, defecating, or sucking, and on the problems each act causes for her adoptive parents. As Pierre says at one point, the men are spending their lives "wiping a baby's ass." "What a fine mess" they have gotten themselves into.

Interestingly, in Walter Kerr's delineation of physical humor, he makes an analogy to a child's first encounters with its mother.

> Low comedy is a birth experience, and for a time traumatic. *It consists in the discovery that we have a backside and that it is going to be slapped.* Total humiliation comes with our first breath of air, is a condition of our breathing. We are embarrassed to have a body that can be subjected to such treatment, and whenever it is subjected to such treatment again—*in a first slap from a mother* . . . we are freshly outraged. (149, my italics)

Thus in dealing with Marie, the men seem to relive and relieve the "humiliation" of their own bodily constraints—limitations that men first associate with women. Perhaps that is why Jacques is impelled to "slap" Sylvia "back into place," or why Hildy Johnson claims that Walter Burns renders women "slaphappy."

Marie's femininity is, decidedly, an issue and is featured in one of the most tasteless bits in the film. On the day she arrives, Michel leaves to buy supplies, and Pierre stays alone with the child. Before Michel can return, Marie has to urinate, and the camera renders a medium shot of her nude genital area with liquid spouting out—a literalization of the smutty joke as "exposure." Rarely in mainstream cinema has the camera focused so unflinchingly on the site of male anxiety. It happens here only because the subject is a child, and the director, a female.

But this revelation of Marie's physiology brings up a related issue: the question of childbirth, an act which is also focused on that physiological terrain. Clearly, the men appropriate the role of mother, and the fact that Marie arrives as a "package" seems parodic of biological delivery, comparable to the visitation of the stork. We are, in fact, reminded of certain traditional comic sketches in which clowns give birth to children. Psychoanalyst Sidney Tarachow discusses a set of etchings, by the eighteenth-century Dutch artist Peter Schenk, of a commedia dell'arte scenario entitled "The Marvellous Malady of Harlequin." The play begins with Harlequin ill. He is visited by the Doctor who gives him an injection in his backside. Harlequin then bears a son, whom he raises with the help of the white clown, Piro. At the end of the sequence, Harlequin is visited by Columbine, who openly mocks his behavior. This act, obviously, prefigures several films already considered: *The Kid*, *Their First Mistake*, and *Three Men and a Cradle*. Significantly, in this last, Pierre, Michel, and Jacques sing a three-part version of "Au clair de la lune"—a classic song about Pierrot/Piro.

Bakhtin's theories are also relevant to this conjunction of comedy and childbirth. For, in surveying the grotesque, he finds its archetypal image "two bodies in one: the one giving birth and dying, the other, conceived, generated and born." Thus, for Bakhtin, the carnivalesque stands on the "threshold of the grave and the crib" (21). Given this view, it is not surprising that he favors a section of Rabelais's writing in which Gargantua's wife delivers a son and dies in the process:

> Gargantua at the age of foure hundred, fourescore fourty and foure yeares begat his sonne Pantagruel, upon his wife named Badebec . . . who died in childe-birth, for he was so wonderfully great and lumpish, that he could not possibly come forth into the light of the world without thus suffocating his mother. (Quoted in Bakhtin, 179)

Bakhtin finds the duality of this primal image (its components of life and death) doubled in Gargantua's emotions, which are split between the joy of fatherhood and the grief of marital loss:

> When Pantagruel was borne, there was none more astonished and perplexed than was his father Gargantua; for on the one side, seeing his wife Badebec dead, and on the other side his sonne Pantagruel borne, so faire and so great, he knew not what to say nor what to do. (Quoted in Bakhtin, 182)

Again, we find parallels to this medieval moment in *Three Men*. For the male protagonists are both distressed by Sylvia's disappearance and elated at the arrival of Marie: like Gargantua, they know not what to feel.

At one point in the film, a commentary erupts on the subject of childbirth and man's appropriation of motherhood. After Marie has been returned to Sylvia, Jacques's life is empty. One night, he becomes inebriated and parades around his apartment with a pillow stuffed under his shirt that makes him look pregnant. It is possible that one thing Jacques envies about motherhood is the fixity of its assignation; his paternity, on the other hand, is continually in question. Eventually, Jacques delivers a speech about Genesis, claiming that if he were God and could remake the world, he would craft Adam out of Eve's rib and not the other way around. Then things would be "clearer," because no one would imagine that a being could emerge from a man's bone. Perhaps, Jacques muses, no one made man believe it; perhaps he simply wanted to.

Although Jacques's speech seems a vindication of woman's maternal role, a realization that men (beginning with Adam) have attempted to replace her, the film ultimately contradicts this reading. First, the phrasing of Jacques's speech is peculiar; despite its revisionist impulse, it implies that the world is really as the Bible represents it. Only if he "were God" could he change the present perspective. Second, he suggests reformulating the creation myth so that Adam issues from Eve's rib—still a denial of the female birth process. Third, if anyone is configured to resemble Eve, it is Sylvia, punished for her sexual knowledge with the social and physical pain of birthing an illegitimate child. Significantly, her daughter is named Marie in honor (one assumes) of Christ's mother, the only woman to have known immaculate conception.

Furthermore, despite Jacques's paean to woman's procreative powers, the film evinces a discomfort with female sexuality. It seems intriguing that when Michel must hide the packets of illicit drugs, he stuffs them in Marie's diaper, perhaps compensating for her genital lack, as Jacques's pillow did for his reproductive incapacity. Moreover, though the men have forbidden cohabitation with women, they have chosen to live with Marie. Thus it is only immature female sexuality that they can tolerate. In the closing scene, when Sylvia collapses in the cradle, they finally have woman where they want her, in a neutralized and infantile position—as child versus parent.

This notion sends us back to the theories of Walter Kerr. In *Tragedy and Comedy*, he delineates the relation between the two genres, which he sees positioned in a particular historical order. For Kerr, tragedy always precedes comedy, and the latter is formed in its image. As he writes: "Laughter is not man's first impulse; he cries first. Comedy always comes second" (19).

Kerr anthropomorphizes concepts to such an extent that he configures tragedy as the *maternal parent* of the comic form: "We insist," he remarks, "upon honoring tragedy as though it were the root, the mother, the matrix" (33). When he notes that modern comedy has veered toward the tragic, he sees the phenomenon, once more, in familial terms. He remarks: "[C]omedy has come home to its source—for which it must inevitably yearn. A child is drawn to its mother even when its survival depends upon its being independent" (248). Kerr asserts that in "returning to its womb . . . Comedy and tragedy become one again"—like parent and child in the generic Imaginary (262).

For Kerr, it is the comic mode that eventually triumphs, slaying tragedy, which is conspicuously absent from the contemporary artistic scene. Thus comedy can be seen as the symbiotic child that fails to separate, the perverse, matricidal offspring that returns to kill (like Owen, in *Throw Mama from the Train*). Comedy can also be seen as Pantagruel—the monstrous generic baby that suffocates the female parent in the throes of childbirth. As Kerr notes: "The clown cannot help himself; he was born to bring ambition down. *He will do it to his own mother*" (334, my italics).

In works like *The Kid* or *Three Men*, mothers are, decidedly, tragic figures. The unwed actress in Chaplin's melodrama is haunted by "her first mistake," and Sylvia in Serreau's film is a maudlin individual. Thus there is a match between Kerr's theory of comedy as subsuming tragedy and those films in which the comic hero (like comedy itself) preempts the role of pathetic mother. Furthermore, as though to replicate the history of the two genres, the recent batch of male maternal comedies supplants a set of "tragic" predecessors: *Kramer vs. Kramer, Ordinary People* (1980), *Table for Five* (1983).

But what, we might ask, is the fate of the female spectator in this scenario of masquerade and annihilation?—a query that has been posed in
the work of Tania Modleski and Mary Ann Doane (Doane, "Film and the
Masquerade"; Modleski, *The Women Who Knew Too Much*). How might
she react to this generic/genetic joke? She might respond to the male
procreative urge with the cynicism of television's Roseanne, who, we suspect, would willingly surrender her maternal role to them. For in one
episode, when facing her own family turmoil, she declared, "I'm gettin'
my tubes tied." Or the female viewer might assume the bemused and
sardonic stance of Columbine, coolly observing the domestic farce enacted by Harlequin and Piro. Or she might approach the male maternal
comic with the superior air that Grotjahn reserves for the comedienne. In
this case, she might paraphrase him, thinking that the comic hero "may
try hard but [he] still is not a [woman]. [He] tries to be what I am. It is
really funny" (99). If the female spectator is transcendent, she may engage the male comic with the composure of Osgood (Joe E. Brown) at
the end of *Some Like It Hot* (1959). For when he learns that his fiancée
is not a woman but a man in drag, he mumbles, generously, "Well, nobody's perfect"—thus inverting clichés of feminine anatomical lack.

Ultimately, however, in the female viewer's reaction we may look for
the spirit of Mary Daly, who prizes the comic sense. Rather than avoid
humor (with a grim feminist propriety), she openly confronts it, valorizing an aggressive, empowered, female response to the masculine grotesque. As she writes: "There is nothing like the sound of women really
laughing . . . roaring at the reversal that is patriarchy, the monstrous
jock's joke . . . this laughter is the one true hope, for as long as it is
audible there is evidence that *someone* is seeing through the Dirty Joke"
(17, my italics). Regrettably, that female "someone" is not filmmaker
Coline Serreau, who is laughing only on the way to the bank. For she
eventually clones her reproduction of mothering in a lucrative American
context—this time (like Sylvia) handing the job over to a man.[4]

Works Cited

Bakhtin, Mikhail. *Rabelais and His World*. Translated by Hélène Iswolsky.
  Bloomington: Indiana University Press, 1984.
Bombeck, Erma. *Motherhood: The Second Oldest Profession*. New York: Dell,
  1983.
Cavell, Stanley. "Psychoanalysis and the Cinema: The Melodrama of the Un-
  known Woman." In *Images in Our Souls: Cavell, Psychoanalysis, and Cinema*,

---

[4] I am, of course, referring again to *Three Men and a Baby* (1987), directed by Leonard
Nimoy.

edited by Joseph H. Smith and William Kerrigan, 11–43. Baltimore and London: Johns Hopkins University Press, 1987.

———. *Pursuits of Happiness: The Hollywood Comedy of Remarriage*. Cambridge: Harvard University Press, 1981.

Daly, Mary. *Gyn/Ecology: The Metaethics of Radical Feminism*. Boston: Beacon, 1978.

Doane, Mary Ann. "Film and the Masquerade—Theorising the Female Spectator." *Screen* 23, nos. 3–4 (September–October 1982): 74–87.

———. "The Film's Time and the Spectator's 'Space.'" In *Cinema and Language*, edited by Stephen Heath and Patricia Mellencamp, 35–49. Frederick, MD: University Publications of America, 1983.

Dozoretz, Wendy. "The Mother's Lost Voice in *Hard, Fast, and Beautiful*." *Wide Angle* 6, no. 3 (1984): 50–57.

Freud, Sigmund. *Jokes and Their Relation to the Unconscious*. Translated and edited by James Strachey. New York: Norton, 1960.

Frye, Northrop. *The Anatomy of Criticism: Four Essays*. Princeton, NJ: Princeton University Press, 1973.

Girard, René. "Myth and Ritual in Shakespeare: *A Midsummer Night's Dream*." In *Textual Strategies: Perspectives in Post-Structualist Criticism*, edited by Josué V. Harari, 189–212. Ithaca, NY: Cornell University Press, 1979.

Grotjahn, Martin. *Beyond Laughter: Humor and the Subconscious*. New York, Toronto, and London: McGraw-Hill, 1966.

Haskell, Molly. *From Reverence to Rape: The Treatment of Women in the Movies*. Baltimore, MD: Penguin, 1974.

Holland, Norman N. *Laughing: A Psychology of Humor*. Ithaca, NY: Cornell University Press, 1982.

Jekels, Ludwig. "On the Psychology of Comedy." In *Comedy: Meaning and Form*, edited by Robert Corrigan, 174–79. New York: Harper & Row, 1981.

Johnston, Claire. "Myths of Women in the Cinema." In *Women and the Cinema: A Critical Anthology*, edited by Karyn Kay and Gerald Peary, 407–11. New York: Dutton, 1977.

Kaplan, E. Ann, ed. *Women in Film Noir*. London: BFI Publishing, 1980.

Kerr, Walter. *Tragedy and Comedy*. New York: Da Capo, 1985.

Kuhn, Annette. *The Power of the Image: Essays on Representation and Sexuality*. London, Boston, Melbourne, and Henley: Routledge & Kegan Paul, 1985.

Leibman, Nina C. "Leave Mother Out: The Fifties Family in American Film and Television." *Wide Angle* 10, no. 4 (1988): 24–41.

Mauron, Charles. *Psychocritique du genre comique*. Paris: J. Corti, 1964.

Mellencamp, Patricia. "Jokes and Their Relation to the Marx Brothers." In *Cinema and Language*, edited by Stephen Heath and Patricia Mellencamp, 63–78. Frederick, MD: University Publications of America, 1983.

Modleski, Tania. "Three Men and Baby M." *Camera Obscura*, no. 17 (May 1988): 69–81.

———. *The Women Who Knew Too Much: Hitchcock and Feminist Theory*. New York and London: Methuen, 1988.

Mulvey, Laura. "Visual Pleasure and Narrative Cinema." In *Women and the Cinema: A Critical Anthology*, edited by Karyn Kay and Gerald Peary, 412–28. New York: Dutton, 1977.

Rose, Jacqueline. *The Case of Peter Pan, or, the Impossibility of Children's Fiction*. London: Macmillan, 1984.

Russo, Mary. "Female Grotesques: Carnival and Theory." In *Feminist Studies/ Critical Studies*, edited by Teresa de Lauretis, 213–29. Bloomington: Indiana University Press, 1986.

Silverman, Kaja. *The Subject of Semiotics*. New York: Oxford University Press, 1983.

Tarachow, Sidney. "Circuses and Clowns." In *Psychoanalysis and the Social Sciences*, edited by Giza Roheim, 3:171–85. New York: International Universities Press, 1951.

7

The Thriller

THE HAND THAT SHOCKS THE CRADLE:

THE MATERNAL THRILLER

Not Home Alone

The anti–day care headlines practically shrieked in the '80s:
"MOMMY, DON'T LEAVE ME HERE!"
 (Susan Faludi)

Walt Disney's *Mary Poppins* (1964), based on the Pamela L. Travers novel (1934), concerns the Banks family and their need of a nanny. Set in turn-of-the-century England, the story concerns a household headed by a workaholic banker, and his wife, an overzealous suffragette—hence neither spends adequate time with the children. Appearing on the scene is the strict but magical Mary Poppins, who creates marvelous adventures for the children and reconciles them with their parents.

Some thirty years later, the image of the nanny that circulates in the cinema is vastly different.[1] Rather than the beneficent Guardian Angel who miraculously materializes to save the day, she is more likely to be envisaged as the Angel of Death who swoops down on families to savage their offspring. As a recent *New York Times* article tells us, "The legend of the nanny as demon thrives in popular movies" ("No Good Nannies?"). It is clear that such screen images are fueled by representations in the broader popular culture. Consider the following murder stories chronicled by contemporary tabloids: the 1991 case of Olivia Riner, a Swiss au pair in Thornwood, New York, accused of setting fire to the infant in her care; or the 1993 proceedings around Ann Franklin, a nanny in Rye, New York, charged with inflicting severe head injuries on the child for whom she baby-sat (Berger, Glaberson). Consider, as well, a December 1991 *U.S. News and World Report* article dramatically entitled "The Nanny Nightmare: How to Weed Out the Bad Seeds before Hiring Live-In Child Care," and another in the *New York Times* called "The Story of a Nanny, from Care to Calamity" (Berger). More

---

[1] While the image of the nanny on-screen has, generally, been pernicious, recently there has been a television sitcom entitled *The Nanny* that is comic.

17. *Mary Poppins* (1964). The strict but magical Mary Poppins (Julie Andrews) creates marvelous adventures for her charges. MOMA

recently, newspapers reported a case in Pennsylvania of a baby-sitter who disciplined her charges by putting them in the clothes dryer ("Girl 13 . . ."). Not surprisingly, Carin Rubenstein describes a parent who "hires a private investigator to check every [child care] applicant for a criminal record." Another article mentions "a California mother [who] hired and dismissed 19 nannies in one year" ("No Good Nannies?"). This paranoia has spread from employers to employees. As one article reports, "[I]t turns out that nannies, too, struggle to find the families of their dreams" ("No Good Nannies?").

When media reports have not focused on the homicidal aspects of Nannydom, they have voiced other concerns. In January 1993 the case of Zoe Baird hit the news. Baird, a lawyer, was proposed for the post of attorney general in President Bill Clinton's cabinet but had to withdraw her name from consideration because she had once employed illegal aliens for domestic help. Shortly thereafter, Clinton's next nominee, Kimba Wood, had to decline the position for a similar reason. The uproar around these stories led Anna Quindlen to quip that "Sitterhood Is Powerful." Others termed the scandal "Nannygate."

Beyond concerns about the legality or criminality of live-in baby-sitters—only 3 percent of the child care sector (Rubenstein)—Americans of the eighties and nineties were consumed with larger problems. Numerous stories emerged of abuse at day care centers: the McMartin Preschool in California and similar questionable facilities in New Jersey, North Carolina, and Canada (Manshel, Howse, "Listen to the Children," "The Child-Abuse Case"). Most commentators treated the incidents as deadly serious, despite the acquittals of many of the alleged perpetrators; some, however, like Alexander Cockburn, saw the events as possibly "imagined" and the media coverage as "hysterical." He writes, "[S]ociety was ripe for a witch hunt . . . and the accumulated energies poised for this end displaced themselves into the virtuous cause of hunting for bodysnatchers of the nation's children" (20).

On a less macabre or sensational note, the national press debated the advisability of early child care—even when the setting was benign. Some studies questioned the placement of children within an extended kinship network. A 1994 newspaper article, entitled "Family Ties May Not Bind When It Comes to Day Care," states that "[p]arents may find some comfort in leaving children with a relative, but the researchers found that a familial tie wasn't necessarily the best predictor for good child care." More essays interrogated day care within an institutional setting. A *New York Times* article in the fall of 1992 is entitled "Too Young for Day Care" (Cherlin), and another is headlined "Learning If Infants Are Hurt When Mothers Go to Work" (Eckholm). A *Newsweek* piece of June 1992 asks, "Who's Minding Our Children?" (Ames), a query mirrored in a subsequent *Fortune* article: "Who's Minding America's Kids?" An earlier article had inquired, "Can Your Career Hurt Your Kids?"—a question clearly addressed to mothers, as fathers' professional commitments are never at issue (Labich). Some essays are more direct in condemning modern female roles. One asks, "Do working mothers imperil their children's inner security and future happiness?" (Eckholm). Here, one is reminded that in *Mary Poppins* the demand for a nanny was spurred by Mrs. Banks's feminist activities. Hence women's rights have always been seen to imperil children.

Perhaps a more recent companion piece to the Disney film is Chris Columbus's *Home Alone* (1990), the story of parents of a large family who inadvertently leave their eight-year-old son in the house when they depart for Paris during Christmas vacation. Typically, the mother seems most to blame for the chain of events: it is she who has forced the child to sleep in the attic as a punishment for his misbehavior, an act that makes him easy to miss in the family's rushed morning preparations and exit. Once deserted, the child is immediately at risk, besieged by two burglars.

The film was hugely successful and instantly interpreted as evincing worries about the fate of our progeny in the postfeminist world—specifically, about the status of "latch-key" children abandoned by working moms. Its reception was followed by national media attention to similar real-life cases: parents who left their children unattended for several days while traveling (Ackerman); a fire in Detroit that killed seven siblings "Left Home Alone" (Grimmer). Other comedies appeared on the same topic: *Don't Tell Mom the Babysitter's Dead* (1991) charts the adventures that befall a set of siblings when the elderly woman with whom their mother has left them suddenly expires and they decide to keep her demise a secret.

Hence America's offspring were seen to be endangered whether left alone—or *not*. If a lack of supervision was often a problem, so was oversight by perverse and destructive caretakers—be they strangers or relatives. The best solution was for Mother, simply, to be there to tend to Hearth and Home. Little consideration was given to the social and economic exigencies that prevented her from doing so (like making ends meet), or to the ways in which child care, now affecting some 55 percent of the population, might be extended and improved (Carroll).

As E. Ann Kaplan has noted, anxiety is prevalent in contemporary maternal discourses, mainly because "there is now a question of whether or not to mother, and of what sort of context for mothering one . . . deems essential" (182). It is not surprising that these apprehensions concerning child care and the working mother should be registered in the cinema—always a medium to tap popular fantasies. A *Fortune* article of August 1992 talked about parents' routinely exchanging "*horror* stories" concerning baby-sitters who allowed "children to sit *zombielike*" all day long ("Who's Minding America's Kids?" my italics). Significantly, it is in the thriller and Gothic modes that these tensions get cinematographically registered, giving those genres a new "maternal" cast.

Noxious Nannies

For the hand that rocks the cradle
Is the hand that rules the world.
  (William Ross Wallace, "What Rules the World")

Out of the cradle endlessly rocking,
Out of the mocking-bird's throat, the musical shuttle.
  (Walt Whitman, *Leaves of Grass*)

One might say that Griffith's devotion to the Cult of Motherhood reaches its apotheosis in *Intolerance*, whose four episodes are linked . . . by stark shots of Lillian Gish, as the im-
passive mother, taking on the full sorrow of history, *her cradle
endlessly rocking.*
  (Scott Simmon, my italics)

No film better exemplifies the emerging genre of "maternal thriller"
than *The Hand That Rocks the Cradle* (1992) directed by Curtis Hanson
and written by Amanda Silver.[2] The film is even mentioned in the *Fortune* article "Who's Minding America's Kids?" as a work with the power
to "unsettl[e] parents." The movie was also the subject of discussion on
several television talk shows (e.g., *The Oprah Winfrey Show*, *Geraldo*)
that examined contemporary child care woes. Finally, its title was embla-
zoned on the cover of the 11 May 1992 issue of *National Review*, accompanied by a picture of Hillary Clinton: the powerful feminist wife of
a presidential hopeful, the working mother par excellence.

   While the film's title references William Ross Wallace's famous lines,
it also calls up D. W. Griffith's *Intolerance* (1916), a work whose four-
part historical structure is sutured by the maternal image of Lillian Gish
and by quotations from Walt Whitman's *Leaves of Grass*. Like the poet's
words (which conjure a musical theme), Griffith's poignant visual trope
positions the innocent madonna *outside* the universe of political injustice. Wallace's verse is of a more cynical tone, implicating motherhood
in the system of corrupt power. *The Hand That Rocks the Cradle* "shut-
tles" (as Whitman would have it) between these two positions: one attached to the biological mother and the other assigned to her surrogate.

   The film tells the story of a yuppie couple, Claire and Michael Bartel
(Annabella Sciorra and Matt McCoy), who live in Seattle and are expect-

---

[2] *The Hand That Rocks the Cradle* was also the title of a 1917 Universal film directed by
Lois Weber. It is a fictionalized account of the arrest of Margaret Sanger for dissemination
of birth control information (Sloan, 341).

ing their second child.[3] When Claire's regular obstetrician is unavailable, she consults Dr. Mott and is distressed when he becomes sexually aroused while examining her. At her husband's suggestion, she reports the physician to the authorities but does so reluctantly. Dr. Mott is disgraced and commits suicide. Mrs. Mott (Rebecca De Mornay), who is in the final stages of pregnancy, goes into shock and miscarries, also suffering a hysterectomy. Her medical emergency is intercut (in Griffithesque fashion) with scenes of Claire's daughter Emma as she joyously feels her mother's fertile belly. When the Bartels' son, Joey, is born, they advertise for a nanny, and Mrs. Mott deviously poses as "Peyton Flanders" to secure the job. It soon becomes clear that her covert intent is to destroy Claire and her standing within the family. What Peyton wants is to replace Claire as mother and wife, thus recouping the stature she has traumatically lost. Janet Maslin includes the film in a contemporary group evincing "personality theft plots." Beyond this, the film seems to reference certain news stories of infant snatchings by deranged barren women. In *The Hand That Rocks the Cradle*, however, it is not only the child who is "stolen" but the role of mother itself. In this regard, one is reminded of an anecdote by Gabrielle Glaser in a recent "Hers" column in the *New York Times Magazine*. She describes having stopped in a crowded urban coffee shop with her infant daughter and ending up sharing a table with another young woman and child. When that woman witnessed the joy with which Glaser's daughter responded to her mother's kiss, the woman remarked, "She really likes you." "I should hope so," Glaser answered, quizzically. "Have you been with her long?" the other woman queried. Puzzled, Glaser said, "Since birth." "Oh," the other woman said, embarrassedly. "You're her *mother*. . . . I only meet other nannies." Curiously, this anecdote replays a scene in the classic film *Imitation of Life* (1959) in which Lora Meredith, a white woman, encounters a black woman taking care of a light-skinned child at the beach. She, too, asks how long the black woman has "been with" the child, only to be told "since birth." In this case, Lora Meredith assumes that the black woman is a Mammy, misreading the fact that the latter's daughter is mulatto. Eventually, the black woman works for Lora, taking care of the Meredith child as well as her own.

While Gabrielle Glaser's anecdote makes light of the substitution of nanny for mother, in *The Hand That Rocks the Cradle*, it is malice that characterizes Peyton's appropriation of Claire's maternal role. (Claire's

---

[3] In "Rich and Strange, or Something This Way Comes: The Yuppie Horror Film," Barry Keith Grant discusses a series of films about yuppies that he considers part of the horror genre. *The Hand That Rocks the Cradle* is included in that group. He describes these works as voicing "[t]he fears and anxieties of the yuppie subculture" (1–2) and calls the character of Peyton a "yuppie gremlin" (12).

friend Marlene in fact, warns her, "Never let an attractive woman take a power position in your home.") This station, however, is precisely what Peyton achieves. She uses her intelligence to diminish Claire's self-esteem and to turn her family against her. Peyton plants one of Claire's stud earrings in the baby's blanket, making Claire seem careless of his safety. Peyton suggests that Michael and Marlene, who are ex-lovers, plan a surprise party for Claire, thereby producing the appearance that they are having an affair. Peyton solicits secrets from Emma, so that she may win the child's preferential trust. Thus, in this film, the hand that rocks the cradle dominates the home.

In part, Peyton's control is realized through access to the gaze—traditionally a male prerogative. An aspect of her intricate plotting involves noticing details, like Claire's lost earring or Marlene's misplaced lighter, which Peyton plants in Michael's pocket. These scenes are rendered in a classic shot/countershot mode, with Peyton as the bearer of the look. Other sequences place her in a male voyeuristic stance. For instance, she and Emma illicitly view scary movies on television as part of their "secret club," which places them in the same position as the audience of the movie they are in. Furthermore, their spectatorship identifies them with a traditionally masculine genre. Throughout these episodes, which highlight Peyton's sight, Claire seems blind.

Beyond vision, Peyton is linked to a masculine position in other ways. When she becomes the object of a workman's gaze, she slaps him. When Emma is troubled by some schoolyard bullies, Peyton intervenes to intimidate them, demonstrating that she can be "one of the boys." She is also sexually aggressive—typically a male stance. In one scene, Peyton appears, unexpectedly, in Michael's office, supposedly to discuss Claire's surprise party. All his coworkers stare at the couple, then later gossip and make snide remarks. On another occasion, Peyton makes a ruckus in the kitchen at night so that Michael will come down. When he does, he finds her in a flimsy, transparent nightgown that displays her breasts. Hence Peyton controls not only Claire but Michael, making a mockery of his rendition of a Gilbert and Sullivan song: "I Am the Captain of the *Pinafore.*" Aside from its patriarchal valence, the tune may evoke the fact that the first American day care facility was founded in 1838 in Boston by a Mrs. Hale, who wanted to provide a nursery for the children of sailors away at sea (Zemal).

Prime responsibility for Peyton's ascendancy in the Bartel home is subtly laid at Claire's feet—those of the ostensibly Good Mother. While Peyton is tied to "masculine" mental acumen and connivance, Claire is easily duped. She is also aligned with the natural, a connection that draws upon familiar dichotomies of nature/culture. She is an amateur botanist who volunteers in a plant nursery. In fact, the reason she requires a nanny is that she plans to build a greenhouse in her backyard. Her project is heavy with implications. On the one hand, the audience may be sympathetic to her, as her horticultural bent is linked to "feminine" nurturing. On the other hand, such a dilettante's enterprise does not seem to "justify" (as would full-fledged employment) a separation from her child. Hence the viewer may resent Claire for dabbling in a hobby and blame her for needlessly shirking her maternal responsibilities. (In fact, she allows herself to be convinced by Michael that she requires help—a notion that she, initially, resists.) On the other hand, she may garner sympathy for not being a "career woman," for assuring Peyton that she will always be close by.

While ostensibly a likable character, Claire's persona is undermined in numerous other ways. Though warranted, her reporting of Dr. Mott ends in disaster; it is her act that leads to the collapse of two families. Moreover, her own inclination is to ignore the incident; only when Michael, with his clear male sense of justice, insists on retribution does she consent to complain. Furthermore, she is depicted as a hysteric whose symptoms take the form of asthma. Her breathing is labored only at heightened moments: after Dr. Mott molests her; when she becomes suspicious and jealous of Michael and Marlene.

While medical literature of the past stressed asthma's "psychosomatic" component, and blamed mothers for its occurrence in children,[4] recent research has downplayed those theories. The film validates the earlier vision of the illness and casts Claire as its victim and stooge. When at the end of the film an asthmatic episode renders her helpless to defend her family against Peyton's murderous attack, she seems doubly at fault. Peyton even derides her by taunting, "You can't even breathe!"

As Claire's stance on working can be read for contradictory meanings ("positive" because she is not a professional; "negative" because she needlessly abandons her child), so can her political position. Prominent in the narrative is the figure of Solomon (Ernie Hudson), a black, retarded workman the Bartels hire through a social service agency to construct a fence on their property. The film, in fact, begins with his mysterious arrival at their home. The Bartels' charitable act labels them as

---

[4] In *Psychological and Allergic Aspects of Asthma* (1965), Michael Hirt mentions how "the 'over-protective' mother has often been associated with the asthmatic child" (243). He also talks of the "faulty mother-child relationship underlying allergic [and asthmatic] disorders" (157). In "The Psychosomatic Approach to Bronchial Asthma," J. J. Groen and J. Bastiaans refer to the literature on the "asthma mother," who has been charged with rejection, maternal overprotection, and loving tyranny (53). Thomas M. French in "The Asthma Attack" quotes research that sees the asthmatic attack as "a reaction to the danger of separation from the mother, or of loss of the mother's love" (34). Furthermore, he sees the asthmatic gasp as equivalent to the cry an infant might emit "upon separation from the mother at birth" (38).

"liberals," as "tolerant" of ethnic, class, and intellectual difference; they tell Emma that Solomon is a "special person." Yet when he first knocks on Claire's door, she instinctively screams, as though she assumes him to be an intruder. Later, her inherent prejudices allow her to fall for Peyton's ploy to undermine Solomon: the planting of a pair of Emma's panties in his bicycle basket. When Peyton choreographs the discovery of the garment, Claire instantly believes that her beloved carpenter is a deranged pedophile. She reports his sexual "misconduct" to the agency, and, for the second time, such a "feminist" act leads to her punishment. Solomon's exit only allows Peyton a more sinister and commanding role. Though banished, this Wise Man, this Divine Fool, stalks the perimeters of the Bartels' universe—keeping watch on the clan. At the end of the drama, he magically appears to foil Peyton's onslaught, ending her reign of terror. Significantly, she falls to her death and is impaled on Solomon's white picket fence.

Given the name of this character, one is reminded of the biblical Solomon and his famous judgment. Two women who have recently given birth to sons come to see Solomon. The first woman claims that when the second woman's baby expired in the night, she exchanged the dead infant for the living one. When the first woman awoke in the morning and found herself beside a dead baby, she realized it was not her own. Solomon is asked to settle the dispute. Dramatically, he orders his servant to bring a sword and divide the surviving child in half, in order to give each mother a part. The first woman drops to her knees and begs Solomon to refrain, even if it means relinquishing her son to another. Solomon wisely decides that she is the true mother, since she is willing to sacrifice her personal happiness for the sake of her offspring (Sellew, 95–97). In *The Hand That Rocks the Cradle*, we have a replay of two mothers who vie for a child after one of their babies perishes. Again, one woman is deceitful, attempting to "steal" a child from another. Solomon (like his biblical namesake) is the character most aware of Peyton's duplicity—long before the Bartels catch on. At the end of the drama, he is allowed to deliver the child to his proper parent.

Curiously, in this black, retarded workman, we find not only reminders of Solomon but nostalgia for the classic Mammy. For, like her, Solomon is the cherished protector of the Bartel children and the savior of the family. While at the beginning of the story Claire requests that he refrain from touching the baby (ostensibly enforcing a rule mandated by his agency), at the end she hands him the infant. With this gesture, Claire symbolically admits her tragic mistake: that her maternal "intuition" has failed, that she was wrong to hire Peyton, that Solomon would have made the best "nanny" (as did Eldin on television's *Murphy Brown*) or, perhaps, the best mom. Even Emma seems to have known more than her mother: in an early discussion of child care options, the little girl had requested Solomon.

Significantly, the number of male nannies is growing in America. As Michele Willen writes, "While still a distinct minority, more men are being hired by parents to take care of their children and more men are eager to get into the field." Perhaps this phenomenon helps to explain not only the popularity of *Murphy Brown* but that of the film *Mrs. Doubtfire* (1993). If inclusion on David Letterman's "Top Ten List" currently signals the ascendancy of an issue to high topicality, this occasion was marked for child care on the night of 10 November 1993, when Letterman asked his viewers to imagine "The Top Ten Signs That the Nanny You Hired Might Really Be a Man."

If, within the dichotomous narrative of *The Hand That Rocks the Cradle*, Claire represents the Good Mother (engaged in a crisis of confidence), Peyton signifies the Bad. Marlene, indeed, recognizes the scent of "Poison" on her as she walks by one evening. With her masculine tendencies, she is—like Mrs. Doubtfire—the archetypal "Phallic Mother," a figure who, according to E. Ann Kaplan, "satisfies needs for power that [the] ideal [mother] function prohibits" (47).

Peyton is every woman's nightmare baby-sitter—a phantom figure that fuels maternal guilt for the sin of independence. We have already discussed Peyton's guileful attempt to supersede Claire, an action that is made plausible by the bizarre circumstances of the plot. But is that not, on some level, the fear of *every* contemporary mother who farms out child care? In an era of nuclear families, we expect the circuit of love and allegiance to be limited. Without extended kinship, we presume the child will bond with its primary caregivers: mother, father, and/or stepparent. The presence of a full-time nanny establishes a triangular relationship that carries its own special tensions. As Susan Chira writes in the *New York Times*, "[M]any women fear they have somehow relinquished their children. 'When I put them in day care, I did feel a pull'; 'I'm not the one raising my children'" (32). In *The Hand That Rocks the Cradle*, this quotidian rivalry is hyperbolized in a tale of grotesque dimensions.

Given recent feminist theory, it is interesting that Peyton's appropriation of Claire's role is signaled by her association with music and voice. When she moves into the Bartel home, she brings a gift of wind chimes—to help the baby sleep, she says. In reality, she will use their sound to mask her secret midnight rambles through the house. On several occasions, when she has set her radio-alarm to awaken her for a feeding, it rouses her with a diva's aria. Hence we may be reminded of Kaja Silverman's notion of the maternal voice as "operatic" (*Acoustic Mirror*, 84–100). In other scenes, music is associated with both Peyton

and Claire, but with the former in a dominant position. As Claire prepares to go out with Michael one evening, she listens to opera as she
dons a sexy red dress that he wishes her to wear. Peyton covertly stains
it with perfume so that Claire must change into a more conservative out-
fit. Thus as the choral music plays, Peyton steals yet another aspect of
Claire's persona: her eroticism. Claire is robbed not only of music but of
vocality: when she succumbs to her asthma attacks, often precipitated by
Peyton, she seems to gasp for voice as well as for breath. The hoarse,
rasping, guttural sounds that she produces contrast with the mellifluous
tones associated with Peyton. Ironically, in the early part of the film
Marlene complains that the woman of today is expected to know how to
cook and to give blow jobs. After Peyton gets done with Claire, the latter is so devoid of sexuality that the only thing she can blow is her in-
haler. At one point Peyton, quite literally, steals Claire's speech. As
Claire talks with Michael in their bedroom, sharing her growing suspi-
cions of their nanny, Peyton listens downstairs through a hidden inter-
com intended for the baby's room.

Certain elements of the story have intriguing historical associations to
traditions of child care. One of the most chilling acts that Peyton perpe-
trates is to *nurse* Joey without Claire's consent or knowledge. In fact,
when she first approaches his cradle in the dead of night and lifts his
pillow, we assume that she will suffocate him; the act she does perform
shocks us nearly as much. Obviously, Peyton can breast-feed because
she has continued to express her own milk following her late-term mis-
carriage. As one would predict, Joey soon rejects his mother's breast,
causing her pain. Peyton's nursing of Joey strikes us as treacherous and
abhorrent since it violates one of the most personal and intimate relationships between mother and child. Yet historically "wet-nursing" was
common and institutionalized. Thus what is a widespread practice in
one era can become abject in another. For centuries, wet-nursing was
associated with high maternal mortality; if the traditional wet nurse replaced a deceased mother, Peyton, "replacing" a living mother, seeks
the latter's death (Fields, 1). In later epochs, wet-nursing constituted a
luxury and convenience for elite families like the Bartels. Often, the
nurse's own child suffered as a result of its mother's care of someone
else's baby. As Valerie Fields notes, "In effect, wealthy parents frequently 'bought' the life of their infant for the life of another" (193).
This exchange of babies invokes Peyton's loss of her own progeny. Furthermore, her precarious mental state has links to the psychology of wet-
nursing. As a Chicago doctor warned in 1923, "There is a grave danger
of mental depression on the part of a woman . . . who, through misfor-
tune or necessity, is forced to seek this means of employment" (Fields,
251). Interestingly, while wet-nursing was phased out in the United

States in the late 1940s, recent times have seen the rise of "cross-nurs-ing," in which women provide breast-feeding services for one another's children without pay. As Judith Z. Krantz and Nancy S. Kupper remark, "Cross-nursing is a logical and practical extension of the resurgence of breast-feeding and may, in turn, . . . make[e] it more attractive to em-ployed mothers" (715). Significantly, the maternal voice is a crucial ele-ment of the breast-feeding experience. Researchers found that cross-nursers could feed another's infant only if they remained silent; if they talked, the baby perceived the dissonance and was disturbed (716).

In one way, *The Hand That Rocks the Cradle* serves as a cautionary tale for the modern mother, alerting her to the disasters that transpire if she is not vigilant on the domestic front. One is reminded of the tabloid stories, years back, of Robin Williams's divorce from his wife and remar-riage to his child's baby-sitter, a woman portrayed "as a home-wrecking nanny" (Williams in Grunwald, 112; Darrach). Ironically, this same woman later served as Williams's manager, acquiring for him the role of Mrs. Doubtfire.

According to one reading, Peyton's characterization as Bad Mother stands outside of Claire's parental self: a separate entity—a m(other)/ other—who can wreak havoc in the Good one's absence. By another in-terpretation, however, the two are "doubles" who form a composite whole. From this perspective, it seems important that Peyton and Claire are both bourgeois women from approximately the same social stratum; they do not enact the typical employer-employee relation, which bridges class. Throughout the film, Peyton dresses in "preppie" clothing that looks as if it was ordered from the L. L. Bean catalog—a mere variation on Claire's slightly more rugged couture. Both Claire and Peyton have carried a son. But while Joey is born healthy, Peyton's son is stillborn. Furthermore, while Claire's asthma renders her somewhat "hysterical," Peyton's behavior marks her as psychotic—her illness ostensibly caused by her simultaneous loss of husband, baby, and uterus. At times, she is clearly delusional. In the closing scene, as she attacks the Bartels, she opens her arms to Emma, shouting, "Mama is here." Both women end the film as Madwomen in the Attic, since the top floor of the Bartel abode is the site of their final struggle. In this sequence, Solomon ap-pears as the Angel in the House, managing to save the family and the day.

The attic locale makes clear the parallels between *The Hand That Rocks the Cradle* and the literary Gothic, a form in which Claire Kahane finds the heroine engaging in "an ongoing battle with a mirror image who is both self and other" (337). Furthermore, Kahane conceives the Gothic as sustaining an inherent maternal discourse: "[L]ocked into the forbidden center of the Gothic . . . is the spectral presence of a dead-undead mother, archaic and all encompassing, a ghost signifying the problematics of femininity which the heroine must confront" (336). The finale of *The Hand That Rocks the Cradle*—with its struggle between maternal "doubles," its demise and resurrection of mothers—is reflective of these observations. So is the fact that Peyton resides in the Bartels' basement, the "forbidden center" of their home.

But there are other elements of the film that are reminiscent of the Gothic—though revised with a twist. As Tania Modleski has noted, "In the typical Gothic plot, the heroine comes to a mysterious house, perhaps as a bride, perhaps in another capacity and . . . starts to mistrust her husband" (59). In *The Hand That Rocks the Cradle*, it is Peyton who comes to the new house in the familiar role of "governess." While the dwelling is safe when she arrives, it becomes threatening under her tenure and residence. While Peyton seems the Gothic heroine, in truth, that figure is Claire. It is she who suffers from the pernicious secrets of the house and begins to mistrust her husband. While in Gothic fiction it is generally the latter who tries "to drive [the heroine] insane, or . . . to murder her" (Modleski, 60), in *The Hand That Rocks the Cradle*, the villain is Peyton, which again places her within a masculine plot space. Critics have also remarked on the Gothic's atmosphere of paranoia and masochism—affects associated with Claire. Modleski notes that "[w]omen in Gothics are persecuted" (82); and Michelle Masse asserts that the "infamous scandal" of the form "is a suffering woman" (41).

Near the end of the film, Claire more obviously fills the shoes of the Gothic protagonist when, suspecting that Peyton is her deceased physician's wife, she tours the vacant Mott home with a real estate agent. When Claire enters the abandoned house, she finds the experience uncanny: she hears a duplicate of Peyton's wind chimes and finds a double of the nursery that Peyton has set up in the Bartel home.

Having posited Claire and Peyton as "doubles," we must take note of prominent psychoanalytic theories which claim that the child divides the mother into "good" and "bad" halves. As Melanie Klein writes: "The baby's first object of love and hate—his mother—is both desired and hated with all the intensity that is characteristic of the early urges of the baby. In the very beginning he loves his mother at the time that she is satisfying his needs. . . . But when . . . his desires are not gratified . . . then the whole situation suddenly alters" (Klein and Riviere, 58). More specifically, Klein identifies this maternal dichotomy with the act of nursing: "[T]he breast of the mother which gives gratification or denies it becomes, in the mind of the child, imbued with the characteristics of good and evil. Now, what one might call the 'good' breasts become the prototype of what is felt throughout life to be good and beneficent, while the 'bad' breasts stand for everything evil and persecuting" (Klein, 291).

In *The Hand That Rocks the Cradle*, we have, quite literally, *two* sets of maternal breasts: Claire's (the legitimate ones) and Peyton's (the felonious ones). But the valence attached to each is complex and shifting. While we might ordinarily associate Claire with the "good breasts" as she is Joey's birth mother, *he* comes to link her to the "bad breasts" when he gets accustomed to, and desirous of, those of Peyton. Even at the end of the film, with the restoration of the family order, it may be too late for Claire to reestablish a nursing bond with Joey.

Interestingly, Peyton's perverse association with milk draws on the folklore of witches, who were believed to have supernumerary nipples (Ravensdale and Morgan, 12) and the power to spoil dairy products. As Nancy Mann Kulish writes, "[M]ythological witches are frequently . . . identified with images of cows and milk, especially ruined or poisoned milk" (394). (In this light, Peyton's choice of perfume becomes doubly significant.) The association between Peyton and witches functions also as another marker of her masculinity. For Geza Roheim, the witch is characterized by such phallic attributes as a tail, beard, and broomstick (362–64). Her association with milk invokes not only the maternal breast but the cow udder, which, for Roheim, is a strangely "phallic nipple" (376).

Klein's notion of the same woman's signifying both Good and Bad breasts to the infant supports the reading of Claire and Peyton as doppelgängers. It also surfaces the Good Mother's worst fear: that she will become the "bad breast" to her own offspring by delegating child care to another.

Witchcraft through the Ages

> Myth transmits and transforms the ideology of sexism and
> renders it invisible.
> (Claire Johnston)

Perhaps the film that most closely resembles *The Hand That Rocks the Cradle* is *The Guardian* (1990), directed by William Friedkin, a work that gives the maternal thriller an *occult* twist. Here, instead of being a banal illegal alien (as were those of individuals in the news), the nanny is a supernatural one—like the "bodysnatchers" Alexander Cockburn ironically predicted. Clearly, we have come a long way from the benign magic of Mary Poppins.

The Guardian opens with a brief prologue depicting a baby-sitter absconding with her charge as the child's parents naively depart for a weekend trip. The sitter flees to the woods and, in a mysterious ceremony, "gives" the child to a tree that "petrifies" it within its bark. A title tells us, "For thousands of years, a religious order known as the Druids worshipped trees, sometimes even sacrificing human beings to them." The main part of the narrative then "reenacts" this scenario with another unsuspecting family.

Phil (Dwier Brown), a graphic artist, and Kate (Carey Lowell), a decorator, move to Los Angeles, where Phil has been hired by an advertising firm called The Belly of the Beast. The couple soon learn that they are expecting a child. When their son is born, Kate seems conflicted about working. "I just want to do what's right for Jake," she tells Phil; "I don't want to miss out on anything." Phil, however, convinces her to work for financial reasons: "We'll do this for two years. Then we'll be solid enough [that] you can do what you want." We assume that what she desires is to be a full-time mom. After interviewing several nanny candidates, the couple choose a young black woman (like the traditional Mammy), but she suffers a freak accident. Instead, they hire Camilla (Jenny Seagrove), who is secretly responsible for the woman's death. Before long, the audience realizes that she is a reincarnation of the same Druid spirit who kidnapped the first infant. Just before Jake meets a similar fate, the couple receives two warnings: from a neighbor, Ned (Brad Hall), who is later murdered by Camilla, and from the mother of the first abducted child. Eventually, Phil kills Camilla by chopping down the magical tree.

The Guardian shares many features with *The Hand That Rocks the Cradle*. While in both films parents hire nannies, the mothers seem highly *ambivalent* about the prospect, thereby maintaining the audience's traditional sympathy. Furthermore, in *The Guardian*, even when Kate ostensibly returns to her job, we never see her work. Yet, on another level, the mothers are both condemned. In *The Guardian*, culpability is attached to the drama's reference to the Hansel and Gretel story, which Camilla always relates to her charges. Since that tale is about parents who heartlessly send their children into the forest to die, it "infects" our attitude toward Kate and Phil, who do not have starvation to justify their "desertion" of Jake. *The Guardian* also places blame on Kate by making Phil the parent who is alert to the dangers of the nanny. While Kate seems oblivious to trouble, Phil has prescient dreams and, after being warned, banishes Camilla from the house. As he does so, Kate seems perplexed, as though she has missed all the menacing signs.

In both films, vegetative imagery is quite important, though it bears opposing meanings. In *The Hand That Rocks the Cradle*, Claire's horticultural bent is endearing, though she is chastised for attending to a plant nursery rather than to her own. But in *The Guardian*, Camilla's worship of trees leads to destruction—no doubt a reference to the Druid practice of human and animal sacrifice (Spence, 104–12). In both films, woman is linked to the earth, but nature is given a genial face in one, a malevolent valence in the other.

In each work, the baby-sitter is an attractive and seductive young woman. In *The Guardian*, Phil awakens one night to noise in the house. When he checks on the baby's quarters, he finds Camilla naked in the adjoining bathroom, bathing the child, with the door flung wide open. Again, this scene fuels fears that a nanny will "steal" not only the affections of a mother's baby but those of her spouse. As Richard Schickel once remarked, the nanny has become "the ultimate Other Woman."

The question of the maternal voice is also at issue in *The Guardian*. Wind chimes are heard in the home of Kate and Phil, and whenever Camilla walks into the baby's room, his musical mobile inexplicably begins to play, invoking the sort of magic with which the Druids were associated (Spence, 145–65). Finally, the maternal breast is a resonant image in *The Guardian*. While Kate nurses her son for a short while, she soon switches to bottle-feeding. When Camilla is hired, she urges Kate to resume nursing, and the latter, guiltily, complies. Again, the paradigm of "Good" and "Bad" mothers (or breasts) is invoked—and reversed.

If *The Hand That Rocks the Cradle* addresses a variety of quotidian maternal fears (the price of reporting sexual abuse, the risk of delegating child care), *The Guardian* operates on a more mystical level. It invokes not only the Druids, and their worship of the oak tree, but also Greek mythology. In her first incarnation, Camilla is aptly called Diana, the name of the goddess of the hunt. Diana is also the keeper of chastity and associated with the moon, imagery that appears in the film. When Ned is attracted to Camilla, and she rebuffs him, he follows her to the woods where she appears as a naked nymph, bathed in moonlight. He is ultimately killed for his voyeurism when she conjures a pack of coyotes to attack him. This seems a reference both to the Druids' alleged powers of bodily transformation and to the Greek myth of Actaeon. The goddess Diana changed him into a stag as punishment for spying on her; he was then devoured by his own hounds. Camilla herself is rendered half-woman and half-animal, and is seen sitting Sphinx-like in the forest. That Phil is employed by a company named The Belly of the Beast seems at this point to have been an ironic forecast.

Central to the film's magical aura is the dual cultural notion of the mother as both creator of life and perpetrator of death (a variation on the Good and Bad breasts). In *The Guardian*, this binary vision is articulated through the structure of the plot. As one set of women bear children, so Camilla kills them. In her own view, Camilla herself embodies the duality, telling one of her victims, "Death gives you life." The belief in the "enchanted" quality of woman is tied to the female's relation to blood. In both menstruation and childbirth, she bleeds but does not die; is "wounded," but does not expire. Hence the import of the forest tree that "bears" the petrified babies and bleeds like a woman when Phil cuts it down.

Significantly, in the era of *The Guardian*'s release, press coverage of child care abuse took a bizarre turn. A *Time* magazine report on a North Carolina nursery stated that "[t]he children spoke solemnly of sodomy, animal sacrifice, fire and snakes." Furthermore, they claimed that their teacher "prayed to the devil" ("Listen to the Children"). Taking a more skeptical perspective on day care scandals, and turning the accusations on the accusers, Alexander Cockburn called the public response to these problems a "witch hunt" and a search "for Satan" (20). Whichever interpretation one chooses to validate, it is clear that occultism was "in the air."

Premonitions

Works like *The Hand That Rocks the Cradle* and *The Guardian* did not spring from nowhere in the 1990s. Earlier periods of film history occasionally produced dramas about the perils of child care—though of a different sort. In *Don't Bother to Knock* (1952), Marilyn Monroe plays Nell, a young woman with a background of mental illness. Unaware of this, a couple staying at a hotel hire her, at the recommendation of the elevator man, to baby-sit their daughter while they go out for the evening. As the night progresses, it becomes clear that Nell is unbalanced. She allows a male stranger into the room, believing that he is an incarnation of her dead lover. When he decides to leave, she blames the child for his departure. She ties her up and threatens to kill her. The girl's mother returns just in the nick of time.

In *The Chalk Garden* (1964), a British film directed by Ronald Neame, Deborah Kerr plays Miss Madrigal, a woman with a secret past who is hired by a wealthy dowager (Edith Evans) to look after her rebellious teenage granddaugher (Hayley Mills). The child's father is dead, and she has been forbidden to see her mother, who has been adulterous. Here, the governess is not initially presented as menacing. Rather, she seems a positive force in the household and makes contact with the misbehaving, alienated child. But as the drama unfolds, we learn that she has just been released from prison, having served a sentence for murder. Though Miss Madrigal has this sordid background, she remains a benign figure and we believe her innocent. Within the context of the narrative, the grandparent stands in for the Bad Mother and Miss Madrigal for the Good, since the former has selfishly kept the child from her parent.

But the closest predecessor to the contemporary maternal thriller is the British film *The Nanny* (1965), directed by Seth Holt. Like *The Chalk Garden*, it was made in the era of *Mary Poppins*. The film stars Bette Davis as "Nanny," a woman employed as a live-in baby-sitter and housekeeper for two generations of an English family. She helps to raise Virginia Fane (Wendy Craig) and then tends to the latter's own children. Tragedy, however, strikes when the Fanes' young daughter drowns in the bathtub. Believing their eight-year-old son responsible for her death, they send Joey (William Dix) away to a special school. The film opens as he returns home after two years at the institution. It is clear that he loathes Nanny: he refuses to eat any food that she prepares; he fears her entering the bathroom while he bathes; he locks his bedroom door against her each night. He requests that his parents fire her, but they refuse. The ensuing tension makes him surly and rebellious—a state of affairs that exacerbates his parents' marital strife.

Mrs. Fane is portrayed as a hysterical woman, entirely incapable of assuming her maternal responsibilities. She continually complains of headaches and is never seen without a drink in hand. She is so terrified of Joey's homecoming that she retreats from meeting him, sending Nanny instead. Throughout the turmoil, Nanny seems stoic and supportive of Joey: refusing to feel insulted by his insolence, trying to comprehend his point of view. When he rejects her welcome-home cake, for example, she says, "Nanny understands; she's on your side." Thus, at first, we fail to fathom the child's hostility toward her. Since Joey's headmaster has warned Mr. Fane (James Villiers) about the boy's penchant for fantasy, we wonder if his fears of Nanny are not hallucinatory or malicious.

It becomes clear, however, that Nanny has an unnatural relationship with Mrs. Fane. Virginia is not only a neurotic female but an immature woman who is dependent upon the nanny who tended her as a girl. Hence when Mrs. Fane is distraught over Joey's behavior, Nanny brushes her hair, reassuring her that everything will be all right. When Joey accuses Nanny of poisoning his dinner, Mrs. Fane is stunned. As Joey leaves the table, Nanny spoon-feeds his mother as one would a toddler, coaxing her to open her mouth.

As the film progresses, and we become identified with Joey's perspective, we begin to feel that he is a reliable narrator. Eventually, he confides in an adolescent neighbor, Bobbie (Pamela Franklin) and describes to her the day his sister died. That afternoon, Nanny suddenly exited the apartment, leaving the children alone in violation of the Fanes' instructions. While she was gone, unbeknownst to Joey, his sister wandered

18. *The Nanny* (1965). Nanny (Bette Davis) with Mrs. Fane and her disturbed son. MOMA

into the bathroom and, in trying to bathe her doll, fell into the tub, knocking herself unconscious. When Nanny returned home, she was distracted. She called the children for a bath, and, without checking the tub, ran the water. She later discovered Suzy drowned. She then tried to hide her mistake by placing the blame on Joey, claiming that he had taken a bath with his sister. As Joey narrates the story, the incidents he details are illustrated by flashbacks.

With Joey released from the institution and back home, Nanny becomes frightened of his power to unmask her. She begins to commit other crimes. She poisons Mrs. Fane to throw suspicion on Joey. When Joey's aunt, Penelope (Jill Bennett), begins to distrust Nanny, the latter withholds Penelope's medicine and allows her to die. Finally, Nanny attempts to smother Joey.

When Nanny feels herself trapped, she recalls the incidents surrounding Suzy's death. The film reprises those events in a second flashback—this time from Nanny's point of view. On that fateful day, Nanny hastily left the Fane household because she received a call concerning her own illegitimate daughter, Janet, of whose existence the Fanes were apparently ignorant. Janet had suffered an illegal abortion and expired from the procedure. When Nanny arrived on the scene, Janet's doctor chided her for the legacy of her transgressive motherhood and scolded her for tending to other people's children at the expense of her own. When Nanny returned to the Fane residence, she was in a daze; hence her failure to check the bathtub. While in the first rendition of the flashback, as told from Joey's vantage point, we failed to witness the discovery of Suzy, in Nanny's version we do see it. What is especially interesting is that her recollection shifts, through editing, between an objective vision of the dead child and a subjective reverie of the girl alive. This explains why, as Joey has recounted, Nanny bathed Suzy's corpse. It is also clear that the traumatic death of Nanny's own daughter had placed her in an unbalanced and regressive state such that her refusal to admit Suzy's demise was tantamount to her reluctance to acknowledge Janet's. In a sense, this introspective sequence humanizes Nanny even as she lets Penelope die. It is a compassionate touch entirely lacking in *The Hand That Rocks the Cradle* or *The Guardian*. At the end of *The Nanny*, after being apprised of her caretaker's derangement and crimes, Mrs. Fane achieves maternal sanity and serenity. Joey assures his mother that he does not "hate" her and sweetly promises to protect her—ostensibly, in Nanny's stead.

What is intriguing about the film is the complex manner in which the poles of Good and Bad Mother align. While Nanny is a monster to Joey (and to Penelope), she is a maternal ideal to Mrs. Fane. But while Nanny succeeds as the latter's nurturing employee, she fails as a biological parent: first, through bearing a bastard child; second, by neglecting her baby; third, by raising a daughter who herself becomes a second-generation unwed mother. Mrs. Fane is an inadequate parent during most of the film—what one critic deemed a "weepingly ineffective mum" ("*The Nanny*"). In fact, for most of the narrative her position is usurped by the teenage Bobbie. Mrs. Fane is, however, allowed to triumph in the final few minutes of the film: as the pernicious Nanny is eradicated from the scene, Mrs. Fane is reborn as the Good Mother.

Unlike the nanny films of the 1990s, in this one the specter of the independent working mother is absent. But that does not save the text from maternal misogyny. Rather, the film condemns the traditional bourgeois mother of *The Feminine Mystique* generation for her privilege, puerility, and psychoneurosis (Friedan). Even when cured of neurasthenia, Virginia is fundamentally an unbalanced child-woman who must be sheltered and nurtured by her own young son. As if to underscore the point, all the adult women of the narrative are ill—not only Virginia but also Nanny and Penelope. When Joey is released from the institution, a physician tells Mr. Fane that his son has an "antipathy to middle-aged females." While in Joey's case that attitude seems directed only to Nanny, the film as a whole universalizes the animosity.

Critics of the era saw *The Nanny* in relation to the Disney film. Philip T. Hartung called Nanny a "ghoulish Mary Poppins," and *Time*'s critic called it an "antidote [for] those who found Mary Poppins too sweet to stomach" ("Bette Meets Boy"). Howard Thompson warned parents that "even if Mary Poppins herself comes a-knocking, call the F.B.I." Within the film itself, Bobbie calls Nanny "Mary Poppins." While the tone of the Disney film was more in keeping with the era, and that of the Holt film something of an aberration, *The Nanny* certainly was a harbinger of things to come.

Crib Death

[I]n order to become a writer a man must both immerse himself in his mother and free himself from her.
   (Wendy Lesser)

Clearly *The Hand That Rocks the Cradle*, *The Guardian*, and *The Nanny* are the archetypal maternal thrillers in that their narratives literally revolve around mothers, babies, and child care. But it is also obvious that a more *submerged* maternal theme has animated other films within the thriller genre. The prototype is, of course, Alfred Hitchcock's *Psycho* (1960), in which the dementia of Norman Bates is tied to his relationship to his mother—a figure whom he keeps, quite like a skeleton in the closet. This theme is revisited in *Dead Again* (1991), in which an aging antiques dealer, who still resides with his mother, is shown to have committed a murder on her behalf decades earlier. In a similar fashion, the male protagonist of *The Eyes of Laura Mars* (1978)—a policeman who is a serial killer—blames his abusive prostitute mother for his mental state and for his crimes. While the psychosis of a murderer in *Peeping Tom* (1963) is blamed primarily on his father, much is made of the killer's morbid nostalgia for his deceased mother. In the political thriller *The Manchurian Candidate* (1962), the enemy of the hero (a brainwashed soldier) is not only the Communists but his villainous, controlling mother, who is in cahoots with them.

In some thrillers, the maternal theme is entirely buried and symbolic. In *Single White Female* (1992), no mother is ever mentioned; but it is clear that Hedra, the deranged young woman who becomes Ally's roommate, is seeking "parental" attention, guidance, and devotion from her. Hedra becomes entirely dependent upon Ally and tries to interject herself into the latter's love affair, as if attempting to replay the Primal Scene.

Misery (1990) is also a thriller with a submerged maternal narrative. Directed by Rob Reiner and based on a Stephen King novel, it tells the story of Paul Sheldon (James Caan), a writer, who, upon finishing his latest novel, embarks on a drive through treacherous Colorado mountains. When a storm overtakes him, he skids and crashes into a gorge. He is found unconscious by Annie Wilkes (Kathy Bates), a middle-aged former nurse who lives alone. She takes him to her secluded home and ministers to his injuries. When Paul awakens and inquires why he is not hospitalized, she lies and tells him that the roads are not navigable. When he asks to make some calls, she claims that the phone lines are down. She confesses to being his "number one fan": a devotee of his romance series, which is set in the 1870s and revolves around a heroine named Misery Chastane. Paul eventually realizes that Annie is lunatic and that she intends to keep him captive. When she learns that he has "killed off" Misery in the last installment of the saga, she lapses into a fury and subjects him to sadistic tortures. Eventually, he kills her and escapes—but only after she has slaughtered the town sheriff who has come looking for him.

On the surface, *Misery* would seem to have nothing to do with the maternal Gothic or thriller; but as one begins to plumb its depths, another view emerges. Like the Gothic, the film is about an innocent individual who enters a pernicious house. While that figure is normally female, in *Misery* it is male—but he, nonetheless, encounters the Gothic's "madwoman in the attic." In this regard, the film also recalls *Sunset Boulevard* (1950), in which a Hollywood writer happens upon an old house inhabited by a neurotic former movie queen. Like Paul Sheldon, Joe Gillis (William Holden) is essentially held "hostage" by Norma Desmond (Gloria Swanson), who offers him a huge fee for his "collaboration" on a screenplay, one that she hopes will assure her screen comeback. As Virginia Wright Wexman has noted, the relationship between Desmond and Gillis (like that of Wilkes and Sheldon) is overlaid with "incestuous attachment" (148).

When Annie rescues Paul and installs him as a helpless invalid in her home, the scenario replicates the birth and care of an infant. She finds him trapped within his bashed-in car and must use a crowbar to dislodge him, as a physician might use forceps to extract a baby. She immediately gives him mouth-to-mouth resuscitation, as a doctor might suction out a newborn's air passages to initiate breathing. With Paul's legs broken and set in Annie's makeshift splints, he is entirely immobile, like an infant. The bed in which he recuperates has bars reminiscent of crib rails. Paul's face, swollen with wounds, looks like the visage of a newborn who has suffered a difficult birth. Annie must tend to Paul's every need: she must feed and bathe him and monitor his bodily functions. As she shaves him, she declares that he looks "just like a baby." While all nursing bears a maternal cast, we find that Annie has been a *maternity* nurse. Moreover, as Paul learns, by surreptitiously examining Annie's scrapbook, she was prosecuted for her alleged role in several neonatal deaths. Here the maternal melodrama meets the maternal thriller.

But there are other elements in Annie's behavior that mark her as a mother-surrogate. She speaks to Paul in a proud, parental fashion, calling him her "genius." She worries over him, advising that he "needs rest before he writes." She is, after all, his "number one fan"—the position occupied by all doting mothers. At other times, she reassures him, in a condescending fashion, that "there's nothing to worry about," and promises to "take good care of" him. When she becomes angry with him for using foul language in his latest manuscript, she scolds him as if he were a misbehaving youth. When he complains of her manhandling his crippled legs, she taunts him, calling him a "crybaby." Before long, there is a martyred tone to her discourse that caricatures the resentful and sacrificing madonna. She complains that she exists to make him happy but gets little in return. When he becomes suspicious of her, she gripes: "I cook your meals; I tend to you twenty-four hours a day. When are we going to develop a sense of trust?" Hence "motherhood" in the film is portrayed as a thankless state of "misery."

As Paul becomes aware of Annie's mania and her intent to hold him hostage, he tries, periodically, to escape when she vacates the house and leaves him Home Alone. Because he is disabled and plagued by pain, he must drag himself slowly from room to room trying to find a means of exit. He is foiled, however, because she continually locks him in. Furthermore, she never stays away for long, so that he must scramble back to his bed in order to keep his forays secret. It is not difficult to discern how the scenario of Paul's leaving and returning replays the basic dynamic of separation between a child and its mother. The youngster repeatedly adventures out into the world, only to retreat home, anxiously, seeking comfort and assurance. Obviously, a good parent allows the child the latitude to experiment and encourages the expansion of his boundaries and confidence. The bad caregiver restrains the juvenile. Obviously, in Annie, we have a grotesque exaggeration of the latter category. When she learns of Paul's expeditions, she ties him to the bed. Comprehending his wish to flee, she becomes depressed and predicts that when his leg is better, he will "want to leave." As Melanie Klein has commented: "Some mothers . . . exploit [the parental] relationship for the gratification of their own desires, i.e. their possessiveness and the satisfaction of having somebody dependent upon them. Such women want their children to cling to them, and they hate them to grow up" (Klein and Riviere, 77–78).

There is a further, more explicit, maternal dimension to this thriller. It concerns the fact that Misery, whom Paul has eliminated in his latest book, dies in *childbirth*. Hence he figuratively *murders a mother*. And it is the "death" of Misery in that volume, published while Paul is Annie's prisoner, which sends the latter into a rage. It is this anger that initiates her sadistic behavior toward him (hobbling his legs), which places Paul in the position of a classic, if reluctant, masochist. As Kaja Silverman has noted, while Freud associated masochism with females, most theorists have thought it more typical of males: "What is to be made of this anomaly, whereby Freud designates as 'feminine' a psychic disorder whose victims are primarily men?" (*Male Subjectivity*, 189). According to Silverman, male masochism is a syndrome that challenges the paternal order and empowers the maternal realm. Paraphrasing Gilles Deleuze, she notes that masochism "is a pact between mother and son to *write* the father out of his dominant position within both culture and masochism, and to install the mother in his place" (211, my italics). Hence by forcing Paul into a masochistic stance, Annie recoups the maternal power of the vanquished Misery. By coercing Paul to pen another volume in the romance series, this time composed on her typewriter and dedicated to her, she requires him to valorize the maternal and to, literally, "write the father out of his dominant position." Significantly, the typewriter she gives him has a defect in the letter *n* that causes it to be omitted from all words. One is tempted to think of the difference between the words "ma" and "ma*n*" as a central one in the discourse of *Misery*.

In discussing *Sunset Boulevard*, Wexman remarks on how the Word is associated with the male writer and the Image with female screen star. To some degree, Gillis's eventual "impotence" is a result of Desmond's having subverted the masculine writing process through her forced partnership with him (148–59). It would seem that a similar process takes place in *Misery*.

For Silverman, male masochism fundamentally involves the assignment to man of a woman's role. Drawing upon Freud, she notes, "[I]t is not only at the level of his sexual life, but at that of his fantasmatic . . . that the male masochist occupies a female position" (*Male Subjectivity*, 209). Hence as punishment for killing Misery, Annie places Paul in his heroine's position—emasculating him in a masochistic masquerade. For Krin and Glenn O. Gabbard, films involving such phallic women feed male masochistic fantasies: "Movies that portray threatening women who castrate and penetrate men may consciously or unconsciously gratify the secret wishes of certain male audience members" (20). Interestingly, given *Misery*'s placement in the thriller genre, Silverman sees "suspense" as "central" to the masochistic scenario (*Male Subjectivity*, 198).

Throughout the film, Annie vacillates between the classic poles of "Good" mother and "Bad," alternately pampering her prodigy and berating him for the despised denouement of his novel; she also *projects* the benign and malevolent paradigms onto him. "I thought you were good," she cries, "but you're not good; you're just another dirty birdy." While her moments as the Bad Mother seem hyperbolic and grotesque, there is a certain maternal "truth" to her anger. As D. W. Winnicott has noted, on one level, "The mother . . . hates her infant from the word go," owing to the extraordinary demands the child places upon her (*Through Pediatrics*, 201). While "[a] mother has to be able to tolerate hating her baby . . . [s]he cannot express it to him" (202). *Misery*'s Annie oversteps the bounds.

If Annie, most often, incarnates the Bad Mother, there is a peripheral figure within the narrative who occupies the space of the Good. Paul's agent, Marcia Sindell (Lauren Bacall), is considerably older than he and takes a supervisory interest in his career. It is she who notices that he has departed from his Colorado lodge but has failed to reach home. In a maternal stance, she acts as a liaison with Paul's daughter, who is expecting her father for a visit. It is Sindell who first contacts the sheriff and urges him to begin a search.

Significantly, Paul has dropped the character of Misery from his novels because he wishes to end the series, which we assume to be in the tradition of Harlequin romances. We surmise that his decision has to do with his wish to quit hack writing and to become a serious author. In the beginning of the film, as he is driving in the snowstorm, he recalls a meeting with Sindell in which he tells her that he "used to" be a writer—pointedly employing the past tense. We deduce that among the reasons for his dissatisfaction with the romance series is that it is a nonprestigious form addressed to a female audience, an audience that Annie embodies. She exemplifies the female reader who is entirely incapable of aesthetic distance (Doane, 12, 32). Annie confesses that in stressful times (her divorce, her trial), she read and reread all of Paul's novels in order to forget her troubles. In atonement for his termination of the Misery series, she requires that he write a *new* volume—one that manages, convincingly, to resurrect the deceased character. *Misery's Return* will be dedicated to Annie, its "Muse." As Paul composes each chapter, she devours it immediately, rejecting sections if they lack narrative coherence. For example, when he tries to base the sequel on Misery's rescue through an experimental blood transfusion, Annie repudiates the plan, reminding him that Misery was buried at the close of the last volume. Hence Annie becomes Paul's harshest critic. Finally, Paul creates a scenario that satisfies her: Misery has not been dead but simply paralyzed by an allergic reaction to a bee sting. Somehow, Paul also concocts a rationale for Misery's disinterment.

From that point out, Annie badgers him constantly for updated plot details, unable to patiently await the arrival of the day's new pages. She is the model of the emotional female reader, consumed by fancy, incapable of separating fact from fiction. She confesses that as a child she was an avid filmgoer, especially fond of serials. At night, we hear the sound of the television blaring quiz shows and dating games. When she turns on the phonograph, she plays Liberace—a singer popular with matronly women.

Let us recall that Paul has attempted to abort the Misery series because of his desire to become a credible *writer*. He regards his prior output as commercial and preliminary to any true literary production. In *His Other Half: Men Looking at Women through Art*, Wendy Lesser argues that a maternal specter haunts the work of *all* male authors: "[T]he mother is the initial woman from whom the male artist has literally to sever himself in order to become both a man and an artist. The mother may, in some disguised form, be the female figure animating the work of all male artists" (23). We have already seen how this obtains in *Misery*, which, in one sense, is a novel about a man's struggle to detach from Mom. Lesser also states that when a man scripts a tale about mothers, it is "bound to be a story about the duality of memory (oneself simultaneously as small child and remembering adult) and about the duplicity of memory ('Is this *really* the way it a happened?')" (24). Again, we find reverberations of these themes in *Misery*. Paul is simultaneously an adult and a child, middle-aged and swaddled in his "cradle." There is also the possibility of "duplicity," or *distortion*, in what transpires. From a certain perspective, the hideous and awesome portrayal of Annie replicates a child's distorted vision of the Bad Mother—a figure with monumental powers over life. Winnicott believes that this misconstrual can lead to a permanent distrust of the female: "Traced to its root in the history of each individual, this fear of WOMAN turns out to be a fear of recognizing the fact of dependence" (*Home*, 125). In a symbolic replay of such fear, at the end of *Misery*, when Paul is lunching with Sindell, he imagines Annie's face in that of the waitress who serves him. Furthermore, the closing credits are accompanied by a rendition of "I'll Be Seeing You," as sung by Liberace. Melanie Klein agrees that children harbor hostile feelings toward their mothers. As she notes, "Hatred and aggressive feelings are aroused and [the child] becomes dominated by the impulses to destroy the very person who is the object of all his desires" (Klein, 306–7). This scenario is realized in the denouement of *Misery* in which Paul, finally, annihilates both Misery and Annie. For Klein, however, the child's full emotional development includes "reparations": "[W]e make good the injuries which we did in phantasy, and for which we still unconsciously feel very guilty." For Klein, "*making reparation* [is] . . . a fundamental element in love and in all human relationships" (Klein, 312–13). Paul, quite literally, undoes the damage he has done to Annie by "making reparations" through Misery's "Return."

In commenting on the male writer, Wendy Lesser claims that he must "immerse" himself in his mother in order to liberate himself from her: "It is to get inside of the woman who once contained you, and then get out" (30). This dynamic of enclosure and escape, reminiscent of the magician's Spanish Maiden, once more reminds us of Paul's entrapment in his car and imprisonment in Annie's house—both of which he evades. Furthermore, he has gotten "inside" a woman, through his role as a writer, by selecting a heroine with whom to identify. Only now is he ready to write a novel as himself, without the guise of a female "cover." Significantly, for Lesser, the male author's growth also involves a wrestling with empathy: "Whenever a man sets out to write a story about a mother . . . it is also, inevitably, a story about the extortion of sympathy. . . . That is to say, it becomes a story both about the sympathy the author had to feel for his mother and about the sympathy we have to feel for him because that other sympathy was forced from him" (23). This tension is replicated in the scenario of *Misery* in which Paul must feign concern for a maternal demon while, simultaneously, soliciting audience concern for his own horrific predicament.

But perhaps the writing process, for men, involves as much a *killing* of the mother as it does her rebirth, a more violent tendency than Lesser allows. Though Lesser does not address this point, her examples from literature focus on authors who imagine or recall a mother's *demise*: Charles Dickens in *David Copperfield*, Harold Brodkey in *A Story in a Classical Mode*, Peter Handke in *A Sorrow beyond Dreams*, and John Berger in *Her Secrets*. Not only does Paul Sheldon kill his Good Mother heroine, Misery (who expires in childbirth), but the murder weapon is his typewriter, which he later uses to bash the head of his Bad Mother, Annie. Perhaps, the "pen" is mightier than the sword. Early on in the film when Sheldon tells Sindell about his new and serious writing project, he says, "I just might have something I want on my tombstone." Hence he associates authorship with death, albeit his own.

Afterword: A Mother Is Being Beaten

Misery is the only thriller discussed to involve a writer-hero, though both Phil and Ned in *The Guardian* are artists. But *Misery* is not the only one to invoke the murder of a "parent." Obviously, in both *The Hand That Rocks the Cradle* and *The Guardian*, the nannies who die are stand-ins for Mom in her "Bad Mother" persona. If Lesser is right, even works without an overt maternal theme may evince this motif. If it is a truism that the thriller routinely selects and punishes a female victim, it is not so common to envision her as Mom. While in *Dead Again* the homicidal character first murders a young woman, he later kills his mother. While in *Psycho* it is Marion Crane who is slashed in the shower, by Norman dressed up as Mom, her death is presaged by that of Mrs. Bates, whose moribund state is never explained. Thereafter, Mom remains mummi-fied (or mommified) among Norman's other taxidermal specimens. Hence the dead mother may be the thriller's "woman in the attic," as the madwoman is the Gothic's.

Works Cited

Ackerman, Jan. "'Home Alone' Father Cleared." *Pittsburgh Post-Gazette*, 24 July 1993.

Ames, Katrine. "Who's Minding Our Children?" *Newsweek*, 8 June 1992, 51.

Barthes, Roland. *The Pleasure of the Text*. Translated by Richard Miller. New York: Hill and Wang, 1975.

Berger, Joseph. "The Story of a Nanny, from Care to Calamity." *New York Times*, 18 April 1993, 40.

"Bette Meets Boy." *Time* 86, no. 101 (29 October 1965): E10.

Carroll, Nicole. "Who Will Watch the Kids? The Child-Care Dilemma." *USA Today*, 9 February 1993, 4D.

Cherlin, Andrew. "Too Young for Day Care." *New York Times*, 17 September 1992, A25.

"The Child-Abuse Case That Left a National Legacy." *U.S. News and World Report*, 29 January 1990, 8.

Chira, Susan. "New Realities Fight Old Images of Mother." *New York Times*, 4 October 1992, 1, 32.

Cockburn, Alexander. "Abused Imaginings." *New Statesman and Society* 3, no. 85 (26 January 1990): 19–20.

Darrach, Brad. "A Comic's Crisis of the Heart." *People*, 22 February 1988, 79–85.

Doane, Mary Ann. *The Desire to Desire: The Woman's Film of the 1940s*. Bloom-ington and Indianapolis: Indiana University Press, 1987.

Eckholm, Erik. "Learning If Infants Are Hurt When Mothers Go to Work." *New York Times*, 6 October 1992, A1.

Faludi, Susan. *Backlash: The Undeclared War against American Women*. New York: Crown, 1991.

"Family Ties May Not Bind When It Comes to Day Care." *Pittsburgh Post-Gazette*, 24 April 1994.

Fields, Valerie. *Wet Nursing: A History from Antiquity to the Present*. New York and Oxford: Basil Blackwell, 1988.

French, Thomas M. "The Asthma Attack." In Thomas M. French and Franz Alexander, *Psychogenic Factors in Bronchial Asthma—Part I*, 33–41. Menasha, WI: George Banta, 1941.

Friedan, Betty. *The Feminine Mystique*. New York: Dell, 1963.

Gabbard, Krin and Glen O. "Phallic Women in the Contemporary Cinema." Unpublished paper. Later published in *American Imago* (50, no. 4 [Winter 1993]: 421–39) under the same title.

"Girl 13, Charged in Case of 2 Tots Punished in Dryer." *Pittsburgh Post-Gazette*, 30 March 1994.

Glaberson, William. "Swiss Au Pair Found Not Guilty of Setting Fire That Killed Baby." *New York Times*, 8 July 1992, A1.

Glaser, Gabrielle. "Hers." *New York Times Magazine*, 20 February 1994, 22.

Grant, Barry Keith. "Rich and Strange, or Something This Way Comes: The Yuppie Horror Film." Paper delivered at the meeting of the Film Society of Canada, Ottawa, June 1993.

Grimmer, Laura. "Fire in Detroit Kills 7 Children Left Home Alone." *Pittsburgh Post-Gazette*, 18 February 1993.

Groen, J. J., and J. Bastiaans. "The Psychosomatic Approach to Bronchial Asthma." In *Psychosomatic Research*, edited by J. J. Groen, 47–70. New York: Macmillan, 1964.

Grunwald, Lisa. "Robin Williams Has a Big Premise." *Esquire*, June 1989, 108–14.

Hartung, Philip T. "The Screen." *Commonweal* 83 (19 November 1965): 217.

Hirt, Michael. *Psychological and Allergic Aspects of Asthma*. Springfield, IL: Charles Thomas, 1965.

Howse, John. "The Martensville Scandal." *Maclean's* 105, no. 25 (22 June 1992): 26–30.

Johnston, Claire. "Myths of Women in the Cinema." In *Women and the Cinema: A Critical Anthology*, edited by Karyn Kay and Gerald Peary, 407–11. New York: Dutton, 1977.

Kahane, Claire. "The Gothic Mirror." In *The (M)other Tongue: Essays in Feminist Psychoanalytic Interpretation*, edited by Shirley Nelson Garner, Claire Kahane, and Madelon Sprengnether, 334–77. Ithaca, NY, and London: Cornell University Press, 1985.

Kaplan, E. Ann. *Motherhood and Representation: The Mother in Popular Culture and Melodrama*. London and New York: Routledge, 1992.

Klein, Melanie. *Love, Guilt and Reparation and Other Works 1921–1945*. London: Hogarth Press, 1975.

Klein, Melanie, and Joan Riviere. *Love, Hate and Reparation: Two Lectures.* London: Hogarth, 1937.

Krantz, Judith Z., and Nancy S. Kupper. "Cross-Nursing: Wet-Nursing in a Contemporary Context." *Pediatrics* 67 (1981): 715–17.

Kulish, Nancy Mann. "Gender and Transference: The Screen of the Phallic Mother." *International Review of Psychoanalysis* 13 (1986): 393–404.

Labich, Kenneth. "Can Your Career Hurt Your Kids?" *Fortune* 123, no. 10 (20 May 1991): 3838–40, 4448, 4452, 4456.

Lesser, Wendy. *His Other Half: Men Looking at Women through Art.* Cambridge, MA, and London: Harvard University Press, 1991.

"Listen to the Children." *Time,* 4 May 1992, 20.

Manshel, Lisa. "Review of *Nap Time: The True Story of Sexual Abuse at a Suburban Day Care Center.*" *Library Journal* 114, no. 20 (December 1989): 145.

Maslin, Janet. "Whose Life Is It, Anyway?" *New York Times,* 16 August 1993, 15.

Masse, Michelle A. *In the Name of Love: Women, Masochism, and the Gothic.* Ithaca, NY, and London: Cornell University Press, 1992.

Modleski, Tania. *Loving with a Vengeance: Mass-Produced Fantasies for Women.* New York and London: Methuen, 1982.

"*The Nanny.*" [Review.] *Playboy* 13, no. 48 (January 1966): 48.

"No Good Nannies? Find a Good Family." *New York Times,* 16 September 1993, C2.

Quindlen, Anna. "Sitterhood Is Powerful." *Pittsburgh Post-Gazette,* 1 March 1993.

Ravensdale, Tom, and James Morgan. *The Psychology of Witchcraft: An Account of Witchcraft, Black Magic and the Occult.* New York: Arco Publishing Company, 1974.

Roheim, Geza. "Aphrodite, or the Woman with a Penis." *Psychoanalytic Quarterly* 14 (1945): 350–90.

Rubenstein, Carin. "Finding a Nanny Legally." *New York Times,* 28 January 1993, C1, C6.

Schickel, Richard. "The Ultimate Other Woman." *Time,* 20 January 1992, 58.

Sellew, Catharine F. *Adventures with Abraham's Children.* Boston and Toronto: Little, Brown and Company, 1964.

Silverman, Kaja. *The Acoustic Mirror: The Female Voice in Psychoanalysis and Cinema.* Bloomington and Indianapolis: Indiana University Press, 1988.

———. *Male Subjectivity at the Margins.* New York and London: Routledge, 1992.

Simmon, Scott. *The Films of D. W. Griffith.* Cambridge, New York, and Melbourne: Cambridge University Press, 1993.

Sloan, Kay. "*The Hand That Rocks the Cradle*: An Introduction." *Film History* 1, no. 4 (1987): 341–42.

Spence, Lewis. *The History and Origins of Druidism.* New York, Melbourne, Sydney, and Cape Town: Rider and Company, 1949.

Thompson, Howard. "Bette Davis as *Nanny.*" *New York Times,* 4 November 1965, 57.

Travers, P. L. *Mary Poppins.* New York: Reynal and Hitchcock, 1934.

Wexman, Virginia Wright. *Creating the Couple: Love, Marriage, and Hollywood Performance.* Princeton, NJ: Princeton University Press, 1993.

"Who's Minding America's Kids?" *Fortune* 126, no. 3 (10 August 1992): 50–54.

Willen, Michele. "Breaking a Stereotype, More Men Are Being Hired as Nannies." *New York Times,* 13 May 1993, C6.

Winnicott, D. W. *Home Is Where We Start From: Essays by a Psycho-Analyst.* Edited by Clare Winnicott, Ray Shepherd, and Madeleine Davis. New York and London: W. W. Norton, 1986.

———. *Through Pediatrics to Psycho-Analysis.* London: Hogarth Press, 1975.

Zemal, Jane. "Let's Talk about Day Care: First Child-Care Center Opened in 1838." *Pittsburgh Post-Gazette,* 9 May 1995, C4.

The Postmodern Film

POSTMODERNITY AND POSTMATERNITY: *HIGH HEELS*
AND *IMITATION OF LIFE*

Remaking a Remake

> Reappropriating existing representations . . . and putting
> them into new and ironic contexts is a typical form of
> postmodern . . . critique.
>   (Linda Hutcheon)

Pedro Almodóvar's *High Heels* (*Tacones Lejanos,* 1991) is a work that
might be placed within the recent genre of "postmodern" film. In fact,
a review of it by Roger Ebert notes how "the writers of New York week-
lies" regularly link that term to the film's director. As Linda Hutcheon
makes clear, one of the hallmarks of the postmodern aesthetic is its radical intertextuality—its tendency to quote and recycle tropes and thematics from the discursive past. Hence *Brazil* (1985) conjures *Metropolis* (1926); *Dead Again* (1991) harks back to *Citizen Kane* (1941);
Wild at Heart (1990) evokes *The Wizard of Oz* (1939); and *Hairspray*
mocks *Rebel without a Cause* (1955).

Almodóvar has acknowledged this inclination toward heteroglossia.
He has deemed himself a creative "mirror with a thousand faces" that
"reflect[s] everything around [him]." While admitting a penchant for
homage, he notes his citations are not merely the "tributes of a cine-
phile." Rather, they arise "in a lively and active way" as organic features
of the text (quoted in Morgan, 28).

It is within this framework that we might envision *High Heels* as a
"remake" of Douglas Sirk's canonical film *Imitation of Life* (1959).
Many have recognized Sirk's influence on Almodóvar's style. The latter
bemoans the devaluation of melodrama and calls Sirk a "genius" (quoted
in Morgan, 29). To characterize Almodóvar's theatrical mode, Roger
Ebert deems it "inspired" by Sirk. David Kehr sees in Almodóvar's
"bold, ironic use of color" a tribute to the Hollywood legend.

Beyond this, there are quite specific aspects of *High Heels* that solicit a comparison to *Imitation of Life*.[1] Both films take a female performer as their heroine. *Imitation* traces a decade in the life of Lora Meredith (Lana Turner), an aspiring actress who eventually achieves success on Broadway and the silver screen. *High Heels* follows the character of Becky Del Paramo (Marisa Paredes), a singer who is already a star when the narrative begins. In both cases, the protagonist has a tense and troublesome relationship with her daughter. In *Imitation*, Susie (Sandra Dee) accuses Lora of parental neglect and becomes enamored of her mother's lover—a circumstance that brings the women's conflict to a head. In *High Heels*, Rebecca (Victoria Abril) makes similar accusations toward Becky and marries (then murders) her mother's ex-lover, Manuel.

In both texts, there is a subplot involving another parent-child dyad. In *Imitation*, it involves the family of Lora's maid, Annie Johnson (Juanita Moore). In *High Heels*, it concerns the ménage of Judge Dominguez (Miguel Bose), the man investigating Manuel's homicide.[2] In both cases, the subplot's child is a performer whose theatricality mocks that of the heroine. In *Imitation*, Sarah Jane (Susan Kohner) becomes a burlesque dancer; in *High Heels*, Dominguez goes "under cover" as a female impersonator. In both instances, the subplot's parent figure is involved with the star performer. In *Imitation*, Annie serves as Lora's backstage confidante and dresser. And in *High Heels*, Señora Dominguez keeps a fan album of clippings on Becky's career.

At times, the parallel between films is even tighter. Both open with sequences involving a beach locale and a lost child. In *Imitation*, Lora frantically searches a Coney Island boardwalk for Susie, who has disappeared. In *High Heels*, as Rebecca awaits the arrival of her mother's airplane, she recalls running away as a youth during a seaside vacation. Both films end in heart-wrenching deathbed scenes. In *Imitation*, it is that of the black domestic; in *High Heels*, that of the heroine.

High Heels's status as a remake is complicated by the intricate "genetics" of *Imitation*. Originally written by Fannie Hurst as a piece of serialized magazine fiction in 1932, it was published as a book in 1933. It was first adapted for the screen by John Stahl in 1934, then later refashioned by Sirk. Hence *High Heels* constitutes a remake of a remake, a copy of a copy, an imitation of an *Imitation*.

---

[1] David Thompson is the only critic I have found to actually compare *High Heels* and *Imitation of Life*, and he does so only in passing.

[2] The character of Dominguez is also known as Eduardo (in addition to his pose as Femme Lethal). Hence it is also possible that he is masquerading as the judge. There is no stable baseline of identity from which to operate.

A Postmodern Simulacrum

Rather than a mere expression of nostalgia, postmodernism
may be seen as an attempt to recover the morphological
continuity of specific culture. The use of past styles in this
case is motivated not by a simple escapism, but by a desire
to understand our culture and ourselves as products of
previous codings.
(James Collins)

Aside from its citation of *Imitation*, there are other reasons why Almodóvar's film constitutes a *postmodern* remake. Its intertextual vision is
highly *parodic*, filled with what Hutcheon has termed "self-conscious,
self-contradictory, self-undermining statement" (1). In the Sirk film,
melodramatic moments often border on comedy, as when the telephone
rings for Lora with a job offer each time she is about to kiss her lover,
Steve (John Gavin). This nascent farce just below the histrionic facade
was apparent to Rainer Werner Fassbinder, whose films were also modeled on Sirk's. Here is an excerpt from Fassbinder's tongue-in-cheek
summary of *Imitation*, which he calls a "great, crazy movie about life
and death . . . [a]nd . . . America": "[The characters] are always making
plans for happiness, for tenderness, and then the phone rings, a new part
and Lana revives. The woman is a hopeless case. So is John Gavin. He
should have caught on pretty soon that it won't work" (Fischer, 244–
55).

In *High Heels* the ironic and melodramatic modes are nearly indistin-
guishable. When Becky and Rebecca are first reunited, they embrace. At
that heightened instant, Rebecca's earring becomes caught in Becky's
hair. When Judge Dominguez asks Becky whether she has killed Manuel, she replies, "You don't do that before a [theatrical] opening."
Later, as Becky is taken away in an ambulance, she tells her homicidal
daughter, "Find another way to solve your problems with men."

Beyond its conjuration of *Imitation*, the film's cinematic references
are quite extensive. With Almodóvar's focus on maternal melodrama,
there are intimations of *Mildred Pierce* (1945), a film that also depicts an
incestuous triangle in which a daughter kills her mother's lover. Like
Becky, Mildred (Joan Crawford) attempts to assume responsibility for
her offspring's crime. (Interestingly, Roger Ebert sees the performance
of Marisa Paredes in *High Heels* as "inspired . . . [or inhabited by] Joan
Crawford" [44].) While *Mildred Pierce* is never mentioned in Almodóvar's film, Ingmar Bergman's *Autumn Sonata* (1978) is. That film,
which concerns a woman's struggle with her renowned pianist-mother,

is cited by Rebecca to explain how she is plagued by Becky's fame. And *High Heels* is not alone among postmodern films in foregrounding a maternal relationship. In *Dead Again*, a killer's dementia is linked to his excessive maternal ties. In *Wild at Heart*, a young woman tries to escape her witchlike mother. In *Hairspray*, the maternal role is assumed by a transvestite. And in *Brazil*, the hero suffers Oedipal delusions as he imagines his lover as his mother in the middle of a sexual encounter.

Alongside the maternal theme, other quotations in *High Heels* issue from Dominguez's pose as a female. As he sings in a nightclub, members of the audience duplicate his every gesture, like spectators of *The Rocky Horror Picture Show* (1975). When Dominguez confesses his love to Rebecca and she rebuffs him for cross-dressing, he replies, "Nobody's perfect." That line replicates one spoken by Osgood (Joe E. Brown) in *Some Like It Hot* (1959) when he learns that the woman he adores is a man.

While *High Heels* circulates in elitist film markets, its citations often derive from mass culture—a fact that distinguishes postmodernist from modernist works. As Almodóvar himself has stated, "I think you can look at genre . . . without making those 'exquisite' divisions of art cinema [and] popular cinema" (quoted in Morgan, 28). That his quotations are often from American movies testifies to the hegemony of Hollywood film in the world economy, as well as to America's more "egalitarian" vision of the arts.[3]

Aside from deconstructing the binaries of high and low culture, the postmodern work has been said to relax the boundaries between fact and fiction. Hutcheon sees the form as enacting a process of hybridization "where the borders are kept clear, even if they are frequently crossed" (37). *High Heels* slyly suggests the "real" in its invocation of a controversy that surrounded the making of *Imitation*: the fatal stabbing of Lana Turner's lover by her daughter, Cheryl Crane, in April of 1958 (Fischer, 216–18). In *High Heels*, this event reenters with a vengeance in Rebecca's twin murders: her childhood killing of her stepfather, by switching his medications, and her later shooting of Manuel.[4] While this subtext can be excavated from *Imitation*, it is on the surface in *High Heels*, which makes crime the central axis of the drama (Fischer, 21–28). Thus *High Heels* partakes in a dual homage: to the fictional narrative of Sirk's film and to the documented tragedy of Turner and Crane. As though to suggest the infamous 1958 tabloid exposé, Almodóvar makes Rebecca a newscaster who confesses her offense during a broad-

---

[3] Morgan discusses the strict distinction between high and low culture in Spanish society (28).

[4] David Kehr also noticed the parallels between the narrative of *High Heels* and the details of the Turner-Crane-Stompanato scandal.

cast. He also has Becky write her memoirs, a detail that alludes to the autobiographies penned by Turner and Crane. If Marisa Paredes reminds us of Joan Crawford, thoughts of *Mommie Dearest* (1981) cannot be far behind.

While *High Heels* accesses the "real" of a Hollywood scandal, it relinquishes the theme of race so prominent in *Imitation*, figuring it only in a flashback of the "natives" who populate the island of Rebecca's childhood vacation. If "passing" is at issue in the film, it is a version devoid of racial overtones that concerns Dominguez and his feminine disguise.[5]

As *High Heels* intermingles fact and fiction, so it crosses genres—much as Judge Dominguez crosses dress. Almodóvar himself states that he does not "respect the boundaries of . . . genre" (quoted in Kinder, "Pleasure," 38). Hence *High Heels* is a "hybrid" of the melodramatic, satirical, and film noir modes. The movie's myriad references to cinema, publishing, and television tap into another postmodern theme—the overwhelming presence of *media* within contemporary culture—producing a vision of existence as the transmission of synthetic images. For Jean Baudrillard, we live in an age in which "production and consumption" have given way to "networks" through which we experience an "ecstasy of communication" ("Ecstasy," 127). Significantly, the life dramas in Almodóvar's film are enacted on TV. Manuel is a network executive. Not only does Rebecca break down during a televised program, but her mother and Judge Dominguez learn of her wrongdoing by watching the show. Likewise, it is by viewing TV that Rebecca discerns her mother is ill. Finally, a narrative twist arises when Rebecca claims the wrong set of prints from a photographic lab—as though to symbolize the rampant confusion of images in the world. Of course, the issue of artificiality is already apparent in *Imitation*, whose title and theatrical setting unavoidably elicit the theme (Affron, Stern).

Other aspects of *High Heels* reveal a postmodern bent. At times, the drama suffers "lapses" at odds with its overall continuity. David Kehr, for example, complains of the film's "strange displacements." When Rebecca is jailed and sent to the prison courtyard, several inmates enact a bizarre, choreographed "production number" reminiscent of those in a Hollywood musical. On another occasion, when Rebecca reads the television news, she laughs as she reports the weekend automobile fatalities, as though to reference Jean-Luc Godard's *Weekend* (1968), which makes the contemporary traffic jam or pileup into a grim sort of "joke." In both cases, the diegesis of *High Heels* is ruptured through homage. At other times, the slippage is produced by an excess of emotion rather

[5] Thanks to Chris Holmlund for pointing out to me the fleeting appearance of the racial theme in *High Heels*.

than by an ironic gap. As Becky, distraught over Rebecca's incarceration, sings in a theater, she kisses the stage floor, whereupon a teardrop falls and lands on her bright red lip print. It is an unlikely moment that functions as a pure icon of sentimentality, like a bird on a branch in a D. W. Griffith film.

"Sign Crimes against the Big Signifier of Sex"

Nothing is less certain today than sex.
  (Jean Baudrillard)

Perhaps the most postmodern aspect of *High Heels* is its presentation of gender. Postmodernism has been known for its decentered and negotiable engagement of subjectivity: both that of its dramatis personae and that of its audience. As Hutcheon explains, subjectivity "is represented as something in process" (39). Privileged in this regard is the genre's depiction of sexuality. According to Arthur Kroker and David Cook, a "reversible and mutable language of sexual difference" is a yardstick of postmodern discourse (20). Elsewhere, they describe the postmodern creator as "committing sign crimes against the big signifier of Sex" (21).

  In *High Heels*, this authorial "larceny," which duplicates Rebecca's, arises in a variety of ways. One of the most transgressive aspects of the narrative is the figure of Judge Dominguez who allegedly goes "under cover" as "Femme Lethal" (a female impersonator), in order to solve the case of a transvestite's murder. As Barbara Creed has noted, the androgyne is a signal figure in today's mass culture (65)—be it Boy George, Michael Jackson, Laurie Anderson, or K. D. Lang. While we assume that Rebecca knows that Lethal is a man, when she follows him into his dressing room, she seems shocked as he disrobes—but perhaps because he has a mole on his penis. While the two become amorous, he does not use his genitals for their erotic caper. Rather, in a more gender-neutral manner, he performs cunnilingus as she hangs from the rafters. What is not revealed at this time is that Lethal is Judge Dominguez, though an astute viewer can surmise it. But when his identity is disclosed, along with his professional rationale for cross-dressing, we are not convinced that it "explains" his behavior; we suspect that his real reasons are "under cover" too. Perhaps he is not what Chris Straayer would term a "temporary transvestite" but one with a more permanent commitment (36). Recalling the parallel subplots of *Imitation* and *High Heels*, we are reminded that Dominguez "stands in" for Sarah Jane—also a nightclub performer—thus accomplishing yet another gender crossing.

To make this issue more slippery, a second sexually enigmatic character appears in the film. When Rebecca is jailed, she meets Chon, an inmate who seems atypically large for a woman. One considers the possibility that she is a male in drag but rejects this theory owing to her exposed, prominent, and seemingly "natural" breasts. Evidently, however, for the Spanish audience the situation is less perplexing. Chon is played by a notorious Spanish transsexual, Bibi Andersson—ostensibly named for the Swedish movie star (Morgan, 29).

The question of gender instability seems encapsulated in an exchange within the film. When Manuel asks Lethal whether he is male or female, the latter replies, "For *you*, I'm a man." Lethal's drag performance thus highlights another element within postmodern discourse: a penchant for the carnivalesque. For Brian McHale, "[P]ostmodernist fiction has reconstituted both the formal and the topical . . . repertoires of carnivalized literature" (173).

In all these cases, the notion of gender is presented as something flexible rather than fixed; it is one more Truth that postmodernism can dismantle. And the cinema is especially adept at executing such a masquerade. For, as Parker Tyler once noted, "With its trick faculties and gracile arts of transformation, the film's technical nature makes it the ideal medium for penetrating a mask, physical or social, and thus for illustrating once more that . . . things are not always what they seem" (210). For Almodóvar, however, the nature of Dominguez's protean sexuality has broader political ramifications: "[F]or me, there is ambiguity in justice and that's why I have given it to the character of the judge. I don't know what the face of justice is—sometimes it's masculine, sometimes it's feminine" (quoted in Morgan, 29). Curiously, in his last remark, Almodóvar implies that masculinity and femininity exist as static and oppositional poles, rather than as the fluid continuum the film seems to imagine.

Beyond remaking a man as a woman, *High Heels*'s postmodernist remake casts Lethal as counterfeiting the theatrical persona of Becky. It is *her* appearance he conjures at the cabaret, and *her* signature musical number that he performs. He later even apologizes to her for his "imitation." This plot device has numerous connotations. It foregrounds the power of the female star as a "role model" not only for women but for men. Specifically, it invokes the gay camp mimicry of such figures as Judy Garland, Barbra Streisand, Cher, Mae West, Joan Crawford, and Lana Turner. Andy Warhol once noted that "drag queens are ambulatory archives of ideal movie-star womanhood" (54). For Rebecca Bell-Mettereau, this object choice bespeaks the "homosexual impersonator's desire . . . to imitate a woman of power and prestige, a professional performer rather than a 'real woman'" (5). Lethal's simulation also reveals

what many theorists have observed about "femininity" within patriarchal culture: that it requires a masquerade even on the part of biological
women—a performance not all that different from drag (Doane, "Film
and the Masquerade"; Johnston). Judith Butler, in fact, sees the engagement of gender as *requiring* a failed imitation of an elusive prototype:
"[T]he repetitive practice of gender . . . can be understood as the vain
and persistent conjuring and displacement of an idealized original, one
which no one at any time has been able to approximate" (2). Significantly, she sees the narrative of *Imitation* as exemplifying this process,
through its focus on the hyperfemale, Lora Meredith.

But the more intriguing element of Lethal's approximation of Becky
is that it places him within the *maternal* position: after all, it is Rebecca's
mother whom he ends up "being." Rebecca even acknowledges this.
When she encounters a poster for Lethal on the street, she tells Becky
that she had gone to see him when she missed her. Thus, in reproducing
himself as a female, Dominguez also becomes the human capable of corporeal reproduction: woman. This facsimile of motherhood becomes
more resonant when one recalls that earlier in the film Rebecca had accused Becky of merely "acting" her parental role—a charge also issued
by Susie to Lora in *Imitation*.[6]

But what are the implications of this narrative move, as regards the
film's overall sexual politics? Typical of postmodernism, it offers us a
multiplicity of readings and subject positions. On one level, the device
seems to raise questions about the relationship between a heterosexual
woman's adult desire for a man and her infantile love for her mother.
According to the prescribed psychiatric script, if a girl is to become heterosexual, she must "shift" her affection from her mother to a male.
While in the traditional literature this turnabout is likened to a substitution, recent views have cast it as a supplementation. The girl does not
relinquish her affection for her mother; she "widens" it to allow for a
man. As Nancy Chodorow observes, "[A] girl develops important Oedipal attachments to her mother *as well as* to her father" (127). The drama
of *High Heels* enacts this move by cementing mother and lover in Dominguez, a man attached to his *own* mother.

The narrative further complicates this odd arrangement by implying
that Dominguez may be gay, given his penchant for drag and his
mother's mention of AIDS. That he makes a female object choice (Rebecca) is not entirely incompatible with that reading. For, as Kaja Silverman has remarked, paraphrasing Marcel Proust, "[T]here are two broad
categories of homosexuals—those who can love only men, and those

---

[6] The parallels between the dialogue in *Imitation* and that in *High Heels* were also noted
by Thompson (62).

who can love lesbian women as well as men" as both occupy a same-sex "feminine psychic position" (381). Interestingly, such homosexuals identify strongly with their mothers, enclosing "a woman's soul . . . in a man's body" (339–88). For Lethal, that soul spills over onto his exterior, in the form of his female attire. Within this framework, Rebecca is a repressed lesbian: a woman who can want a man only if he appears to be a woman—the primal woman at that. For Marsha Kinder, Rebecca's conduited maternal desire is liberating: "This film . . . boldly proclaims that motherlove lies at the heart of all melodrama and its erotic excess" ("*High Heels*," 40).

The film further investigates the problematic rapport between mother and daughter. If Rebecca is haunted by a nostalgia for the Imaginary, so is Becky, whose signature torch song is entitled "You'll *Recall*." She returns to Madrid *specifically* to acquire the basement flat in which she was raised. At the end of the film the two women's regressions merge. As Becky lies in her childhood apartment dying, Rebecca pulls the curtains of the high window that faces the street above. As pedestrians stroll by, she watches their legs and feet. She remembers how, as a child, when Becky went out, she would anxiously await the sound of her mother's high-heeled footsteps returning—hence the film's literal title: *Distant Heels.*

Though this scene is poignant, it is undercut by earlier parodic moments of the film. Within the context of the myriad "perversions" the text invokes (patricide, transvestism, incest), the notion of *foot fetishism* unavoidably comes to mind; indeed, the syndrome is signaled in the work's title. For Freud, this symptomatology is tied to the young boy's shock at seeing his mother's lack of a penis. As Freud notes: "[W]hat is possibly the last impression received before the uncanny traumatic one is preserved as a fetish. Thus the foot or shoe owes its attraction as a fetish . . . to the circumstance that the inquisitive boy used to peer up the woman's legs towards her genitals" (217). In *High Heels*, Lethal's platform shoes are very visible in his cabaret number, an act that imagines a mother *with* a penis. And when he and Rebecca make love in his dressing room, she is afraid to jump from the rafters because she is wearing high heels. These ironic moments involving shoes "infect" the denouement, giving Rebecca's yearning for her mother's footsteps a masculine and "unnatural" cast. It is significant that she looks *up*, from a basement window, at people walking by on the street—as though to actualize Freud's vision of the male fetishist-to-be, gazing up women's skirts.

Given Becky's desire to return home, Rebecca's melancholy and nostalgic angst seems a remake of her parent's, adding to the problematic, tendentious portrayal of mother-daughter symbiosis. But Rebecca is a replica on more levels than one. Her name is a variant of her mother's: "Re-Becca" remakes "Becky." She marries her mother's ex-lover and then considers wedding her mother's male doppelgänger. Furthermore, during the course of the film, Rebecca becomes pregnant, by her maternal look-alike, thus approaching the matrilineal position herself. Hence within the film "the reproduction of mothering" goes berserk. But its vertiginous chain of duplication should not surprise us, for, as Hutcheon notes, "commitment to doubleness or duplicity" (1) is a benchmark of postmodernism. *High Heels* engages this trope within both the style and the thematics of the film: it is a remake about the process of remaking.

Polymorphous Perverse

> The postfeminist play with gender in which differences are elided can easily lead us back into our "pregendered" past where there was only the universal subject—man.
>   (Tania Modleski)

While the mutable world of postmodernism has been applauded in some critical circles and heralded for its progressive thrust (Hutcheon, 141–68), in other arenas it has been treated with suspicion. Feminists have been loath to relinquish the category of "woman" for fear that the act subverts their analysis of patriarchal culture. E. Ann Kaplan notes that "much of what people celebrate as liberating in . . . postmodernism is . . . an attempt to sidestep the task of working through the constraining binary oppositions, including sexual difference" (43). And Barbara Creed observes that the "postmodern fascination with the . . . 'neuter' subject may indicate a desire *not* to address problems associated with the specificities of the oppressive gender roles of patriarchal society, particularly those constructed for women" (66).[7]

It is clear how this debate might inform the case of *High Heels*. No doubt, the film entails gender fluidity—but, we might inquire, fluidity for whom? Ultimately, it is *man* who has that prerogative, not woman. Almodóvar can dabble in the "woman's picture." Dominguez can imitate a female. And Chon can "become" one. The only hint of movement in the opposite direction is the androgynous demeanor of Marisa Paredes as Becky. But what she resembles is not so much a man as a man impersonating a woman, like Dominguez as Lethal. Hence what passes for difference is, ultimately, the same, as in Luce Irigaray's notion of the

---

[7] See also Straub for a discussion of the dangers of postmodernism for feminism.

Freudian "dream of symmetry" (11).[8] B. Ruby Rich makes a similar point in her observations on postmodernism: "In all the talk about transvestitism and transsexualism there's little acknowledgement that even the world of gender-bending is male dominated—it's just that here men rule in the guise of women" (73).

There is also a fetishistic strain to *High Heels* that works against the film's claims for an unconventional vision of sexuality, despite Kinder's deeming such fetishism "fetching" ("*High Heels*," 41). In addition to shoes, the theme privileges the prop of earrings: pendulous objects seen to hang from a women's body, as though in "compensation" for that which does *not*. In the opening scene of the film, as Rebecca awaits Becky's arrival, she remembers how her mother bought her earrings on a childhood trip. We learn that they were made of horn, a substance associated with *male* animals and, metaphorically, with their erections. It is this jewelry that Rebecca fondles and wears on the day of her mother's return, and that gets tangled in Becky's hair. Later, when Rebecca takes her mother to the nightclub, Lethal and Becky exchange mementos: she donates one of her earrings (a stand-in for the lost penis) and he offers one of his "tits." In the later scene of Becky's performing onstage, she wears huge, dangling earrings that graze her shoulders. In all these cases, Becky seems linked to a fetishistic object that "substitutes" for the male genitalia. This bespeaks a masculine view of woman as signifying a distressing physiological "Lack." Only a man like Dominguez (in drag) can constitute a woman who is "fully equipped."

Rebecca, too, seems haunted by a phallic Lack, which is overcome by her appropriation of a gun, a familiar symbol. In the film's opening credits, drawings of high heels and guns are juxtaposed, linking the two fetishistic items. Furthermore, a *Sight and Sound* cover announcing a review of *High Heels* inside reads "Almodóvar's *Stiletto* Heels"—again coupling shoes with a phallic weapon, this time a knife (Thompson). Rebecca hides the gun in the chair in which Manuel used to sit, emphasizing the physical and semiotic proximity of the firearm and the phallus. It is this gun that she delivers to the dying Becky, so that her mother may mark it with her own fingerprints and false guilt.

In forcing the gun on Becky, Rebecca turns her parent into the archetypal Phallic Mother, a classic figment of the male child's imagination. Freud refers to this fantasy in 1928, while discussing the fetishist's inability to accept his mother's genital "omission." But Freud implies that the fabrication is present in *normal* masculine development. As he notes, "[T]he fetish is a substitute for *the . . . (mother's) phallus which the little*

---

[8] In talking of the "old dream of symmetry," Irigaray is characterizing Freud's constant tendency to imagine female development as parallel to and/or "symmetrical" with that of the male.

boy once believed in and does not wish to forego" (215). Thus Rebecca is placed in the position of a "transvestite" daughter whose psychic essence is male. Obviously, she finds the ultimate Phallic Mother in Lethal and his masquerade as Becky.

Clearly, this fantasy is equally powerful for Dominguez, who, in his role as cross-dresser, makes a similar maternal disavowal (Kulish, 394). His problematic relation to his own bedridden mother surfaces in scenes in which he is depicted in her home. The narrative context is unclear, but it is entirely possible that they still live together.

But need the fetishistic drift of the film be read as masculine? While some feminists have raised the possibility of *female* fetishism, it bears a different cast from the male variety. In an article on lesbianism, Elizabeth A. Grosz makes the point that rather than disavowing the "castration" of their mothers, young girls may deny their *own* (47). It is *this* disavowal that is translated into female fetishism. The "narcissistic" woman may compensate for her own perceived "lack" by vainly making a fetish object of herself through excessive costume, makeup, jewelry, and the like. The "hysterical" woman will compensate by selecting a part of her body for fetishistic "disabling" (e.g., paralysis). The "masculine" woman will disassociate herself from femininity by seeking out women with whom she can act "like a man" (47–52). None of these cases of alleged female fetishism is dominant in *High Heels*, where women are linked to phallic objects—a configuration more closely tied to men.

We find the same male bias in the writing of a critic who pioneered discussions of transvestism and film: Parker Tyler. In *Screening the Sexes*, he sees male cross-dressing as replicating the symbolism of sexual intercourse, which he describes from a masculine perspective: "When, with the surrogate of his penis, a man penetrates a woman, *he wears her body*. The penis dons the vagina via the vulva and wears the womb as a headdress. . . . In dynamic terms a curious kind of transsexuality has taken place" (217). Hence male cross-dressing is appropriate, as he already, like some hatted Ziegfeld girl, "wears [woman's] body" in coitus. (The notion of a man's "wearing" woman's body is extrapolated to the most disturbing extent imaginable in *The Silence of the Lambs* [1991].) When Tyler talks of conception, his metaphors are somewhat modified:

> In "planting the tree" of his body, the male *transplants* it . . . duplicates his own penis in the opposite direction. . . . [T]he woman, as the penetrated one, herself senses this exchange of penis orientation as a transference, or "transvestism." Hence at the crux of the act of potency, *she* becomes the penised one and, as such, one who wears, has donned, her own vagina. (217–18)

Thus it is only through access to man's penis that the woman can "wear" her own organs—which are, otherwise, worn by him.

In many ways, *High Heels* replicates Parker's scenario. It is Dominguez who makes love to and "wears" Rebecca's vagina in the dressing room of the club in which he cross-dresses. It is he who will later implant his "tree" and "seed" in her, thus "permitting" her to wear her own sexuality.

Postmaternity

[T]he crisis of the master narratives may not necessarily benefit women . . . gynesis, as written by men, could well prove to be a "new ruse of reason."
   (Barbara Creed)

Clearly, *High Heels* remakes *Imitation* and the star scandal surrounding it. But how does it reproduce motherhood? Elsewhere, I have shown how the Sirk film charts the impossibility of female parenting: if Lora is damned as uncaring, Annie is guilty of overprotecting; if Lora is faulted for putting profession before home, Annie is chastened for making a career of domesticity. While the narrative begins by establishing Annie and Lora as Good versus Bad mothers, it ends by equalizing them in failure (Fischer, 14–21). Whenever the women have troubles with their daughters, Steve steps in. When Lora departs on a film shoot, Steve is left in charge of entertaining Susie. When Annie wishes to pursue Sarah Jane, Steve makes the travel arrangements. "It's so nice to have a man around the house . . ."

While this masculine takeover is subtle in *Imitation*, it is strident in *High Heels*, which adopts what we might deem a "*postfemale*" stance. This position requires the figure of Dominguez—a man who imitates and supplants a woman. Jean Baudrillard has argued that "[t]he strength of the feminine is that of *seduction*" (*Seduction*, 7, my italics). This act is based on "artifice" and stands in opposition to the masculine reality principle. As he writes, "The only thing truly at stake" in seduction "is mastery of the strategy of appearances, against the force of being" (10). If femininity is associated with surface, as distinct from masculine "depth," it follows that the female body holds no particular truth or weight. As Baudrillard states, seduction knows "that *there is no anatomy* . . . that all signs are reversible" (10). According to this logic, the *transvestite* (like Lethal) becomes the ultimate "woman" because of his exaggerated play with the codes of femininity: "What transvestites love is this game of signs, . . . with them everything is makeup, theater, and seduction" (12–13). While championing this mimicry, Baudrillard admits that it may bear a critical tone: "The seduction . . . is coupled with a parody in which an implacable hostility to the feminine shows through and which might be interpreted as a male appropriation of the panoply of female allurements" (14). In *High Heels*, this translates into a cruel joke on the negation of anatomy as destiny.

Beyond valorizing a postfemale world, *High Heels* offers a "post-*maternal*" one, envisioning a universe in which men (like Dominguez) make the best Moms, as Tootsie once made the best feminist. For it is he who functions as maternal hero(ine) or surrogate mom, a role vacated by Becky through her parental ineptitude. It is he who loves and comforts the hysterical Rebecca, who arranges for a rapprochement within her family, who finesses her release from jail, who bares the maternal "breast" (albeit a "falsie"). Meanwhile, all that Becky manages is to reproduce her neuroses in her daughter and to visit her maternal sins upon her child.

Hence what we find in *High Heels* is the kind of questionable "male mothering" so prevalent in contemporary cinema—a phenomenon that I have critiqued in an earlier chapter.[9] While, superficially, this trope seems to express a benign male nurturant impulse, it arises at the *expense* of woman, causing her to feel a monumental postpartum depression.

Writing on the film, Kinder notes that Almodóvar's project began as a narrative about two sisters who kill their mother. In an interview with her, Almodóvar claims that "[w]hen you kill the mother, you kill precisely everything you hate, all of those burdens that hang over you" ("Pleasure," 43). While Kinder admits the misogyny of Almodóvar's abandoned scenario, she sees the final film as an "inversion" of that paradigm, in which "the . . . goal [is] no longer to destroy the maternal but . . . to . . . empower it" ("*High Heels*," 39). Earlier, I have used the term "matricide" for the male diegetic appropriation of maternal space. Unlike Kinder, I find it applicable to the fate of Becky in *High Heels*—a fate that indicates a return to Almodóvar's original theme. For Becky's demise seems linked as much to Lethal's "voodoo" *replacement* of her as to Rebecca's heinous behavior. As Baudrillard observes, "To seduce is to die as reality and reconstitute oneself as illusion" (*Seduction*, 69). As Becky expires, Lethal triumphs as the seductive maternal Imago.

In cataloging various attacks on postmodernism, Hutcheon notes that its contradictory and multifarious discourse has been found "*empty at the center*" by critics who decry the vacuity of its myriad interpretive scenarios (38).[10] This image of the *void* might well apply to Dominguez, who can emulate the maternal surface but never be "fully equipped" at the maternal core/corps. It might also apply to Almodóvar, who "empties" *Imitation* of its maternal weight.

---

[9] See also Modleski, 76–89.

[10] Though Hutcheon catalogs the objections to feminism's appropriation of postmodernism, she ultimately rejects that position.

Curiously, for Baudrillard, it is masculinity that is aligned with "production" and femininity with its absence: "All that is produced, be it the production of woman as female, falls within the register of masculine power. The only and irresistible power of femininity is the inverse power of seduction" (*Seduction*, 15). What this vision accomplishes is to deny any mode of female agency. It negates production as maternal *reproduction*, once again declaring woman's body null and void. Furthermore, it deems man (like Adam) the creator of "woman as female," leaving her entirely out of the semiological and biological loop.

One suspects that Almodóvar chose the name "Femme Lethal" to highlight the cultural cliché of the Femme Fatale. Since *High Heels* invokes film noir, this archetype is especially apt.[11] According to Mary Ann Doane, the stereotype arose with the Industrial Revolution, at "the moment when the male seems to lose access to the body which the woman then comes to *overrepresent*" (*Femmes Fatales*, 2). By 1991, however, the female is underrepresented, and her being subsumed by the allegedly "disembodied" male. For Doane, the femme fatale is "the antithesis of the maternal—sterile or barren, . . . produc[ing] nothing in a society which fetishizes production" (2). In this sense, the figure finds her true incarnation in the corpus manqué of Lethal. Hence while Almodóvar (in feminist drag) may have meant to mock female stereotypes with the name "Femme Lethal," we can also read his epithet "against the grain." Perhaps it reveals that the postmodern posture may be "lethal" to the women who deem it progressive, who are "seduced" by it. Doane wisely remains skeptical of the femme fatale as a "resistant" figure: "[I]t would be a mistake to see her as some kind of heroine of modernity. She is not the subject of feminism but a symptom of male fears about feminism" (2–3).

Elaine Showalter once observed that "[a]cting as a woman . . . is not always a tribute to the feminine" (138). Ultimately, what is "under cover" in *High Heels* is not only a male judge but a male *judgment* latent in the euphoric "polymorphous perversity" of the postmodern pose.

Works Cited

Affron, Charles. "Performing Performing: Irony and Affect." In Fischer, 207–15.

Baudrillard, Jean. "The Ecstasy of Communication." In *The Anti-Aesthetic: Essays on Postmodern Culture*, edited by Hal Foster, 125–34. Port Townsend, WA: Bay Press, 1983.

---

[11] Thompson mentions the film noir atmosphere in *High Heels* (62).

_____. *Seduction*. 1979. Translated by Brian Singer. New York: St. Martin's Press, 1990.

Bell-Mettereau, Rebecca. *Hollywood Androgyny*. New York: Columbia University Press, 1985.

Butler, Judith. "Lana's 'Imitation'": Melodramatic Repetition and the Gender Performative." *Genders*, no. 9 (Fall 1990): 1–18.

Chodorow, Nancy. *The Reproduction of Mothering: Psychoanalysis and the Sociology of Gender*. Berkeley, Los Angeles, and London: University of California Press, 1978.

Collins, James. "Postmodernism and Cultural Practice." *Screen* 28, no. 2 (Spring 1987): 11–26.

Creed, Barbara. "From Here to Modernity: Feminism and Postmodernism." *Screen* 28, no. 2 (Spring 1987): 47–67.

Doane, Mary Ann. *Femmes Fatales: Feminism, Film Theory and Psychoanalysis*. New York and London: Routledge, 1991.

_____. "Film and the Masquerade: Theorizing the Female Spectator." In *Issues in Feminist Film Criticism*, edited by Patricia Erens, 41–57. Bloomington and Indianapolis: Indiana University Press, 1990.

Ebert, Roger. "Story Looks Stylish in *High Heels*." *Chicago Sun Times*, 20 December 1991, 44.

Fassbinder, Rainer Werner. "Six Films by Douglas Sirk." Translated by Thomas Elsaessar. Excerpted in Fischer, 244–49.

Fischer, Lucy, ed. *Imitation of Life*. New Brunswick, NJ: Rutgers University Press, 1991.

Freud, Sigmund. "Fetishism." In *Sexuality and the Psychology of Love*, edited by Philip Rieff, 214–19. New York: Colliers, 1974.

Grosz, Elizabeth A. "Lesbian Fetishism?" *differences* 3, no. 2 (Summer 1991): 39–54.

Hurst, Fannie. *Imitation of Life*. New York: Collier & Son, 1933.

Hutcheon, Linda. *The Politics of Postmodernism*. New York and London: Routledge, 1989.

Irigaray, Luce. *Speculum of the Other Woman*. Translated by Gillian C. Gill. Ithaca, NY: Cornell University Press.

Johnston, Claire. "Femininity and the Masquerade: *Anne of the Indies*." In *Psychoanalysis and Cinema*, edited by E. Ann Kaplan, 64–72. New York and London: Routledge, 1990.

Kaplan, E. Ann, ed. *Postmodernism and Its Discontents*. London and New York: Verso, 1988.

Kehr, David. "Almodovar Takes a Melodramatic Turn in *High Heels*." *Chicago Tribune*, 20 December 1991, F7.

Kinder, Marsha. "*High Heels*." *Film Quarterly* 45, no. 3 (Spring 1992): 39–44.

_____. "Pleasure and the New Spanish Mentality: A Conversation with Pedro Almodovar." *Film Quarterly* 41, no. 1 (Fall 1987): 33–44.

Kroker, Arthur, and David Cook. *The Postmodern Scene: Excremental Culture and Hyper-Aesthetics*. New York: St. Martin's Press, 1986.

Kulish, Nancy Mann. "Gender and Transference: The Screen of the Phallic Mother." *International Review of Psychoanalysis* 13 (1986): 393–404.

McHale, Brian. *Postmodernist Fiction*. New York and London: Methuen, 1987.

Modleski, Tania. *Feminism without Women: Culture and Criticism in a "Postfeminist" Age*. New York and London: Routledge, 1991.

Morgan, Rikki. "Dressed to Kill." *Sight and Sound* 1, no. 12 (1992): 28–29.

Rich, B. Ruby. "Gender Bending." *Mirabella*, December 1992, 71–75.

Showalter, Elaine. "Critical Cross-Dressing and The Woman of the Year." *Raritan* 3, no. 2 (Fall 1983): 130–49.

Silverman, Kaja. *Male Subjectivity at the Margins*. New York and London: Routledge, 1992.

Stern, Michael. "*Imitation of Life*." In Fischer, 279–88.

Straayer, Chris. "Redressing the 'Natural': The Temporary Transvestite Film." *Wide Angle* 14, no. 1 (1992): 36–55.

Straub, Kristina. "Feminist Politics and Postmodernist Style." In *Image and Ideology in Modern/Postmodern Discourse*, edited by David B. Downing and Susan Bazargan, 273–86. Albany: State University of New York Press, 1991.

Suleiman, Susan. *Subversive Intent: Gender, Politics, and the Avant-Garde*. Cambridge, MA, and London: Harvard University Press, 1990.

Thompson, David. "*High Heels*." *Sight and Sound* 1, no. 12 (1992): 61–62.

Tyler, Parker. *Screening the Sexes: Homosexuality in the Movies*. Garden City, NY: Doubleday, 1972.

Warhol, Andy. *The Philosophy of Andy Warhol*. New York: Harcourt Brace Jovanovich, 1975.

9

The Nonfiction Film

"THE REPRODUCTION OF MOTHERING":
DOCUMENTING THE MOTHER-DAUGHTER BOND

Docu-*men*-tation

> Truth . . . lies in . . . seizing the individual unawares rather as
> you may discover the real face of a woman in the early morn-
> ing on the pillow beside you.
>   (Louis Marcorelles)

Within the history of cinema, the documentary impulse has long been
associated with the masculine. The cover of Erik Barnouw's survey of
the genre boasts a still from a Dziga Vertov film in which a male cinematographer peers through a viewfinder that reflects (and doubles) his
image. The title of Vertov's opus—*The* Man *with the Movie Camera*
(1929)—says it all. When one enumerates the luminaries of the field,
they are predominantly male: Robert Flaherty, John Grierson, Hum-
phrey Jennings, Frederick Wiseman, Jean Rouch, Ken Burns, Ross
McElwee.[1] Furthermore, such artists have favored masculine themes:
Nanook of the North (1922), *The Man of Aran* (1934), *A Diary for Tim-
othy* (1945), *Showman* (1962), *Salesman* (1969), *Law and Order*
(1969), *Basic Training* (1971), *Sherman's March* (1985), *The Civil
War* (1990). In its linkage of masculinity and truth, the documentary
mode has tapped into broader cultural tenets. For Jean Baudrillard, the
female is linked to the synthetic and the male to the authentic. As he
writes, "[T]he immense privilege of the feminine is . . . [that] of having
never acceded to truth . . . and of having remained absolute master of
the realm of appearances" (8).

In some nonfiction texts, woman's domain tentatively emerges, as it
did in Muybridge's protocinematic motion studies. Amid the machismo
scenes of war and labor on a reel of French primitive "views," we have
the domestic vignette *Feeding the Baby* (1895), which depicts Mama and

---

[1] There are, of course, certain important female documentarists recognized in film history, including Esther Shub, Jill Godmilow, and Helen Frank.

Papa Lumière and their precious offspring. The scene is obviously staged, and one suspects that the entrepreneurial paterfamilias was not always present at the breakfast table. Similarly, in a compilation of films of the 1890s, we discover Edison's *Morning Bath* (1896) among the sagas of male toil (rescuing animals, driving trains, sawing wood). Here, a black woman washes her child in a basin of water, as he bemoans, in perpetuity, the soap in his eyes. While *Nanook of the North* privileges masculine tasks like igloo building and walrus slaying, brief glimpses of the Eskimo wife and child are permitted. The maternal haunts the frame of the documentary text, periodically stalking its borders.

19. *Morning Bath* (1896). A rare example of maternal labor in the documentary form. MOMA

Given such containment, it is crucial to examine the rare documentary that places maternity at its center. One such text is David and Albert Maysles's *Grey Gardens* (1976), a film about a bizarre mother and daughter duo.[2] One suspects that this topic was intriguing primarily because the pair was invested with tabloid notoriety as the eccentric aunt and cousin of Jacqueline Bouvier Kennedy Onassis. They were not simply a family but "news."

Specifically, "Grey Gardens" refers to a decaying, twenty-eight-room Long Island mansion inhabited by eighty-year-old Edith Beale and her fifty-nine-year-old daughter, Edie. The two women emerged from obscurity when local newspapers reported their home condemned by the

[2] Credits for *Grey Gardens* indicate that it was codirected by Ellen Hovde and Muffie Meyer; but it is known as a "Maysles film," and the two women are often forgotten in discussions of the work or are thought of as mere editors.

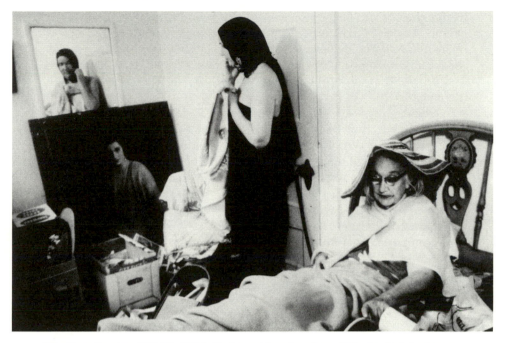

20. *Grey Gardens* (1976). Edith Beale and her daughter, Edie, in their bedroom. MOMA

Board of Health. This proved an embarrassment to the Bouvier clan who offered funds toward the estate's renovation (Knight). The Maysleses gained access to the women through Onassis's sister, Lee Radziwill, who commissioned them to make a film about her childhood. When Radziwill saw the Maysleses' footage, she was appalled and forced them to relinquish the material. Obsessed with their subjects, the Maysleses returned to Grey Gardens as its first outside visitors in twenty years and fashioned their own film (Antonini and Feder, 92; Hovde in Rosenthal, 376–77). It was shot in five weeks with the brothers in residence. Two years were spent on its editing under the supervision of codirectors Ellen Hovde and Muffie Meyer (Roud).

In its style, *Grey Gardens* is a classic of the cinema verité school. While filmmakers have claimed a heightened "truth" for that mode, with its pursuit of life registered "unawares," critics have seen it as one more documentary *style*—one with conventions as manufactured as those of the *March of Time*.[3] Among the hallmarks of the verité tradition are the use of portable sound gear, fast film, and lightweight, handheld cameras,

---

[3] The debates around the "realism" of the verité style are discussed in Noël Carroll's work.

technologies that allow filmmakers to shoot on-location and bypass the studio. As Peter Graham notes, "With this equipment they can approximate quite closely the flexibility of the human senses . . . they can follow their subjects almost anywhere, and because of their unobtrusiveness . . . people soon forget the presence of the camera and attain surprising naturalness" (34).

Verité documentaries shun prescripted scenarios, reenacted vignettes, voice-over narration, and theme music—"theatrical" touches seen as inappropriate. The outright interview format is often avoided, replaced by the extended monologue. Here, the subject speaks directly to the camera in protracted long-takes. In some works, the filmmaker appears onscreen, while in others the director is merely an implied presence. The rhetoric of verité also seeks to delimit the "interpretive" role of the artist. Rather, it endeavors to let events "spontaneously" unfold, with the viewer imposing a subsequent reading.[4]

Much of *Grey Gardens* conforms to this model. All material is shot on the mansion premises with the camera immersed in the action, adjusting its views with perceptible dollies, pans, and zooms. The only music heard is that of the Beales' singing or playing the phonograph and radio. While neither Maysles brother is explicitly depicted, their presence is assumed. At one point, a mirror inadvertently reflects the image of the Maysleses filming, while at another, a male voice intones in the background. Though the film creates the illusion that the women are extemporaneously speaking, we know that an interlocutor hovers offscreen. At times, Edie addresses one of the Maysleses by name or makes pointed comments to the men with the movie cameras. "David," she asks at one moment, "do you think I should have gotten into nightclub work?" And later, she chides him: "You're wasting your film on this!" While the goal of such techniques is to position the spectator as a secret observer of an unmediated "slice of life," Hovde reminds us that assertive editing reduced some eighty hours of footage to a mere ninety-four minutes. Clearly, a structuring hand was always there. Hovde herself mocks the utopian "axioms" of the male verité pioneers: "They were all cameramen, and they . . . really objected to tampering with reality. Reality to them means you photograph it as it happened and you do not cut it. . . . It is just patently untrue . . . all those films were *always* cut" (quoted in Rosenthal, 384).

Beyond the film's documentary position, questions arise as to its ideological project. Though the Maysleses were possessed by the Beales, Hovde reports that "[t]hey really had no idea why they were interested

---

[4] Cinema verité (as a style with specific characteristics) is discussed by Carroll, Graham, and Hall.

in these people" (quoted in Rosenthal, 377). As one apprehends the film, the brothers' raw, inchoate fascination comes through, and their stance seems quasi-voyeuristic (Knight). This term seems apt because of the perverse quality of the universe the Beales inhabit and to which the viewer is privy. On one level, its decadence is physical. The house is cluttered, filthy, decrepit, and repulsive, overrun by cats, whose litter boxes and rotting food cans are omnipresent. One feline, in fact, defecates behind an oil portrait of Mrs. Beale. The women are unkempt and frequently immodest: Mrs. Beale wears skimpy halters, and her daughter is bedecked in campy, décolleté outfits made ingeniously from towels, scarves, or scraps of fabric. Louis Marcorelles would be interested to learn that the women wear no makeup and regret the camera's harsh scrutiny. The mansion grounds are strewn with leaves and weeds; the attic is infested with raccoons. Hence Grey Gardens is a Gothic "house of horrors," and we sense a prurience in our perusal of it. The estate's material degeneration would not terrify us were it not an emblem for the women's mental state. For what is both chilling and compelling about *Grey Gardens* is the Beales' individual and collective insanity.

Their dementia has a strong cultural component that reverberates with stereotypes of the feminine. Edie's sexual exhibitionism—her strutting in bathing suits and miniskirts—is perceived as improper because she is middle-aged. It would not be scandalous for her to be a sexpot; it is only unsavory because she is an elderly and, hence, parodic one. Critic Charles Michener referred to her as a "self-made nun in heat." Furthermore, frequently depicting the women gazing into mirrors, the film foregrounds their "female" narcissism. In one sequence, Mrs. Beale hands Edie a looking glass, before which the latter poses provocatively. Here again, Edie's cosmetic self-absorption is presented as pathetic, mainly because she is too old to reap its benefits. Critic Walter Goodman, who calls the women "a pair of grotesques" (169), remarks on Mrs. Beale's "flabby and creased" arms as well as on Edie's "heavy thighs" (168). Similarly, Richard Eder notes how the camera is "unsparing of [the women's] old sagging flesh" (21).

Hovde has commented on the Maysleses' seeming intent to depict Edie as vain, even when she diverged from this pattern. They shot Edie discoursing on politics but refused to include the material, despite their codirectors' protestations: "[T]he real reason why we wanted it was that it showed Edie in a moment that was not narcissistic. She was showing that she did read, that she was aware of public events . . . we did feel strongly that the scene should be in. In fact, we were constantly putting it in, and David was constantly taking it out." According to Hovde, he "was never able to explain . . . satisfactorily why he wanted [the footage] out" (Rosenthal, 380).

The film's necrophilic fixation on decay is articulated in its morbid intercutting of the aged Beales with photos of their gorgeous, youthful selves. We wonder if the Maysleses would have found the women's lives quite so tragic had they never been beautiful. But despite the women's decline, they can still serve as objects for male "seduction." At one point Edie exclaims, "Darling David, where have you been all my life?" At another, she confesses, "I wish I had David and Al with me before this." These moments led critics to charge the work with exploitation. Marjorie Rosen, for example, asked whether the filmmakers were encouraging us "to gawk at a goon show," and Goodman questioned whether the work constituted a "sideshow" (168). Eder stated that "[t]o watch *Grey Gardens* is to take part in a kind of carnival of attention with two willing but vulnerable people who had established themselves . . . in the habit of not being looked at" (21). While the Maysleses denied such accusations, Hovde admits that during the making of *Grey Gardens* she was concerned about "exposing [the Beales] to ridicule from people who wouldn't understand them." The Maysleses, however, "felt that everything that had gone on was all right, and that if the Beales revealed themselves completely," it was "fine" (quoted in Rosenthal, 381).

But perhaps the most provocative aspect of *Grey Gardens* is its vision of "matriarchy." For if the Beales are individually unbalanced, it is in their *relation* that they are truly disturbed. Again, the portrayal of their plight reinforces cultural fears about the mother-daughter bond—a liaison that has been seen as dangerously symbiotic. Nancy Friday calls her book on the subject *My Mother, Myself*, indicating the potential for nefarious duplication between mother and daughter. And Simone de Beauvoir remarks that "[i]n her daughter the mother . . . seeks a double" (577). While sons similarly imitate their fathers, the traditional family offers boys limited time with them; hence the risk of mirroring is reduced.

There can be no more emphatic vision of mother-daughter attachment than that presented in *Grey Gardens*. The publicity material even refers to the women as "Big" and "Little" Edie. As evidence of the latter's fusion with her parent, she still resides in Mrs. Beale's home and refers to herself "as Mother's little girl." Ultimately, the women's bedroom—where they cook, eat, and entertain—stands as a metaphor for the Lacanian Imaginary, identified with infancy and the maternal. There, Edie remains psychically and spatially trapped in a "time capsule" (Antonini and Feder, 92). This parasitic motif resounds throughout the film, especially in Edie's discourse. She asks, "When am I gonna get out of here?" and vows that she will not spend "another ten years" in Grey

Gardens. To explain the vacancy of her life, she claims that she "never had a chance because Mother wasn't well."

Edie, however, is not the only one driven by compulsive need. Whenever the camera finds the younger woman alone, Mrs. Beale's shrill and demanding voice shrieks in the background, as though she cannot let her daughter out of her audiovisual range. Here we have a sense of the maternal voice as an "umbilical net" that encloses and restricts the child.[5] Whenever the women are together, their voices compound. As one of them recounts a story, the other "dubs" over her version—or monopolizes the discussion when the first one takes a breath. This echolalia caused problems in the film's postproduction, when the editors could not find a silent moment on which to cut. Hovde recalls that "[a]s one conversation finished and you wanted to say, bam that's the end of the scene, the other voice would begin" (quoted in Rosenthal, 384). To remedy this, they asked the women to rerecord certain phrases, imposing a break at the end of their statements, and thus violating purist verité codes.

The Beales' mutual dependence is encapsulated in the image of their room with its matching twin beds. It is a parody of the conjugal boudoir, underscoring Edie's failure to leave and marry. Mrs. Beale herself foregrounds this failure: in one of her reminiscences, she quips, "France fell [in World War II], but Edie didn't." When Mrs. Beale, who once was a singer, renders her versions of "Tea for Two," "You and the Night and the Music," "Night and Day," and "People Will Say We're in Love," the irony of the women's incestuous "romance" reverberates. While the "operatic" maternal voice is, generally, an icon of bliss and plenitude, here it has a depraved edge.[6]

The women's emotional entanglement is highlighted by their competition over men, thus reinforcing notions of mother-daughter rivalry (Beauvoir, 579). Edie chastises Mrs. Beale for eliminating each of her eligible suitors "in fifteen minutes flat." She also refers to her father as "*Mr.* Beale," marking an uncomfortable distance from him, and the women's conversation places Edie at the center of her parents' marital strife.

The women's interaction is predominantly hostile and venomous, making the film a "fugue of . . . recrimination" (Roud). Sometimes, their antagonism emerges verbally, as when Mrs. Beale claims that Edie is driving her to drink. At other moments, their resentment surfaces in

---

[5] Kaja Silverman talks of a paranoid vision of the maternal voice (in the "umbilical night") in her *Acoustic Mirror* (72–100).

[6] Silverman also discusses the more benign ("operatic") vision of the maternal voice. Ibid.

physical ways, as when the women wrestle over family photographs. At certain points, their friction is embedded in their psychic interaction. When Edie sings, infringing on her mother's "territory," Mrs. Beale unleashes a spate of criticism, mocking Edie's handling of the lyrics, her grimacing, her mispronunciation.

It seems crucial that both women are theatrical. While Mrs. Beale aimed to be a chanteuse, Edie aspired to be a model and actress. One of Edie's greatest resentments stems from an incident when Mrs. Beale summoned her home from Manhattan on the eve of an important audition. Throughout the film, the Maysleses focus on the women as performers: Mrs. Beale singing, Edie executing a drum majorette's routine. Once more, this vision taps into certain myths of the female as embodying disingenuity. This focus on the "masquerade" did not escape the critics. Marjorie Rosen notes: "[M]other and daughter perform before the camera as though they've been waiting in the wings for 25 years. This is their moment before the kleig lights." Although it is unstated, a reference to *Sunset Boulevard* (1950) seems implied, with the Maysleses standing in for William Holden and Cecil B. DeMille. Rosen describes the scene at the New York Film Festival premiere, where Little Edie appeared "with the aplomb of a prima donna, [and] threw roses to her audience." Kenneth Robson finds the women's lives "like a series of discontinuous takes or rehearsals" (44).

In *Grey Gardens*, the Beales enact the "worst-case scenario" of the mother-daughter "plot."[7] Significantly, no *social* perspective is brought to bear on their biography. Rather, the women seem as hermetically sealed in the text as they do in the home from which its name derives. We do glean hints of their patrician background—through the arcane grandeur of the estate, through anecdotes, newspaper clippings, and photographs. Evidently, Hovde and Meyer wanted to emphasize this cultural framework, but the Maysleses refused:

> [We] wanted to start the film with a dolly shot down Lily Pond Lane where the Beales live. On that road are enormous houses with espaliered trees, and fancy gravelled driveways—they are very elegant. And we thought it would be wonderful to just go right past those houses and come to the Beales' house. You would be immediately saying a lot. *You would be putting them in a context.* Now both David and Al were adamant about that they would never do that shot. Al said, "I don't care where this house is, it could be in the middle of Harlem, and the story would be the same." Muffie and I [didn't] agree at all; *we [thought] the story ha[d] very much to do with the society and . . . the class they c[a]me from and how they deviated from that.* (Quoted in Rosenthal, 380–81)

[7] I am referring to the title of Marianne Hirsch's book.

Neither does the viewer have a sense of the *gendered* world the women inhabit and how it may have facilitated their mother-daughter entrapment. It might have been stressed, for example, that in the era of Edie's youth, careers for women were not encouraged, that "spinsters" were denigrated, that daughters were expected to tend their ailing parents. We hear mention of her brother, but it is never considered that he might have come home to help. Such cultural insights might have made the Beales more sympathetic, their plight less pathological or idiosyncratic. Thus the film, in its psychological focus, replicates the role of psychoanalysis in the construction of motherhood. As Monique Plaza asserts of psychoanalysis, "[O]ne of its first ideological tasks was to camouflage the *history* of the maternal function in *psychobiologizing* it . . . creating the concept of 'mother-child symbiosis' in order to naturalize the social relation that exists between a woman and the child she has brought into the world" (79).

Curiously, though the Maysleses initiated the film, it was their female coauthors who grasped its meaning; and, as Hovde reports, the team's views split along lines of sexual difference. While the Maysleses saw the Beales' drama in terms of plot and climax ("[W]ould Edie leave or not"?), Hovde and Meyer comprehended its equilibrium: "We felt absolutely certain that Edie had no intention of leaving." For them the issue was not novelistic resolution but psychological enigma: "Why were mother and daughter *together*?" (quoted in Rosenthal, 379). Even the crew's postproduction experience followed traditional gender expectations. While the Maysleses went out into the world to earn more money (on commercials, commissioned films, industrials), Hovde and Meyer edited on the home front.

As I have mentioned, at one moment in the film, one of the Maysleses' images is accidentally caught in the Beales' mirror; the footage remains as a gesture of self-reflexivity. Yet although Albert and David Maysles had studied psychology (Antonini and Feder, 92), according to Hovde they had little understanding of their motivation for making the film. For help, they turned to Hovde and Meyer, who acted like analysts for the creative endeavor:

> [W]e suggested to Al that he was interested in Big Edie because she was rather like his mother, and that struck a chord in him. He was very involved with his mother, who had recently died. David said that it was maybe because he identified with Little Edie because he too was afraid of getting married, and was very attached to family. But that was as far as they could come with any reasons for making the film. (Quoted in Rosenthal, 377)

In *The Reproduction of Mothering* Nancy Chodorow explains how a girl raised in the traditional family learns to *connect* with people through imitating her mother, while a boy learns to *separate* from others through a process of maternal *dis*identification. In the *content* of *Grey Gardens* we see the perils of the mother-daughter union—when "empathy" is taken to extremes. Instead of leading to affiliation, such overidentification results in annihilation. In the *making* of the film, we see a different phenomenon, one that is readable along gender lines. While the male filmmakers blindly track their artistic obsession, without a clue as to the nature of their preoccupation, the women filmmakers provide the tools for self-knowledge. While the men remove themselves from the Beales—like psychologists "interested in observing people" (Antonini and Feder, 92)—the women struggle with the implications of the Beales' relation to the Maysleses and with the ethics of disturbing the Beales' uneasy peace. If "the reproduction of mothering" fails in the film, its legacy tentatively succeeds in the process, with Hovde and Meyer attempting to save their creation from its makers.

"The Great Unwritten Story"

> Women have been *both* mothers and daughters, but have
> written little on the subject; the vast majority of literary and
> visual images of motherhood comes to us filtered through a
> collective or individual male consciousness.
>   (Adrienne Rich)

While Hovde and Meyer were able to influence the construction of *Grey Gardens*, it remains a work formulated by men. It was the Maysleses who selected the Beales as suitable subjects, and it was they who decided what the film was to include and what not. For Adrienne Rich, such male oversight is endemic to the historic representation of mothers and daughters.

Given this context, it is not surprising that a young generation of women filmmakers, empowered by feminism of the 1970s, turned to this topic in their own documentary work. For as Rich comments, "Th[e] cathexis between mother and daughter—essential, distorted, misused—is the great unwritten story" (226). As though to signal this move, the final chapter of Rita Mae Brown's influential seventies novel *Rubyfruit Jungle* (1973) concerns a female artist who breaks film school protocol by shooting a documentary about her mother.[8]

Early films of the era sketched portraits of mothers or grandmothers, as an homage to matriarchy: *Nana, Mom and Me* by Amalie Rothschild, *An Old Fashioned Woman* by Martha Coolidge, and *Yudie* by Mirra

---

[8] Thanks to John Groch for this observation about *Rubyfruit Jungle*.

Banks, all made in 1974. But the seminal text was Michelle Citron's *Daughter Rite* (1978).[9] Breaking ranks with its realistic predecessors, *Daughter Rite* forged an experimental style, interweaving home movie footage with staged material. Like *Grey Gardens, Daughter Rite* disclosed a dark side to the mother-daughter dyad. But it declined an omniscient narratorial position to advance a voice track clearly identified with the *daughter*. No "real" or "single" child was implied in the text. Rather, Citron, who interviewed numerous women, drew a composite picture of the mother-daughter bond from her subjects' collective experience. In its psychoanalytic thrust and fixation on the parent, *Daughter Rite* inscribes a process that Jane Flax finds in her female patients: "Much time at the beginning of therapy may be taken up with a description and analysis of the mother's history and problems" (35).

With *Daughter Rite*, a "cinema of matrilineage" was born—a genre simultaneously formulated in the other arts. Nan Bauer Maglin lists five defining features of its literary incarnation:

1. the recognition by the daughter that her voice is not entirely her own;

2. the importance of trying to really see one's mother in spite of or beyond the blindness and skewed vision that growing up together causes;

3. the amazement and humility about the strength of our mothers;

4. the need to recite one's matrilineage, to find a ritual to both get back there and preserve it;

5. and still, the anger and despair about the pain and the silence borne and handed on from mother to daughter. (258)

Given the youth of these filmmakers, their identification with the *daughter*'s viewpoint is understandable. In *The Mother/Daughter Plot*, Marianne Hirsch remarks on this phenomenon in literary studies: "[M]uch of feminist theory situates itself in the position of daughter and at a distance from the maternal" (25).[10] For Hirsch, there are clear reasons for this trend, given the artists' maturation during the women's movement: "Mothers—the ones who are not singular, who did succumb to convention inasmuch as they are mothers— . . . bec[a]me the . . . primary negative models for the daughter" (11). Hirsch finds this situation regrettable as it "collude[s] with patriarchy in placing mothers into the position of object—thereby keeping mothering outside of representation" (163). She urges women to begin listening "to the stories that mothers have to tell," and to create "the space in which mothers might articulate" those tales (167).

---

[9] *Daughter Rite* has been extensively discussed; see, for example, E. Ann Kaplan's *Women and Film*, 181–88.

[10] Kaplan makes a similar point in *Motherhood and Representation*, 46–47.

Home and the World

> Our personalities seem dangerously to overlap with our
> mothers'; and, in a desperate attempt to know where mother
> ends and daughter begins, we perform radical surgery.
>   (Adrienne Rich)

Some nonfiction film and video makers have begun to navigate this un-
charted territory, clearing a zone for the maternal. In *News from Home*
(1976), Belgian artist Chantal Akerman documents her move to New
York by rendering visual images of the city while reading letters from her
mother on the audio track. The film participates in the brand of "displaced autobiography" that Janet Bergstrom finds characteristic of Akerman's oeuvre (Bergstrom and Doane, 97).

Specifically, *News from Home* offers footage of urban locales, photographed by Babette Mangolte: automobiles, streets, diners, warehouses,
highways. The visuals are drawn from *public* space, with the only interi-
ors being those of subway cars or restaurants as seen through their win-
dows. Acoustically layered over these *communal* images is a sound track
that utters *private*: maternal thoughts, as rendered in the daughter's vo-
calization, requiring us "to distinguish between the voice itself and the
words it utters, a distinction which the classic text would work hard to
erase" (Silverman, "Disembodying," 319–20). Judith Mayne has commented on the crucial dichotomy between public and private realms in
women's lives:

> The task of rendering ourselves visible has . . . entailed a process of re-reading
> the very notion of history: not as a series of Grand Events in the public do-
> main, but as a constant interaction of the realms of private and public life. For
> women have always participated in public life, although most frequently
> through the mediation of domestic life. (Quoted in Kaes, 153–54)

In *News from Home*, the mother's homespun monologue is painful to
hear. As Akerman herself admits, its discourse is rather untutored: "My
mother didn't learn to write, she quit school at 11, and then there was
the war. She writes as she can, she formulates her feelings in an unso-
phisticated way" (quoted in Silverman, "Disembodying," 320). Her
mother's words speak of maternal desire, of a lost union with the child,
of melodramatic suffering. Indeed, Akerman calls the epistles "love letters" (Silverman, "Disembodying," 320). Specifically, Mother pleads
for news from her offspring and details of how she is doing: "Write
often; it's all I ask of you." She begs to be remembered: "We only ask
one thing, that you don't forget us." Her discourse reveals an overin-
vestment in parenthood: "I live to the rhythm of your letters. Don't

21. *News from Home* (1976). The visuals of New York City are drawn from public space. BFI

leave me without news." She is haunted by dreams of her daughter and mentions symptoms of fatigue, insomnia, dizziness, and depression. While her verbiage is inherently histrionic, it is delivered in a hurried monotone that nullifies its sentimental aura. It is the *script* of the maternal melodrama without the genre's affect—a woman's picture without the tears.

Troubling aspects of the mother-daughter bond continually surface. Mother sometimes infantilizes her child, calling her "my dear little girl." She smothers her from a distance, ending her letters with "hugs and kisses." Guilt is marshaled in the epistolary diatribe as she stoically claims to accept her daughter's unannounced flight to America. Martyrdom is invoked as she promises to eschew selfishness, to seek what is best for her child. Frequently, she sends cash, as though to bribe her daughter to write. As Mother's letters relate gossip of family and friends, her pointed anecdotes mask complaints and jealousies: she mentions her husband's business worries, her community's engagements, marriages, and pregnancies. Ultimately, all of the communiqués begin to sound alike and tawdrily clichéd.

While some aspects of the maternal dialogue are disturbing, others are salutary. Though obsessive, the mother's voice exhibits warmth and concern: "Be careful; don't go out at night." She urges her daughter to phone American relatives, attempting to extend the kinship network abroad. While it is clear that the mother's bourgeois existence is at odds with her daughter's bohemian ways, she takes interest in her child's career and tries to conjure the proper enthusiasm. Though distressing, her melancholy is touching and testifies to the crucial role her daughter has played in her world.

While the maternal sound track is one of emotional excess, the visuals are minimalist. The scenes depict barren vistas, rendered in sparse long-shot/long-takes, seemingly photographed at dawn. Critics have compared these bleak, deserted views to the "elegiac" cityscapes of Edward Hopper (Holden). The film's omission of the daughter's verbal response comes to seem a psychic withholding, from both the mother and the audience that witnesses her grief. But while Akerman refuses to share her own words, her imagery connotes a desolation not unlike her parent's. As Stephen Holden notes, "By the end of the film the repetitive familial banalities and the images of urban dehumanization have merged and begun to suggest parallel worlds, one small, the other large, that are equally stultifying."

Although Akerman's cinematic style is spare, it resonates with meaning. Angela Stukator has seen the film's imagery as "reclaiming and reworking attributes of primitive cinema" (170). Hence one might argue that the film "regresses" on both personal and historical levels. If *Grey Gardens* is a film about mother-daughter symbiosis, this is a work about detachment, about the child's break from home. The rift between mother and daughter is embedded in the filmic form through the "radical surgery" between sound and image, tracks that resist being synchronized or merged.[11] Yet in the editing the two are brought together, striking a restive balance—like magnets with opposite poles.

It is curious that, in a film about moving, most shots are static, with an occasional pan—a fact that ironizes the nature of Akerman's voyage. At times, the content of images seems subtly relevant to the broader subject. In various street scenes, U.S. Mail trucks pass; a mother and child sit on a subway bench; the Port Authority is seen. Several of Mother's letters mention snapshots (sent or requested); later, a photo lab is glimpsed in a subway mall. The final shot of the film, depicting lower Manhattan as seen from a departing boat, conjures images of returning to Europe.

In her book on mother-daughter fiction, Hirsch criticizes Freud for failing to examine how the female parent experiences the rupture with her child: "If the story of individual development . . . rests on a process of separation from the mother, then the mother's own part in that process remains absent, erased from theoretical and narrative representa-

---

[11] Silverman has spoken of the import of asynchronous sound as a strategy for feminist film (*Acoustic Mirror*, 141–86).

tion" (169). We might think of *News from Home* as restoring that dele-
tion, as inscribing maternal discourse into film language. Though
Mother's thoughts, with their sentimentality, pathos, and manipulation,
may be "improper," they are nonetheless expressed. If Hirsch urged
women to listen "to the stories that mothers . . . [would] tell," she did
not promise they would be uniformly inspiring or uplifting (167).

While *News from Home* takes a tentative step toward rendering a maternal viewpoint, that enunciation is highly qualified. The maternal
voice is inflected with the daughter's judgmental outlook, an unavoidable consequence of its placement in her film. In an act of aesthetic passive aggression, the sound mixing frequently drowns out the maternal
monologue: sometimes Mother's voice is incomprehensible as it fades
into a scene; other times, it is drowned out by ambient noise. At moments, Akerman's dissemination of her mother's letters seems a breach
of privacy. As Jane Flax notes, "Women tend to feel guilty that they are
somehow betraying their mother in an attempt to resolve and terminate
the symbiotic tie" (35).

On one occasion, it is implied that Akerman has sent her mother the
script of another film she is making. Her mother strives to be positive
but admits to finding it "sad," "dreary," and "social." Ironically, the
same words might apply to *News from Home*, but without the negative
connotations. While Akerman's stark portrayal of maternal consciousness is sometimes "sad" and "dreary," revealing the potential for desperation at the maternal core, its distanced delivery foregrounds the "social." Stripped bare of a fictional scenario, or of verité voyeurism, the
film highlights the hazards of traditional motherhood where the only
news is old. Akerman has left that universe, and her film documents the
spatial and psychic journey she has taken; but it also reveals the poignant
pull of hearth and home.[12]

Motherhood and History

> Our family is in fact constituted by and in the general move-
> ment of History, but is experienced, on the other hand . . . in
> the depths and opaqueness of childhood.
>   (Jean-Paul Sartre)

While a societal framework is absent from *Grey Gardens* and contingent
in *News from Home*, it is prominent in a series of feminist experimental
documentaries of the 1980s and 1990s. Again, they are made from the

---

[12] For a further discussion of the maternal theme in Akerman's work, see the writing of
Brenda Longfellow.

22. *The Ties That Bind* (1984). Filmmaker Su Friedrich and her mother. MOMA

filial stance, but they evince a developing respect for the maternal position. The first text to signal this move is Su Friedrich's *The Ties That
Bind* (1984). It presents an extended interview with the artist's mother,
Lore Bucher Friedrich, who came of age in Germany during the Third
Reich, then emigrated to the United States with her GI husband after
the war. Specifically, the film inquires about Bucher's experience of Nazism and of her German ancestry—phenomena that have bedeviled both
mother and child. Rather than conceive the mother-daughter dyad in
some essentialist Imaginary space, as does *Grey Gardens* and even *News
from Home*, the film locates the mother within *history* (or *her*story) and
inquires how such a placement affects the matrilineal line. This strategy
squares with Miriam Hansen's notion of creating an oppositional discourse: "[C]onceptualizing an alternative tradition requires a concept of
experience which not only is the opposite of socially constructed signs
and systems of representation but, rather, mediates between individual
perception and social determinations, and emphatically entails memory
and an awareness of its historical diminishment" (quoted in Bergstrom
and Doane, 172).

Friedrich employs several techniques that work against the realist pull
of the documentary text, positioning her film in an avant-garde vein.
Sometimes, images are decelerated or frozen. Instead of being synchronized with the picture, her mother's narration accompanies disparate

visuals: a contemporary setting (home or office), her photographic past, an abstract montage (mountaintops, toothpaste commercials). At points, these shots relate to Bucher's commentary, as when her words about German expansion are juxtaposed with images of men boxing, but at other times they do not. Bucher's face is often segmented in extreme close-up, which prevents a sentimental audience response. At times, Friedrich's choice of imagery seems almost random, as when she focuses on her mother's feet. But, ultimately, these shots seem a reference to *Rubyfruit Jungle*. As its heroine muses: "I filmed [my mother] through the week . . . and she was thrilled that I could work a camera. It didn't take her long to figure things out because when I took a shot of her revving up her rocker she snapped, '*What are you doing taking pictures of my feet? People wanna see my face not my feet*'" (Brown, 180–81, my italics).

While Friedrich does not appear in *The Ties That Bind*, Bucher refers to her daughter, whose questions and remarks are "vocalized" through intertitles scratched into the emulsion in the manner of Stan Brakhage. At one point a title inquires of Bucher, "How old were you then?" and at another, "Can you tell me more about the [American] occupation?" On other occasions, Friedrich's words label something (like the German "cross of honor"). In its refusal of synchronized sound, the text shares with other feminist works a tendency to grant the disembodied female voice a new authority (Silverman, *Acoustic Mirror*, 141–234).

Ostensibly, Friedrich imposes a "silence" on herself in order to highlight her mother's words. But Friedrich's titles betray a certain power and insistence. Because they are handwritten, in what David Edelstein deems a "quivery grade-school scrawl," they reassert the filial stance. Furthermore, they periodically seem to "shout," despite their apparent muteness. When Bucher claims that people were unaware of the murders in the concentration camps, a capitalized intertitle declaims "NO!" In an interview, Friedrich explains that "[i]t made [her] extremely uncomfortable to behave as if [her] mother was lying, but . . . when it was necessary . . . to contradict her [mother's] version of . . . history, [she] did." Thus "the film is meant as a dialogue" (Friedrich). But Barbara Kruger finds it more "like a court transcript of a mother brought to trial (albeit kindly) by her own daughter."

On another level, Friedrich's stance shares much with that of the *oral historian* as she interviews her subject and transcribes the latter's life story. But rather than conform to conventional models, Friedrich invests the procedure with a feminist bent. Kristina Minister has noted how male oral historians have favored a linear/chronological approach: preparing a set of topics and compelling the subject toward addressing them. Furthermore, their queries have focused on people's concrete actions rather than on their emotional response to events. For Minister, the feminist must discard such a framework, which is at odds with how women have been socialized to communicate: "[F]eminist interviewers [must] adopt their narrators' time frame, shifting gradually to new issues only after old ones have been developed" (39). And researchers must relinquish claims of objectivity: "Before oral history can build subjective records of women's lives, interviewers must position themselves subjectively within the discourse" (36). While Su Friedrich does not claim to be a feminist oral historian, her filmmaking mode seems informed by Minister's dictates—in its fluid temporal structure, in its anecdotal and emotional tone, in its suppression of the interviewer's voice, in its assertion of the latter's affective connection to her subject.

The tale that Friedrich extracts is one of contained resistance within a system of "ties that bind." While Bucher and her parents were antifascist, they were not martyrs; they simply attempted to survive the era with minimal complicity. Though Bucher was friendly with members of the political underground (like the White Rose), she did not join them. As she admits, they "did what [she] would not do." Rather, her rebellion took the form of helping Jewish students in school, or refusing to shout "Heil Hitler."

The structure of the film asserts explicit connections between mother and daughter in relation to their sociohistorical positioning. Friedrich intercuts newspaper headlines about political dramas of her day, like nuclear war, that rival the Nazi threat. She includes documentary footage of protests she has attended, such as a 1983 women's antiwar march, evincing the need for continued vigilance. Finally, she photographs a stack of political mail from such organizations as Amnesty International. At times, her intertitles try to envision her *own* response to the German menace. One reads, "I just can't imagine it," and another asks what she would have done. At other moments, they suggest how she has repressed her mother's background and experience: "I can't remember the war stories she told me when I was young." This lacuna is explained by the stigma Friedrich feels about her ethnic heritage: "[M]y own shame at the legacy of the Germans kept me from finding out more about the war when I was younger" (Friedrich). Her mother expresses a similar sentiment as she talks of feeling "embarrassed" about being Teutonic: "It is a persecution to the end of my life and I don't deserve it."

As Bucher is honest about her timidity, Friedrich confesses her romantic desire for a more intrepid mother who could have "done something" about Nazism. When Molly Haskell first formulated the notion of the "woman's film," she spoke of the ordinary woman who becomes extraordinary (161). Friedrich uses similar language to describe the theme of *The Ties That Bind* but minimizes the valorous tone: "The

[film] presents the life of an 'ordinary' woman living through extraordinary times—not in order to make her a hero, to investigate how fascism and war are formed by and affect daily life" (Friedrich).

The text also signals how war and womanhood interrelate, a continuation of what Scott MacDonald has called Friedrich's "attempt to rethink gender" (36). A title introduces the image of "the cross of the German mother," as we hear how childbirth was encouraged for nationalistic reasons. The theme of women's patriotism is highlighted by a clip, earlier in the film, of a turn-of-the-century American movie showing an American woman dancing with a flag. But while the American woman's relationship with the symbol of her country seems one of spectacular adornment, the German woman is uged to serve in a maternal role.

Intercut throughout the film is footage of Friedrich's journey back to Ulm, Germany, in 1982, to find the house in which her parent was raised. In this respect the work is similar to Christa Wolf's *Patterns of Childhood* (*Kindheitmuster*), originally published in 1976, in which a woman returns to the town where she grew up and experienced Nazism. In other respects, *The Ties That Bind* invokes Helma Sanders-Brahms's *Germany, Pale Mother* (*Deutschland, Bleiche Mutter*, 1980). In that dramatic film, a woman relates, through voice-over narration, the tale of her ordeal as a child in war-torn Germany, when her father was sent off to battle, and she and her mother had to survive on their own.[13]

In *The Ties That Bind*, when Friedrich voyages to Germany, a title tells us how she "saw [her] mother's home for the first time" and located the "room [that] had been hers." She also documents the process of assembling a miniature cardboard house in the style of a European chalet. Barbara Kruger finds this focus on the home suggestive of "its place as the site of women's presence [and] . . . interiority."

Through the journey motif, Friedrich proclaims the positive aspects of mother-daughter doubling—of "the ties that bind." It seems requisite that she retrace the steps of her parent, inhabit her residence, see out the same window. But this bonding bears no trace of symbiosis, for it is strength that Friedrich learns from Bucher. Jessica Benjamin argues that female desire must be imagined "intersubjectively," in terms of connection versus disengagement: "Woman's desire . . . can be found not through the current emphasis on *freedom from*: as autonomy or separation from a powerful other, guaranteed by identification with an opposing power. Rather, we are seeking a relationship to desire in the *freedom to*: freedom to be both with and distinct from the other" (97–98).

---

[13] Some other fiction films about mothers and daughters include *The Thin Line, Autumn Sonata* (1978), *Malou* (1983), *Imitation of Life* (1934, 1959), *Mildred Pierce* (1945), and *Stella Dallas* (1937).

While Bucher is not idealized, she is portrayed as a woman who maintains autonomy. This fact is crucial for the maternal relationship, for as Adrienne Rich has stated, "The quality of the mother's life—however embattled and unprotected—is her primary bequest to her daughter, because a woman who can believe in herself, who is a fighter, is demonstrating to her daughter that these possibilities exist" (250–51). Bucher survives incarceration in a German work camp, where she is impounded for secretarial service. Later, she endures divorce and life as a single, working parent. While she has faced personal and historical constraints (the war, the death of her parents, the termination of her education), she has overcome them. She mentions her childhood wish to take music lessons and her husband's failed promise to provide them. The film ends by revealing that she has purchased a piano and begun to "practice scales." Throughout the film, we see shots of Bucher swimming, images of release and liberation. She confesses that one day she might "swim out so far" that she "can't come back." Again, Rich's words illuminate this trope of a borderless terrain: "The most important thing one woman can do for another is to . . . expand her sense of actual possibilities. . . . It means that the mother herself is trying to expand the limits of her life. *To refuse to be a victim* and then go on from there" (250). The women in *The Ties That Bind* "refuse to be victims"—either of their historical circumstances or of patriarchy's malign mother-daughter plot.

Voices from the Attic (1988) is another work in which a daughter confronts her mother's wartime existence. However, this time the parent is a clear victim rather than a potential "oppressor." Debbie Goodstein returns to the Polish village in which her Jewish mother was hidden, as a child, during the town's occupation by the Nazis. The film begins inside the attic in which her mother was sequestered, as Goodstein attempts to visualize her family's plight: "I try to imagine sitting in a ten-by-fifteen-foot space with fifteen other people. The room is hot (about one hundred degrees). There's no electricity, also no plumbing, no lighting of any kind. We can't bathe or brush our teeth. We sleep on straw and go to the bathroom in a pot." While her film seeks to uncover her mother's past, which has been shrouded in secrecy, an aunt acts as a maternal surrogate, since her parent refused to make the trip. In the opening monologue, Goodstein makes clear that the voyage is a search for her own identity as well, since she has always felt that the attic shaped her life. Once in Poland, she feels that she is "*re*living things never seen and stories never heard." "Being there," she states, "felt like being back."

In making the film, Goodstein joins a group of minority artists focused on the maternal theme. As Natalie M. Rosinsky has noted: "Members of racial, ethic . . . and economic minority groups . . . have deline-

23. *Voices from the Attic* (1988). The filmmaker's mother, who did not make the trip to Poland.

ated their apprehension of the social forces which intervene between mother and daughter. Perhaps because the added oppression of minority group membership exacerbates this often painful relationship, these writers seem particularly aware of its tragic destructiveness" (280).

Voices from the Attic blends numerous types of documentary imagery. Some sequences comprise interviews with members of Goodstein's family (aunts, uncles, cousins), apparently shot in their New York City homes. Her mother appears momentarily on camera, but her repressed presence subtends the entire film. Periodically, Goodstein's voice emerges on the sound track, offering some reflection or insight.

Most of the footage concentrates on Goodstein's aunt, Sally Frishberg. It is she who has had the courage to confront the past by returning to Poland, perhaps because she was older than Goodstein's mother when the trauma transpired. She tells us about her childhood in the village prior to the Holocaust: about her warm domestic life, her schooling, the religious prejudices faced by her family. At first, the onset of the war did not seem to threaten them. Like other Poles, they took a German soldier into their home. It was he who hinted that they might be in danger. As Frishberg notes, "I was, in a way, saved by a German officer." It is characteristic of her consummate generosity that she can see a Nazi as her deliverer.

Interspersed with such interviews is archival material of Jewish life in Poland from the turn of the century through World War II, images that establish a broader context for the personal tale we hear. Considerable footage is included of the family's return to Poland: their search for Frishberg's home, their reunion with the family who hid them, their hunt for the local Jewish cemetery, their interaction with the villagers, their tour of Auschwitz.

While the homecoming has the triumphant quality of a survivor's conquering her past, incidents disturb the victory. As the family walks down a road, a youth yells, "Heil Hitler!" When they return to the cottage of Frishberg's childhood, they find a freshly painted swastika on its exterior. When Frishberg is reintroduced to Maria Grocholska, the wife of the farmer who hid her, the woman comments on how "*well* [Frishberg] is doing," indicating continuing resentments of Jewish success. We also learn that Grocholska did not cloister Frishberg's family out of altruism or idealism, but in return for all their modest furs and jewels.

Throughout the pain and dislocation of this cultural "reentry," Frishberg is dry-eyed, stalwart, and affirmative—happy to be home despite its devastating associations. She breaks down only twice: when she discusses her Uncle Naftali's death and when she relates her mother's abandonment of her sickly infant daughter (Frishberg's sister) on a church doorstep, in the hopes that someone would save her. The child died, and Frishberg's mother was wracked by guilt for her "choice" (like Sophie's in William Styron's novel). When Frishberg cries, she apologizes to Goodstein for doing so.

Frishberg's stoic attitude seems especially remarkable given that, upon emigrating to the United States, she vowed to forget her past and to lose her foreign accent. She admits that things became more complex with the birth of her children. It was difficult to hide from them her recurrent sadness, and she would often have to leave the room when her eyes welled up with tears. When Frishberg's daughter witnesses her mother's emotional collapse, she comforts her and tells Goodstein, "The woman who [is] crying on the sofa today is not the woman who raised me as a small child." Though she had known she had an aunt who died as a baby, the circumstances had always been cloaked in mystery.

Frishberg is, clearly, a heroine: someone who has not simply overcome tragedy but has done so with her spirit intact. If someone had scripted her into a fictional film, she would have seemed too wise and noble to be credible. Yet, as a woman, she has kept her experience secret—unlike men, who traditionally share their "war stories." In fact, Frishberg relates her narrative in the *name* of her deceased Uncle Naftali, who her father had assumed would transmit family history. When

Goodstein, in the name of her mother, brings Frishberg's drama to the screen, she thereby retrieves and voices the silenced maternal tale. In this respect, Goodstein resembles poet Alfonsina Storni, who imagines that all her verses express

> what was never allowed to be . . .
> what was hidden and suppressed
> from woman to woman, from family to family.

(20)

Motherhood and Race

> As focal point of cultural consciousness and social change,
> writing weaves into language the complex relations of a sub-
> ject caught between the problems of race and gender.
>   (Trinh T. Minh-ha)

While *The Ties That Bind* and *Voices from the Attic* have raised issues of nationality, religion, and ethnicity, they have taken *Caucasian* women as their subject—the "norm" for Western cinema. In recent years, however, female artists have examined mothers and daughters of other races. In *History and Memory* (1991), Rea Tajiri pursues a family "secret": her relatives' internment as Japanese Americans in a relocation camp during World War II, a situation that in some ways parallels the cloistering of Goodstein's family. While the resettlement experience affected both of Tajiri's parents, it is upon her mother that she concentrates, and a recurrent image is that of the latter drawing water from an outdoor faucet in camp. The scene is reenacted by Tajiri, indicating the filmmaker's identification with her parent. As Tajiri tells us, "I don't know where this [image] came from but I just had this fragment, this picture that's always been in my mind."

She feels that her mother repressed her wartime ordeal, accomplishing an "erasure of one part of her life."[14] As Judith Arcana has noted, our mothers often fail "to remember the painful, frustrating aspects of their living as women" (36). "In that forgetting," she continues, "our mothers lie to us" (37). This dishonesty becomes a lapse for Rea, too, who hears only vague whispers of the camps in her youth: "I remember having this feeling growing up that I was haunted by something—that I was living within a family filled with ghosts. There was this place they knew about; I had never been there. Yet I had a memory for it." The

---

[14] Tajiri said this at a talk she gave at the Carnegie Museum of Art (Pittsburgh) on 1 October 1992.

24. *History and Memory* (1991). Filmmaker Rea Tajiri reenacts her mother's role in the relocation camp.

video becomes Rea's quest: to research the internment and to reconfig-
ure the deleted recollections.

History and Memory is an experimental text that mixes archival footage of government newsreels, family photographs, documentary sequences, dramatized scenes, and clips from Hollywood films. Linking
these together is Tajiri's narration, which recounts aspects of her family
story. Again, synchronous sound is avoided, except for the excerpts
from *Yankee Doodle Dandy* (1942), *From Here to Eternity* (1953), *Come
See the Paradise* (1990), and *Bad Day at Black Rock* (1954). Tajiri includes the last of these films because it concerns the murder of a Japanese American in a small Western town. As she notes, "Kimoko's disappearance from Black Rock was like our disappearance from history."
Tajiri identifies not only with Kimoko but with the male hero (played by
Spencer Tracy) who investigates the crime. She feels most like him when
she arrives by train in Poston, Arizona—the site of her mother's imprisonment. Her productive use of *Bad Day at Black Rock* is especially interesting given the debates around the female spectator's "transvestite"
identification with the masculine screen protagonist (Mulvey, 32–33).

Tajiri continually foregrounds the interrelation of quotidian and cinematic life. In one sequence, she describes her sister's collection of film

star "glossies," to which she adds those of her beaus. In another, Tajiri muses, "I often wondered how the movies influenced our lives." Elsewhere, she intercuts footage from patriotic films like *Yankee Doodle Dandy* with wartime newsreels.

Throughout the video, there is a tension between extant and imagined images. At one point Tajiri states, "There are things that have happened in the world with cameras watching—things we have images for." We then see shots from a wartime documentary. As Anton Kaes has noted, "History . . . returns forever—as film" (quoted in Friedberg, 8). A few moments later, Tajiri adds, "There are other things that have not happened that we restage in front of cameras to have images of." We next see a clip from *December 7* (1942), a John Ford film depicting a manic kamikaze pilot. Sometimes Tajiri indicates that the distinction between fact and fiction breaks down: she includes a 1941 newsreel of the attack on Pearl Harbor, in which a witness says, "It certainly *looks* real . . ."—as though he had some doubt.

At one point, Tajiri muses, "There are things which have happened for which there have been no observers except the spirits of the dead." She then presents a rolling title that describes a scene of workmen uprooting, uplifting, and disposing of a house. She imagines this rape of her ancestral home as witnessed by her deceased grandfather, the only relative not then interned. The figure of her house recurs throughout the film and holds the same centrality as Bucher's residence in *The Ties That Bind*, the loft in *Voices from the Attic*, and the mansion in *Grey Gardens*.

Finally, Tajiri tells us, "There are things which have happened, the only images for which exist in the minds of the observers present at the time." These are the memories she suspects are locked in her mother's consciousness and emerge only erratically. Toward the end of the film, Tajiri confesses that she has one remembrance of her mother speaking of camp: "I overhear her describing it to my sister—this simple action—her hands filling a canteen out in the middle of a desert." This matches the image we have of Tajiri, in the role of her mother, at a faucet. Earlier, Tajiri spoke of the need to create images "where there are so few." This scene is her attempt to reconstruct a crucial detail of her family narrative: "For years I've been living with this picture without the story . . . not knowing how they fit together. But now I found I could connect the picture to the story." Thus Tajiri reveals that the film is an attempt to *contextualize* this reminiscence—to complete its historical and personal frame. Significantly, when she returns to Poston, the town sign is missing the letter *S*. For Tajiri, though, Poston is not a site of absence but one of completion, as she learns her family history and "forgive[s] [her] mother her loss of memory."

The water imagery (associated with the vision of Tajiri's mother at a faucet) is significant on another level, as well. Japanese Americans were known, at the time, for their agricultural skills. Even while interned in the desert, they worked to make plants grow. Tajiri, in fact, discovers the fruits of their horticultural labor in the contemporary landscape of Poston, Arizona, when she visits the site of her mother's relocation camp.

Like Friedrich and Goodstein, Tajiri has been troubled by her parent's long-term silence and has made the film to force her to "talk." As Flax remarks, speaking of the therapeutic situation, "Women . . . often feel as if they must rescue their mother in order to and before they can work on their own problems (35). While Bucher speaks willingly and is heard and seen often, Tajiri's mother (like Goodstein's) is reluctant; she does not appear and is heard only once. Nonetheless, the film asserts her symbolic "voice," while respecting her concrete need for privacy.

It is significant that Tajiri feels she must "forgive" her mother her historical "amnesia"—a posture that might, at first, seem smug and harsh. But the film functions less as an absolution than as a *cure*, providing her mother a lost memory trace in the form of a celluloid simulacrum. Relevant to this "medical discourse" is the fact that Tajiri's mother witnessed an internee "lose her mind," and apparently submerged her own trauma to save her sanity.

But more than a "cure," the film seems a gift: a loving tribute from daughter to parent. Tajiri reveals that she has gone to Poston to photograph the locale *for* her mother, who (like Mrs. Goodstein) has been unable to face the scene herself. During the course of the film, Tajiri recalls and displays a carved wooden bird that her mother kept in a jewelry box, an object with which Tajiri was forbidden to play. As part of her archival research, Tajiri miraculously unearths a photograph of her grandmother in a bird-carving class in camp—an image that helps her make retrospective sense of the treasured artifact. As the bird was a precious artisanal token from one generation to the next, signifying the loss and triumph of internment, so the film is a gift from Tajiri to her mother, honoring the pain and pride of her matrilineage.

It seems likely that *History and Memory* was influenced by Janice Tanaka's *Memories from the Department of Amnesia* (1989).[15] The latter is an elegiac meditation upon the filmmaker's recently deceased mother, who had been interned in a Japanese relocation camp during World War II. Again, the work focuses upon a woman's memory loss—on her obfuscation of the conditions of her abuse.

---

[15] In a talk at the Carnegie Museum of Art in Pittsburgh (25 September 1993), Tanaka talked of knowing Tajiri and of having given Tajiri a credit on her film *Who's Going to Pay for These Donuts, Anyway?* (1992).

Tanaka's film begins with an abstract, poetic section that depicts a garishly colored, surreal dreamworld, resembling the interior of a diner. As a man rides around on a bicycle, the handheld camera moves haphazardly, sometimes looking at the ceiling, sometimes shooting at eye level. The image renders extreme close-ups of the bicycle wheel, of a glass of water. Strange and ominous electronic tones accompany the visuals, punctuated by fragments of music and choral singing. Tanaka intended this section to encapsulate the disorientation she felt upon her mother's demise. The bicycle, a child's vehicle, symbolizes the roots of her emotional turmoil in youth. The diner conjures a host of similar establishments to which her working mother often took the family for the evening meal.[16]

At a certain point, a figure in surgical garb appears within the diner mise-en-scène, introducing a relevant medical gaze and discourse into the film: Tanaka's mother expired of complications resulting from an operation. At other times, the physician figure floats in a voidlike vacuum. Finally, fleeting photographic images of a Japanese woman materialize.

As the screen fades to white, we hear the voice of Tanaka's daughter, Rebecca, talking about her grandmother. Tanaka herself chimes in with comments and anecdotes. As the women converse, the frame is divided into two areas. On the left, a hand places one matched photograph over another, the top one registered in negative. On the right, a continuous montage of family snapshots unfolds, ostensibly those of Mrs. Tanaka and her relations. On the left, captions demarcate various stages of Mrs. Tanaka's life: her birth, her abandonment by her mother, her molestation by her father, her marriage, her childbearing, her internment in Manzanar relocation camp, her husband's insanity, her divorce, her hysterectomy, her nervous breakdown, her death. Meanwhile, the women's commentary provides details about Mrs. Tanaka's persona: her distraction, her eccentricity. The conjunction of the doubled screen and the sound track leads us to construct a picture of a woman devastated by personal and political shocks: by childhood hardships and by wartime racism. We learn that in 1979 she located her birth mother, but the woman failed to acknowledge any kinship.

For Tanaka the multilayered text allows her to "define the complexity of a human being" without "creating a movie with a narrative structure." She sees the printed statistics as conveying "the dry fact of chronology," while the photographs and conversation evoke resonant remembrance.[17]

---

[16] Tanaka made these points about the film in introducing the work at the Carnegie Museum of Art in Pittsburgh (25 September 1993).

[17] Again, this information derives from Tanaka's introduction to the film at the Carnegie Museum of Art in Pittsburgh (25 September 1993).

Like Tajiri, Tanaka sees memory loss as a major matriarchal problem. Hoping to purge themselves of the past's disturbing reverberations, women refuse to transmit their personal and cultural recollections to daughters and granddaughters. Tanaka's title implies that her film seeks to resurrect the reminiscences that have been repressed by the maternal "department of amnesia."

In *My Mother Thought She Was Audrey Hepburn* (1989), Sharon Jue confronts the issue of her self-image as a Chinese woman within American society. Through her voice-over narration, we learn that she has always denied her background. As she wryly asks, "Why be Chinese when you can be White?" Elsewhere she calls herself a "banana": "White on the inside and Yellow on the outside." To dramatize this situation, she interviews a Chinese-American woman and her Caucasian friends, friends who claim that they disregard their acquaintance's race. Jue's narration (like Tajiri's) relates details of her youth: how she was the only Chinese girl in her grade school class; how fellow students automatically paired her with the one Asian boy; how her teacher failed to see the humor in having her participate in the "game" of matching students with their baby pictures.

As the film's title indicates, Jue's identity is tied to that of her mother, who, alternately, considers herself a look-alike for Audrey Hepburn and Jacqueline Kennedy. Jue's link to the maternal Imago leads to "racial self-hatred": she has her hair permed, her eyes tucked; she feels like "Twiggy trapped inside [a] short, squat Chinese girl." As Judith Arcana has noted, utilizing an image from Chinese culture: "A mother's victimization does not merely humiliate her, it mutilates the daughter who watches her for clues as to what it means to be a woman. Like the traditional foot-bound Chinese woman, she passes on her affliction. The mother's self-hatred and low expectations are the binding rags for the psyche of the daughter" (13). While Jue's tone in the film is comic, her monologue invokes a catalog of pain: of interracial dating (a boyfriend's family assumed that she was related to the local laundry owner), of ethnic jokes (made at the expense of Chinese drivers), of political affronts (the supposition that she was a Maoist).

Jue notes the near absence of Chinese Americans in the media. When she informs her family that she will major in mass communication, they want her to be another Connie Chung. She observes how the Chinese are deemed the "model minority," presumably for their high achievement and social docility. She also focuses on how her female ancestors were paragons within this exemplary community. Her grandmother succumbed to an arranged marriage, then came to the United States and worked at the Del Monte food plant. While Jue's mother set herself a

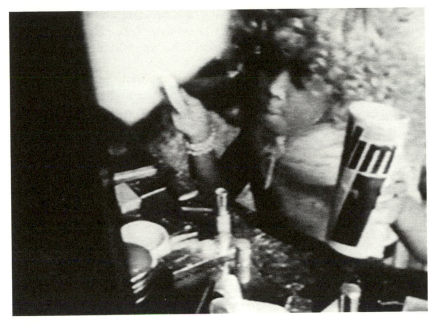

25. *Coffee-Coloured Children* (1988). A young girl of mixed race makes up at a mirror.

higher goal—to become a scientist—she relinquished her plans and attended secretarial school at her mother's request. Civil service jobs were considered the pinnacle for that generation of Chinese-American female. Later, she attended night school and became a microbiologist. As Jue notes, her mother "worked very hard and achieved her own version of the Chinese-American dream." Thus the thrust of the film is contradictory: Jue is distressed at her racial self-loathing, at her wish that her mother really *were* Hepburn or Kennedy; but she is proud that her family has successfully assimilated and succeeded. In the film's final shot, of her grandmother's grave, Jue confesses that she never knew whether the matriarch had "bound feet." Clearly, she is proud that both she and her mother do not.

Another film that confronts motherhood and race is Ngozi Onwurah's *Coffee-Coloured Children* (1988), made in Great Britain. It follows the pattern established by other experimental feminist documentaries. A female voice, presumably the filmmaker's, tells us about the discrimination she faced growing up as an interracial child in a Caucasian British neighborhood. The visuals reenact such horrendous events as skinheads smearing excrement on her family's front door. They also present mock home-movie footage of a little mulatto girl dressing up in a white voile gown, like the blonde princesses she knew from fairy tales—attempting to "pass" in a racial masquerade. Like Jue's, her childhood is lost "in a blur of aching self-hate."

We also witness the girl and her brother scrubbing themselves in the bathtub, trying to bleach the pigment from their bodies. As the voice-over notes, the cleanser "wouldn't clean [our] skin because [our] skin wasn't dirty." At points, the monolithic subjectivity of the sound track is violated by the presence of a male voice, ostensibly that of the film-maker's brother.[18] Both siblings wonder whether society is a "melting pot" or an "incinerator"—a question that foregrounds the violence in metaphors of assimilation. At the film's end, they create a conflagration to burn the icons of their subjugation: costumes and cleansers.

Central to the film's discourse is the mulatto daughter's difficulty identifying with her white mother—the opposite of the dilemma in *Imitation of Life* (1959), where the light-skinned Sarah Jane rejects her dark-skinned mother, Annie. While Ngozi's brother presumably experienced the same racial disjunction as she, since his black father was absent, he would have seen himself as separate from the mother who raised him. For Ngozi, it was more complex, given her developmental need to "reproduce mothering."

At the end of the film, Onwurah confronts this issue head-on. As the bonfire burns, she queries whether she has constructed the text for her "unborn daughter" or for "that little girl who was me as a child." She concludes that they are "one and the same—intertwined and interchangeable." She then muses: "The man I love may be white but the father of my child will be black. For I have not yet enough courage to throw my child into the great big melting pot knowing that it is so hot she may have her coffee-colored skin burnt red—so uncomfortable that she may spend her childhood not being able to look at her own reflection." Interestingly, Ngozi can only envision herself as the parent of a female child, which indicates the centrality of the mother-daughter relationship in her life. Yet implicit in her statement is a certain condemnation of her own mother. Onwurah, clearly, sees herself as black, despite the fact that she is half-white. Thus she identifies with her absent father, rather than with her present mother, as Sarah Jane identified with her missing dad, who was "practically white." In truth, Ngozi's decision is also dictated by social attitudes, according to which even a minute percentage of African blood is sufficient to warrant the label "black." Hence she does not imagine the possibility of a dark-skinned daughter

---

[18] The film does credit a Simon Onwurah.

who might reject *her* mulatto self. Furthermore, she implies that her mother heedlessly "threw" her into the fiery flames of bigotry—an act that Ngozi refuses to inflict upon her own potential offspring. When she recalls her inability to confront her "reflection" as a child, we suspect that she is really addressing the impossibility of conceiving herself as her mother's "double."

We began our discussion of the documentary tradition with a mention of Edison's *Morning Bath*, a one-minute film in which a black woman washes her infant. Though soap gets in his eyes, which he vehemently protests, she continues to scrub him, and the audience laughs. Until recently, I thought that the humor of the piece lay in her obtuseness; but recently the possibility of a racial slur was raised to me.[19] Given turn-of-the-century attitudes, part of the "comedy" may have been the notion of a black mother's trying to cleanse her baby of his negritude. In *Coffee-Coloured Children* and its vision of mulatto children scouring themselves in the tub, we return to documentary's primal scene: this time, with the children trying desperately to purge themselves of race and racism in a valiant attempt at maternal identification. As ever in our society, this desire for the mother is represented as a disabling, even masochistic, process.

Coda: The Woman at the Window

When Su Friedrich locates the apartment building of her mother's youth, she frantically pans its exterior, searching for the window from which her parent would have gazed, behind which she occupied a "room of her own." This image of "the woman at the window" is a familiar cultural icon. While men are thought to produce and experience history, women are thought merely to observe it: to wait and watch inside as the world goes by. This metaphor is apparent in a series of posters from the First World War. In an English one captioned "Women of Britain Say—Go!" (Paret, Lewis, and Paret, 52), a mother and her children stand by an open window as soldiers parade by. All the woman can do is to spur them on. In an American one (Paret, Lewis, and Paret, 56), a man stands inside a room looking out the window, as a caption asks intimidatingly, "On which side of the window are you?" The query (addressed, specifically, to men) marks the interior space as feminine and the exterior as masculine—hence its use to encourage enlistment. As

---

[19] The reading of this "joke" was proposed to me, some years back, by a black undergraduate student of mine in a course on women and film.

critics have noted, the image of the woman at the window has also had great currency in the cinema: be it Maya Deren looking out in *Meshes of the Afternoon* (1943) or Barbara Stanwyck, in *Stella Dallas* (1937), looking in. As the latter scene suggests, the quintessential watching woman is the mother who has the dual mission of witnessing the lives of both her husband and her child.

While the fiction film has frequently posed mothers at the window, depicting their apprehending the world as a distanced tableau, it has also restrained their viewpoints, as is evident from the iron bars and police surveillance that attend Stella's vista of her daughter's wedding. Rather than abandon the woman at the window, feminist experimental documentarists have attempted, through a cinema of matrilineage, to reclaim her agency and vision, to reveal her as an active participant in the sociohistorical universe.

Within the theory of the realist cinema, the screen has been configured as a "window on the world"—ironically, the only such portal at which woman is not entirely welcome. By deforming the codes of realism, by distorting Baudrillard's masculine Truth, feminist filmmakers have expanded the cinematic horizon to accommodate a maternal outlook. If Rea Tajiri's mother did not recognize herself in the government footage she screened, she *might* in *History and Memory*. In this respect, feminist filmmakers have made the screen not only a window but a mirror. But it is not the regressive lens of the Lacanian Imaginary, nor is it the patriarchal looking glass that captures the narcissistic Beales or the voyeuristic Maysleses. Rather, it is one that reflects the image of mother and daughter as positioned within the frame of gender, race, and nation. In this respect, the works correct the "blindness and skewed vision" of which Nan Bauer Maglin spoke—achieving what we might term a "dark victory."[20]

Works Cited

Antonini, Anita, and Dan Feder. "A Road Less Traveled." *Stop*, 1991, 92–96.
Arcana, Judith. *Our Mother's Daughters*. Berkeley: Shameless Hussy Press, 1979.
Barnouw, Erik. *Documentary: A History of the Non-Fiction Film*. London, Oxford, and New York: Oxford University Press, 1974.

---

[20] The following are additional films/videos that may be interesting in relation to the topic of feminist documentaries regarding the mother-daughter or daughter-grandmother relation: Gunvor Nelson's *Red Shift* (1984) and *Time Being* (1991); Jan Oxenberg's *Thank You and Goodnight* (1991).

Baudrillard, Jean. *Seduction*. Translated by Brian Singer. New York: St. Martin's, 1990.

Beauvoir, Simone de. *The Second Sex*. Translated by H. M. Parshley. New York: Vintage, 1974.

Benjamin, Jessica. "A Desire of One's Own." In *Feminist Studies/Critical Studies*, edited by Teresa de Lauretis, 78–101. Bloomington: Indiana University Press, 1986.

Bergstrom, Janet, and Mary Ann Doane. "The Spectatrix." Special issue of *Camera Obscura*, nos. 20–21 (1990).

Brown, Rita Mae. *Rubyfruit Jungle*. Toronto, New York, Sydney, and Auckland: Bantam, 1988.

Carroll, Noël. "From Real to Reel: Entangled in Nonfiction Film." In *1983 Philosophic Exchange*, 5–46. Rockport, NY: The Center for Philosophic Exchange, 1983.

Chodorow, Nancy. *The Reproduction of Mothering: Psychoanalysis and the Sociology of Gender*. Berkeley, Los Angeles, and London: University of California Press, 1987.

Edelstein, David. "Serious Fun." *Village Voice*, 9 April 1985, 56.

Eder, Richard. *"Grey Gardens."* *New York Times*, 27 September 1975, 21.

Flax, Jane. "Mother-Daughter Relationships: Psychodynamics, Politics, and Philosophy." In *The Future of Difference*, edited by Hester Eisenstein and Alice Jardine, 20–40. New Brunswick, NJ: Rutgers University Press, 1985.

Friday, Nancy. *My Mother, Myself: The Daughter's Search for Identity*. New York: Delacorte Press, 1977.

Friedberg, Ann. *Window Shopping: Cinema and the Postmodern*. Berkeley, Los Angeles, and Oxford: University of California Press, 1993.

Friedrich, Su. *"The Ties That Bind."* Publicity material.

Goodman, Walter. *"Grey Gardens*: Cinema Verité or Sideshow?" *New York Times*, 19 February 1976, 168–69.

Graham, Peter. *"Cinema-Verité* in France." *Film Quarterly* 17, no. 4 (Summer 1964): 30–36.

Hall, Jeanne. "Realism as a Style in Cinema Verité: A Critical Analysis of *Primary*." *Cinema Journal* 30, no. 4 (Summer 1991): 24–50.

Haskell, Molly. *From Reverence to Rape: The Treatment of Women in the Movies*. New York: Holt, Rinehart and Winston, 1974.

Hirsch, Marianne. *The Mother/Daughter Plot: Narrative, Psychoanalysis, Feminism*. Bloomington and Indianapolis: Indiana University Press, 1989.

Holden, Stephen. "Beauty amid the Beastliness in Portraits of Manhattan." *New York Times*, 11 July 1989, C16.

Kaes, Anton. *From Hitler to Heimat: The Return of History as Film*. Cambridge, MA, and London: Harvard University Press, 1989.

Kaplan, E. Ann. *Motherhood and Representation: The Mother in Popular Culture and Melodrama*. London and New York: Routledge, 1992.

———. *Women and Film: Both Sides of the Camera*. New York and London: Methuen, 1983.

Knight, Arthur. "*Grey Gardens.*" *Hollywood Reporter* 240, no. 22 (2 March 1976).

Kruger, Barbara. "Su Friedrich, *The Ties That Bind.*" *Artforum* 23, no. 2 (October 1984): 89.

Longfellow, Brenda. "Love Letters to the Mother: The Work of Chantal Akerman." *Canadian Journal of Political and Social Theory* 13, nos. 1–2 (1989): 71–90.

MacDonald, Scott. "From Zygote to Global Cinema via Su Friedrich's Films." *Journal of Film and Video* 44, nos. 1–2 (Spring–Summer 1992): 30–41.

Maglin, Nan Bauer. "'Don't Never Forget the Bridge That You Crossed Over On': The Literature of Matrilineage." In *The Lost Tradition of Mothers and Daughters in Literature*, edited by Cathy N. Davidson and E. M. Broner, 257–90. New York: Ungar, 1980.

Michener, Charles. "Film Festival Preview: Charles Michener on *Grey Gardens.*" *Film Comment* 11, no. 5 (September–October 1975): 38.

Minh-ha, Trinh T. *Woman, Native, Other: Writing, Postcoloniality and Feminism.* Bloomington and Indianapolis: Indiana University Press, 1989.

Minister, Kristina. "A Feminist Frame for the Oral History Interview." In *Women's Words: The Feminist Practice of Oral History*, edited by Sherna Berger Gluck and Daphne Patai, 27–41. New York and London: Routledge, 1991.

Mulvey, Laura. *Visual and Other Pleasures.* Bloomington and Indianapolis: Indiana University Press, 1989.

Paret, Peter, Beth Irwin Lewis, and Paul Paret. *Persuasive Images: Posters of War and Revolution.* Princeton, NJ: Princeton University Press, 1992.

Plaza, Monique. "The Mother/The Same: Hatred of the Mother in Psychoanalysis." *Feminist Issues* 2, no. 1 (Spring 1982): 75–99.

Rich, Adrienne. *Of Woman Born: Motherhood as Experience and Institution.* New York: Bantam, 1977.

Robson, Kenneth. "The Crystal Formation: Narrative Structure in *Grey Gardens.*" *Cinema Journal* 22, no. 2 (Winter 1983): 42–53.

Rosen, Marjorie. "*Grey Gardens*: A Documentary about Dependency." MS. January 1976.

Rosenthal, Alan. *The Documentary Conscience: A Casebook in Film Making.* Berkeley, Los Angeles, and London: University of California Press, 1980.

Rosinsky, Natalie M. "Mothers and Daughters: Another Minority Group." In *The Lost Tradition: Mothers and Daughters in Literature*, edited by Cathy N. Davidson and E. M. Broner, 280–90. New York: Ungar, 1980.

Roud, Richard. "Germane Maysles." *Manchester Guardian*, 29 October 1975, 10.

Silverman, Kaja. *The Acoustic Mirror: The Female Voice in Psychoanalysis and Cinema.* Bloomington and Indianapolis: Indiana University Press, 1988.

————. "Disembodying the Female Voice." In *Issues in Feminist Film Criticism*, edited by Patricia Erens, 309–27. Bloomington and Indianapolis: Indiana University Press, 1990.

Storni, Alfonsina. "It May Be." In *The Other Voice: Twentieth Century Women's Poetry in Translation*, edited by Joanna Bankier, Carol Cosman, Doris Earnshaw, Joan Keefe, Deirdre Lashgari, and Kathleen Weaver, 20. New York: Norton, 1976.

Stukator, Angela. "Feminist Film Criticism: An Investigation of the Textual Strategies in the Films of Chantal Akerman." Ph.D. diss., University of Bristol, 1991.

Wolf, Christa. *Patterns of Childhood*. Translated by Ursula Moniaro and Hedwig Rappolt. New York: Farrar, Straus and Giroux, 1984.

10 _____

Epilogue

MATERNITY AND THE ARTIST: "A REMARKABLE ZOOLOGICAL SPECIES"

> Mothers don't write, they are written.
>   (Susan Rubin Suleiman)

> [T]he woman of letters is *a remarkable zoological species*:
> she brings forth, pell-mell, novels and children. . . . But
> make no mistake: let no women believe that they can
> take advantage of this pact without having first submitted
> to the eternal statute of womanhood. Women are on the
> earth to give children to men; let them write as much as
> they like. . . . One novel, one child, a little feminism,
> a little connubiality.
>   (Roland Barthes)

The "Childless Goddess of Fertility"

In the previous chapter, we found that a series of feminist documentaries created from the perspective of the daughter provided some of the most compassionate portraits of the mother that exist in the history of cinema. But does it remain for the artist-daughter to ventriloquize her parent? Is it only she who can speak for the mother within the realm of creative discourse?

  In past eras, our answer to that question might have been affirmative. As Tillie Olsen has noted:

> [U]ntil very recently almost all distinguished achievement has come from childless women. . . . Most never questioned, or at least accepted (a few sanctified), this different condition for achievement, not imposed on men writers. (Webber and Grumman, 58–59)

Though "barren," these artistic women—whom Muriel Rukeyser deemed "childless goddess[es] of fertility" (Webber and Grumman, 52)—were all, nonetheless, daughters and hence could create, as did

Virginia Woolf, sensitive (but perhaps distanced) literary depictions of the mother.

In recent decades, however, women writers have more frequently incorporated parenthood into their life plan, allowing the maternal voice to emerge more convincingly in literary discourse. As Olsen inquires:

> What possible difference, you may ask, does it make to literature whether or not a woman writer remains childless . . . especially in view of the marvels these childless women have created. Might there not have been other marvels as well, or other dimensions to these marvels? Might there not have been present profound aspects and understandings of human life as yet largely absent in literature? (Webber and Grumman, 59)

It is, precisely, such insights that are now asserting their presence.

But the news is not all good. As Sandra M. Gilbert and Susan Gubar have established, Western culture has long perceived an "incompatibility" between the female and authorial positions. "If the pen is a metaphorical penis," they ask, "with what organ can females generate texts?" (7). If the implied answer to that query is "the womb," it is assumed that a woman who chooses the organ's "proper" function will have children and, having performed that procreative act, will have no use for writing. As Susan Stanford Friedman notes: "Male paternity of texts has not precluded their paternity of children. But for material and ideological reasons, maternity and creativity have appeared to be mutually exclusive to women writers" (75). On the same note, Paula Rabinovitz states, "For a woman to produce a literary text, to enter the (masculine) terrain . . . she must step out of her gender and therefore, ironically, *out of bounds*" (68, my italics).

But what of the rebellious women who demand both acts—who require biological *and* intellectual creativity within their universe? For Friedman, their responses form a continuum ranging from "a fundamental acceptance of a masculinist aesthetic that separates creativity and procreativity" to "a defiant celebration of (pro)creation, [and] a gynocentric aesthetic based on the body" (86). In Friedman's view, much is revealed about such writers when one examines their use of the "birth metaphor" as a way of conceptualizing literary work. As she notes, such tropes

> are often figurative expressions of the strategies by which their authors confront the double bind of the woman writer: how to be a woman and a writer within a discourse that has steadfastly separated the two. Consequently, where men's [birth] metaphors tend to perpetuate the separation of creativities, women's metaphors tend to deconstruct it. (86)

Not surprisingly, most women who document their maternal/authorial lives emphasize the *struggle* of their bifurcated existence. As Ann Tyler remarks, in imagery reminiscent of the Humpty Dumpty story,

> I have spent so long erecting partitions around the part of me that writes—learning how to close the door on ordinary life when it's time to start writing again—that *I'm not sure I could fit the two parts of me back together now.* (Sternburg, 7, my italics)

For Olsen, the author-mother lacks neither drive nor ability but the social conditions conducive to writing:

> In motherhood, as it is structured, circumstances for sustained creation are almost impossible. Not because the capacities to create no longer exist, or the need . . . but . . . the need cannot be first. . . . Motherhood means being instantly interruptible, responsive, responsible. (Webber and Grumman, 60)

Frustrations aside, most author-mothers find that maternity provides an invaluable experience for their creative endeavors. Alice Walker talks of how she "was changed forever" by the birth of her child, an event that brought "the incomparable gift of seeing the world at quite a different angle than before" (Sternburg, 126). Similarly, Ann Tyler comments:

> [S]ince I've had the children, I've grown richer and deeper. They may have slowed down my writing for a while, but when I did write, I had more of a self to speak from. . . . My life seems more intricate. Also more dangerous. (Sternburg, 9)

Many author-mothers conclude that maternity has enabled them to reject male standards of writing. As Alicia Ostriker states:

> If the woman artist has been trained to believe that the activities of motherhood are trivial, tangential to the main issues of life, irrelevant to the great themes of literature, she should untrain herself. The training is misogynist, it protects and perpetuates systems of thought and feeling which prefer violence and death to love and birth, and it is a lie. (Daly and Reddy, 8)

As Friedman has noted, many female authors come to see their creation in human reproductive terms, reclaiming for women a metaphor long appropriated by men. In "The Poet in the World," Denise Levertov compares the process of writing to childbirth:

> The poet is in labor. She has been told that it will not hurt but it has hurt so much that pain and struggle seem, just now, the only reality. But at the very moment when she feels she will die, or that she is already in hell, she hears the doctor saying, "Those are the shoulders you are feeling now"—and she knows the head is out then, and the child is pushing and sliding out of her, insistent, a poem. (Webber and Grumman, 85)

In a similar manner, Marie-Elise imagines "diapering a poem":

Here:
This poem is clean
    and dry.
Would you like to hold it
till it starts to cry?

                                        (Webber and Grumman, 441)

As her final query indicates, the poet also envisions a darker side to mothering in which production is thwarted:

Diapering this poem,
    I listen to my hands
        folding fatigue,
        creating silence.
I never smile while self-exiled:
    following a blind muse
    like a whining child

                                        (Webber and Grumman, 441)

If, for Marie-Elise, the poem suffers in the world of the author-mother, for others, the victim is the child. As critic Barbara Johnson notes, "It is as though male writing were by nature procreative while female writing is somehow by nature infanticidal" (198).

Out of Bounds

While there have been few female "auteurs" in the history of the cinema, and even fewer who were parents, the film medium has often dramatized the struggle of the artist-mother, reinforcing cultural notions of the incongruity of maternity and creativity in women's lives. Most often, this maternal figure has been imagined as a performer: be it the vaudeville dancer in *Applause* (1929), the actress in *Imitation of Life* (1959) or *Persona* (1966), the pianist in *Autumn Sonata* (1978), the opera singer in *Luna* (1979), the ballerina in *The Turning Point* (1977). Less frequently, the mother-artist has been a creator (versus an interpreter) of texts, like the painter in *The Sandpiper*. Generally, the films in which she appears have been directed by men, be it Rouben Mamoulian, Douglas Sirk, Ingmar Bergman, Bernardo Bertolucci, Herbert Ross, or Vincente Minnelli.

In these works, the conjunction of art and maternity has been seen as an unlikely, if not impossible, scenario—one fraught with distress and failure. In *Applause*, a stripper must exile her daughter to a convent

26. *Applause* (1929). A burlesque queen (Helen Morgan) with her daughter.
MOMA

school to shield her from burlesque's sleazy atmosphere. In *Imitation of
Life*, the ambitions of a stage and screen star lead her to alienate her
child. In *Persona*, a classical actress, who has tried to feign enthusiasm
for motherhood, experiences a breakdown and existential "nausea." In
Autumn Sonata, a renowned female pianist makes inordinate demands

27. *The Sandpiper* (1965). The artist-mother (Elizabeth Taylor) with her son and lover (Richard Burton). MOMA

upon her adult daughter, thereby damaging the latter's self-image. In *Luna*, a selfish and vain diva makes incestuous moves on her teenage son, exacerbating his drug addiction. In *The Sandpiper*, a painter—an unwed mother—must confront behavior problems exhibited by her son at prep school, ostensibly a result of her having raised him as a free-spirited bohemian. In *The Turning Point*, an ex-ballerina, Dee Dee (Shirley MacLaine), must come to terms with her choice of a domestic path at the moment when her daughter decides to devote her life to dancing. Dee Dee's distress is worsened by the fact that her daughter comes under the tutelage of Emma (Ann Bancroft), an old ballet friend of Dee Dee's who has chosen performance over parenthood. At one point, the two women vent their mutual envy and rage in a scene that is emblematic of the cultural schism this genre of film announces. Dee Dee shouts to Emma, "You got nineteen curtain calls!" as Emma retorts, "You got pregnant!"

In numerous works of this sort, a man comes to the rescue of the troubled and driven maternal artist. In *Imitation of Life*, the actress's lover is a confidante to her daughter—a situation that eventually leads to a tense love triangle. In *The Sandpiper*, the school's headmaster (also the painter's lover) intervenes with authorities on behalf of her son.[1] In *The Turning Point*, Dee Dee's husband reaffirms the value of their marriage, quelling her regretful tendencies.

In recent years, women filmmakers have wrestled with the subject of motherhood and creativity.[2] Some, like Claudia Weill, have crafted narratives quite similar to those outlined above. In *Girlfriends* (1978), a poet relinquishes her writing to raise a family and type her husband's dissertation. Significantly, however, rather than continue to portray female artists who have uneasily assumed the maternal position, women directors have chosen heroines who have *rejected* that option—perhaps a more honest (and less melodramatic) stance on the situation.

An early foray into this territory was Gillian Armstrong's *My Brilliant Career* (1979), based on an autobiographical novel by Australian author Miles Franklin. The film concerns Sybilla (Judy Davis), a young woman who lives in the outback with her impoverished family. While her mother grimly tends to a horde of offspring, Sybilla rejects her parent's life path and desires to become a writer. In the course of the narrative, Sybilla is continually frustrated with the nurturing roles society thrusts upon her as a female, be it as mother's helper, baby-sitter, or school-

---

[1] Some other films (directed by men) that are relevant to this topic are *Evergreen* (1934, Victor Saville), *Mommie Dearest* (1981, Frank Perry), *Ladies on the Rocks* (1983, Christian Braad Thomsen), and *Blonde Venus* (1932, Josef von Sternberg).

[2] Some other films (directed by women) that are relevant to this topic are *Joyce at 34* (1973, Joyce Chopra and Claudia Weill), *Schmeerguntz* (1966, Gunvor Nelson and Dorothy Wiley), *Riddles of the Sphinx* (1977, Laura Mulvey and Peter Wollen), *Entre-Nous* (1983, Diane Kurys), *Sheer Madness* (1984, Margarethe von Trotta), *This Is My Life* (1982, Nora Ephron), *The Girls* (1969, Mai Zetterling), *One Sings, the Other Doesn't* (1977, Agnes Varda). For discussions of *The Girls* and *Riddles of the Sphinx*, see Fischer, 80–88, 49–62.

marm. By the end of the drama, she has rejected romance and marriage and the maternal role that both imply.

But it is in Armstrong's later work *High Tide* (1987) that the film-maker directly addresses the issue of the artist-mother. In that drama, Judy Davis stars as Lily, a small-time singer, who, we learn, gave up her baby following her husband's untimely death. Years later, she accidentally encounters her teenage daughter Allie (Claudia Karvan) while stranded in an Australian beach town, having been fired from a traveling band.

In the beginning of the film neither we nor the characters know the details of the complex circumstances. Rather we follow, through parallel editing, Lily's arrival in town and Allie's outings with friends. It is only later, after Lily and Allie have met at their trailer park, that Lily realizes their relation: she recognizes Allie's caretaker, Bet (Jane Adele), her former mother-in-law. This discovery precipitates a crisis whereby all three women must grapple with the convoluted situation.

On one level, *High Tide* perhaps reinforces notions of maternity as "natural." In the intercutting between mother and daughter that opens the film, the disgraced mother is associated with artifice (the theater); the innocent child is linked with nature (the ocean). When we first see Lily onstage, performing as a backup singer for an Elvis impersonator, she wears a slinky sequined dress and a platinum blond wig and is glimpsed through a shiny blue vinyl curtain. Alternately, we find Allie floating transcendently in the waves. The event that allows Lily to discover motherhood and her daughter is her termination as a performer and her forced sojourn at the beach. This contrastive theme returns throughout the film in the comparative editing of tracking shots of the highway versus moving camera shots along the sand. In the continual picturing of Allie in the ocean, sometimes filmed partially underwater, we get not only a vision of nature but an intimation of fetal life in the amniotic "sea."

While the film establishes such an opposition, it violates its own facile binary framework by depicting the maternal position as complex, shifting, and ambiguous. In the segment prior to the startling genetic revelation, Lily is portrayed as a strident rebel. Though part of a sleazy lounge act, she rejects the authoritarian control of her Elvis-mentor. She does not wear makeup offstage, as he would like her to, and is the only singer not to throw kisses to the audience. When she wins a chicken in a saloon raffle one night, she immediately gives it away, indicating her lack of domesticity. This theme is highlighted again later in the film: when Allie asks her where she lives, she says, "I travel." But her traveling is interrupted when, after being fired, Lily discovers that her car is stalled. She then gets roaring drunk, and it is in this condition that she first encounters her daughter.

28. *High Tide* (1987). Judy Davis plays a singer who is reunited with the child she abandoned. BFI

After Lily learns Allie's identity, she is not immediately stricken with maternal instinct; rather, she backs away. This stance is encouraged by Bet, who has grown passionately attached to Allie, and who blames Lily for her parental desertion. Bet offers Lily a bribe to leave town, then threatens to kill her, an act that would realize her assertion to Allie that her mother is dead. Lily's first response is to bolt, but her efforts are thwarted by the excessive cost of her car repair. She is, however, so desperate to depart that she momentarily entertains the notion of prostituting herself to the garage mechanic.

Forced to hang around town, Lily tries to avoid Allie but finds herself compulsively "stalking" the girl. When Lily discovers Allie taking a shower in the public bathroom, she wistfully notices that Allie is shaving her legs—an indication of the onset of puberty. As Lily voyeuristically peers at the shower stall, Bet comes in and banishes her. At a later point, Lily secretly peers at Allie through a window as the girl tends her surfboard. Again, Bet chases her away. Only when Bet is out of town does Lily dare to invite Allie to have a meal. As they dine, Lily becomes emotional and leaves the table to cry in the bathroom.

Despite her sentiments and curiosity, Lily would seem to have no intention of proclaiming herself Allie's mother. The girl learns of her parentage only because Lily entrusts her secret to a man, and he, in a paternalistic gesture, decides that it is best for everyone that the girl know. Perhaps, in this respect, he is her savior—like the men who populate other maternal melodramas.

Then, it is Allie who pursues Lily. When she confronts her mother to tell her she loves her, Lily responds, "You don't know me." When Allie asks whether Lily ever searched for her, the latter refuses to give her the answer she desires, emphatically stating, "I gave you away." As though to fulfill Bet's vision of her, Lily becomes inaccessible and stops visiting. Bet comforts Allie: "Never mind her. I could've told you. . . ." But, like her mother, Allie has an obsessive need to spy on her newfound relation, and she locates her in a most transgressive pose. In order to earn money to retrieve her car, Lily agrees (for the first time in her career) to do a striptease. It is during this act that Allie happens upon her while she is wandering through a bar. In many ways, this scene replays one in *Applause* in which the daughter of a burlesque queen witnesses her mother onstage the day she leaves her sheltered life in a convent school.

While in a more conventional film such an episode would disqualify a woman as a proper maternal figure—especially since Lily stripped to escape, not to support her child—in this film, Allie is not deterred. Rather, her mother's iconoclasm seems to make her *more* attractive in her daughter's eyes. When Allie finds Lily packing her car to leave town, she runs to embrace her, and Lily, spontaneously, asks if she wishes to go along. The girl responds affirmatively, and the two set off. Hence, in accessing her maternal role, Lily takes Allie away from nature and on the road—usually a male terrain. Furthermore, while in other movies this might have been the happy end of the film, Armstrong includes a second, more unsettling denouement. When, that night, the two stop in a restaurant to eat, Lily excuses herself, ostensibly to go to the toilet. We, however, see that she has snuck back outside to the car. We witness her panicked impulse to flee and then her tentative decision to stay. Thus the film leaves us in limbo, without the moral or narrative assurance that the family circle has been permanently restored. Clearly, Lily will make no conventional accommodations. Before she spilled her maternal secret to him, her paramour had asked her to marry him and help him start a small business. While this would have provided the safe way back to motherhood and domesticity, Lily refused his offer, chastising him for his bourgeois "slave mentality." She is no martyr—neither to men nor toward her daughter. Indeed, even the "Good Mother" in this drama, Bet, is no Angel in the House. Like Lily, she is a performer, singing ballads on amateur night in the local pub, and, on several occasions, she drinks excessively. Furthermore, though she has a steady boyfriend, she succumbs to a one-night stand with an itinerant country-western singer. All this from a woman in her early sixties! In some respects, she is reminiscent of the grandmother in *The Chalk Garden* (discussed in chapter 7). For Bet's devotion to Allie masks a selfish need—one that Lily recognizes and Bet acknowledges toward the end of the film.

Interestingly, the beach town in which *High Tide*'s encounter takes place is called Eden, and the trailer park, The Mermaid Caravan. Many issues seem symbolically bundled into these names. While on one level Allie seems the mermaid, often pictured half in and half out of the water, it is also an image that attaches to Lily. She is a sexually attractive female, a kind of provocative siren—normally not an acceptable position for mothers to claim. Furthermore, she comprises many aspects, as a mermaid is half-fish and half-human: she is mother, artist, woman. The "Caravan" of the park's name refers to the Australian word for trailer but also reminds us that this is a "road movie," one in which the woman is allowed to collect her child and still go on her way. Furthermore, like Eve in Genesis, Lily has been punished for her spunk and eroticism through the pangs of a childbirth that has produced great psychic pain. Finally, while at the end of the film mother and daughter drive off into the sunset, Armstrong has been bold enough to render their future no Paradise Regained, no blissful Garden of Eden.

Mirroring *High Tide* on a documentary level is *Finding Christa* (1991) by Camille Billops, a black independent filmmaker, and coauthored by James Hatch. While earlier nonfiction films privileged the perspective of the daughter, *Finding Christa* bespeaks an aesthetic more consonant

29. *Finding Christa* (1991). Camille Billops's daughter Christa, given up for adoption. Camille Billops/James Hatch

with one imagined by Marianne Hirsch. What she envisions is a pose that bridges filial and maternal positions: "Through the voices of daughters speaking for their mothers, through the voices of mothers speaking for themselves . . . and eventually, perhaps, through the voices of mothers and daughters speaking to each other, oedipal frameworks are modified by other psychological and narrative economies" (8). No other film so embodies Hirsch's ideal as *Finding Christa*.

While earlier documentaries had the daughter "ventriloquize" the mother, *Finding Christa* speaks directly in the maternal voice. Furthermore, it delineates a transgressive parental act (as did *High Tide* and *Voices in the Attic*): the abandonment of a baby—next to infanticide, the ultimate female taboo. Specifically, the film explores Billops's pregnancy as a young, unmarried woman and her later decision to put her four-year-old daughter up for adoption. The film was precipitated by that child's successful attempt, in her early twenties, to contact Billops. In this fluid mixture of maternal and filial agency, we are reminded of Elizabeth Cowie's notion of the cinema as a fantasy requiring multiple subject positions. Among those she delineates are "active or passive . . . child or parent, *mother or daughter*" (Cowie in Bergstrom and Doane, 129, my italics).

Unlike Anna's in *Way Down East*, Billops's unwed motherhood is not treated as high tragedy. Though she faced social disapproval and risked losing her teaching job, she was not ostracized by her family, nor was she driven from the community. Rather, she relinquished her daughter by choice to give her child a conventional family and to pursue her own artistic ambitions. As she has stated: "I wasn't poor, I wasn't broke, I just didn't want to be a mother. I wanted to go back to the crossroads and change it" (lecture). In reality, *that* wish brands her more "sinful" than any heroine Griffith could have imagined.

While Billops's daughter contacted her in 1981, *Finding Christa* was not made until a decade later. In between, Billops shot another work that bears traces of maternal concern and consciousness. In *Suzanne, Suzanne* (1982), Billops and Hatch craft a filmic portrait of the troubled relationship between Billops's sister and her daughter, Suzanne. In addition to having drug problems, Suzanne suffers from not resembling her glamorous mother, a fashion model. Rather, she favors her late father, an abusive man who abandoned them years back. *Suzanne, Suzanne* makes clear Billops's obsession with works about family. She herself calls her films "one long-running soap" (lecture). Her films also depict and celebrate what Barbara Lekatsas has termed the "female network within [the] Black middle-class": "Men in the films constitute the absent center. Even when present, they seem not to be there, as women talk around and about them" (396).

Suzanne, Suzanne also imagines what Billops's life might have been like had she not bypassed the maternal "crossroad" (an option denied to Dee Dee in *The Turning Point*). As Lekatsas notes, the film "juxtapos[es] [Billops's] fate, her odyssey outward, to the domestic entrapment of her sister . . . expos[ing] two life styles and their aftermath" (408). But the central focus of *Suzanne, Suzanne* is the mother-daughter bond, and Billops's own mother enters the drama as a player as well. Most of all, the film seems an unconscious "rehearsal" for *Finding Christa*; Christa's vocals are even used on the sound track.

Significantly, the first voice that we hear in *Finding Christa* is that of Billops's daughter asking her, "Why did you leave me?"—a query later repeated in an intertitle. The film is an attempt to address that poignant question, and it does so with a minimum of piety or remorse. For the first half of the piece, Billops interviews those who saw her through her travail: a cousin who raised her, a longtime friend, her mother's acquaintance. They are allowed to proffer harsh theories about Billops's motivation. Her cousin alleges that Billops abandoned Christa to placate Hatch, her future husband—an opinion that Billops denies. Intercut with this material is home-movie footage of her pregnancy and her early days raising her daughter. Intermittently, we hear Christa's voice describing relevant events, like the devastating morning she was left at the Children's Home Society.

In dramatized scenes set in her studio, Billops talks with friends about Christa's search. One of them relates her own story of adoption and foster care, and her attempt to track her mother down. In one sequence, a tape is played of Christa performing a song she has written for Billops. Also incorporated are droll fantasy sequences in which Billops "auditions" for a mother-daughter recital.

Midway through the film a title inquires, "Christa, where were you?" It is spoken from Billops's perspective and symmetrically parallels the earlier question from Christa. The film then focuses on Christa's adoptive mother, Rusty Carlyle, as she relates the details of her cherished daughter's childhood. We see shots of Christa amid her affectionate siblings. Carlyle talks of how she wanted to adopt a baby because she had once relinquished a child of her own. She confesses that she imagined a girl with a dark complexion, like hers, and was somewhat nonplussed at Christa's light skin. The issue of color disparity becomes part of the family's legacy and humor, indicating how the question of racial difference arises in an all-black group. Carlyle recalls that although Christa was a happy youth, she hungered for a biological parent with whom to identify. It was Carlyle who suggested that Christa look for Billops, a proposal that her daughter enthusiastically endorsed.

The film provides documentary footage of Camille and Christa at their first meeting and covers their reunion with Billops's extended family. It also contains staged sequences of mother and daughter examining old photos of the girl's father. At points, Christa's narration details Billops's distancing strategies: her refusal to be touched, her treatment of her daughter as a demanding "octopus." Christa also admits the complex pull she experiences as the child of two assertive mothers. However, her musical creativity flourishes with her maternal reunion, and she composes songs on the theme of the "child who returns." We sense the excitement she feels at discovering her own artistry presaged, doubled, and validated in her mother's talent. Thus while Suzanne had suffered from underidentification with her mother, Christa experiences the pleasures of maternal mirroring.

Sometimes Billops speaks, admitting fears of being "caught again" by her child. To the end, she rejects sentimentality. She has said of Christa: "I'm not her mother and I'm not her friend. I'm a third term. I'm her gene pool" (lecture). In an interesting parallel, in *High Tide* it is the hereditary aspects of motherhood that most intrigue Lily. She tells Bet that she has noticed traits of her husband in Allie. And she tells her lover that she feels compelled to scan Allie for signs of her parentage.

In *Finding Christa*, the only maudlin note emerges when Hatch reads Billops's distraught diary entry for the day she surrendered her daughter. While for Christa finding her mother has "saved [her] life," Billops waxes less poetic. She stands behind her original choice and concludes, "I did better and she did better."

For Marianne Hirsch, traditional narrative can change only "if the feminist daughter becomes a feminist mother who can tell her feminist daughter about that process of becoming" (160). This is precisely the position that Camille Billops "finds" in the act of "finding Christa." But in truth it is Christa who finds *her* and, in so doing, locates a complex and ambivalent maternal role model.

In *High Tide* and *Finding Christa*, the artist-mother ultimately devises the means to combine the two sides of her self, if only provisionally. Unlike the protagonist of *Applause*, she need not die, and unlike that of *Persona*, she need not go mad. Unlike Dee Dee in *The Turning Point*, she need not select one or the other. Contrary to the message of *Autumn Sonata*, she need not take blame for her offspring's pain, and contrary to *Luna*'s, she need not witness her child's descent into self-destruction. This is not to say that *High Tide* and *Finding Christa* present the conjunction of artistry and motherhood as a project of pat solutions and joyful resolutions. Rather, it is depicted as a venture of monumental strain and negotiation. What the films demonstrate, however, is that the coupling of motherhood and artistry—while challenging—need not be suicidal or infanticidal.

In writing about this issue, poet Carolyn Kizer initially mocks the tradition of the "childless goddess of fertility":

> I will speak about women of letters, for I'm in the racket,
> Our biggest successes to date? Old maids to a woman . . .
>
> . . . .
> Middle-aged virgins . . .
> With continuous periods.
>
> (Webber and Grumman, 95)

But later she notes, optimistically, that "[w]e're emerging from all that" (Webber and Grumman, 96). More important, however, she ends by encouraging all mother-poets to "believe in the luck of [their] children":

> Whom we forbid to devour us, whom we shall not
> devour.
>
> (Webber and Grumman, 96)

Works Cited

Barthes, Roland. *Mythologies*. Translated by Annette Lavers. New York: Hill and Wang, 1972.

Bergstrom, Janet, and Mary Ann Doane. "The Spectatrix." Special issue of *Camera Obscura*, nos. 20–21 (1990).

Billops, Camille. Lecture. The Carnegie Museum of Art (Pittsburgh), 14 January 1995.

Daly, Brenda O., and Maureen T. Reddy, eds. *Narrating Mothers: Theorizing Maternal Subjectivities*. Knoxville: University of Tennessee Press, 1991.

Fischer, Lucy. *Shot/Countershot: Film Tradition and Women's Cinema*. Princeton, NJ: Princeton University Press, 1989.

Friedman, Susan Stanford. "Creativity and the Childbirth Metaphor: Gender Difference in Literary Discourse." In *Speaking of Gender*, edited by Elaine Showalter, 73–100. New York and London: Routledge, 1989.

Garner, Shirley Nelson, Claire Kahane, and Madelon Sprengnether, eds. *The (M)other Tongue*. Ithaca, NY, and London: Cornell University Press, 1985.

Gilbert, Sandra M., and Susan Gubar. *The Madwoman in the Attic: The Woman Writer and the Nineteenth-Century Literary Imagination*. New Haven: Yale University Press, 1984.

Hirsch, Marianne. *The Mother/Daughter Plot: Narrative, Psychoanalysis, Feminism*. Bloomington and Indianapolis: Indiana University Press, 1989.

Johnson, Barbara. *A World of Difference*. Baltimore: Johns Hopkins University Press, 1987.

Lekatsas, Barbara. "Encounters: The Film Odyssey of Camille Billops." *Black American Literature Forum* 25, no. 2 (Summer 1991): 395–408.

Rabinovitz, Paula. *Labor and Desire: Women's Revolutionary Fiction in Depression America*. Chapel Hill and London: University of North Carolina Press, 1991.

Sternburg, Janet, ed. *The Writer on Her Work*. New York and London: W. W. Norton, 1980.

Webber, Jeanette L., and Joan Grumman, eds. *Woman as Writer*. Boston: Houghton Mifflin, 1978.

Index

About the Author

LUCY FISCHER is Professor of Film and English at the
University of Pittsburgh, where she directs the film
studies program. Her books include *Shot/Countershot:
Film Tradition and Women's Cinema* (Princeton), *Imitation of Life*, and *Jacques Tati*. She has worked as a curator at The Museum of Modern Art in New York City
and at the Carnegie Museum of Art in Pittsburgh.